MEANING AND VALUE IN A SECULAR AGE

PRAISE FOR
MEANING AND VALUE IN A SECULAR AGE

"Paul Kurtz has widened the scope of scientific humanism to include the last frontier of inquiry, arguing the essential continuity of political and ethical conduct and bringing both under the efficacy of reason. His original work has earned him the leadership in American pragmatism. Nathan Bupp has collected Kurtz's best work in a volume that confirms his undisputed role in the world affairs of human culture and the significance of eupraxsophy."

—John P. Anton,
Distinguished Professor of Philosophy,
University of South Florida

"It is a relief to learn that a secular age may be achieved without contempt for religion. Paul Kurtz writes with wisdom and tolerance about a topic that today is often engulfed in polarizing debate. Having set out on this road long before most everyone else, he stresses the universal need of the human species for meaning and hope."

—Frans de Waal, author of *The Age of Empathy*

The Writings of
PAUL KURTZ

MEANING AND VALUE IN A SECULAR AGE

ᐁ WHY EUPRAXSOPHY MATTERS ᐁ

Edited by NATHAN BUPP

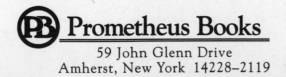

Prometheus Books

59 John Glenn Drive
Amherst, New York 14228–2119

Published 2012 by Prometheus Books

Cover image © 2012 Media Bakery
Cover design by Jacqueline Nasso Cooke

Inquiries should be addressed to
Prometheus Books
59 John Glenn Drive
Amherst, New York 14228–2119
VOICE: 716–691–0133
FAX: 716–691–0137
WWW.PROMETHEUSBOOKS.COM

16 15 14 13 12   5 4 3 2 1

Library of Congress Cataloging-in-Publication Data

Kurtz, Paul, 1925–
    Meaning and value in a secular age : why eupraxsophy matters : the writings of Paul Kurtz
/ edited by Nathan Bupp.
        p. cm.
    Includes bibliographical references and index.
    ISBN 978–1–61614–231–5 (pbk.)
    ISBN 978–1–61614–279–7 (ebook)
    1. Humanism. 2. Religion. I. Bupp, Nathan, 1971– II. Title.

BL2747.6.K873 2012
191—dc23
                                                                    2012004777

Printed in the United States of America on acid-free paper

Philosophy recovers itself when it ceases to be a device for dealing with the problems of philosophers and becomes a method, cultivated by philosophers, for dealing with the problems of men.

—John Dewey

We are interested in cognitive and ethical questions, in achieving, especially at the present juncture, a cultural renaissance or cultural reformation. We offer a distinctive set of intellectual and normative values. We emphasize the importance of reason and critical thinking, and we wish to use these methods in order to reformulate and refashion our values, and to raise the quality of taste and the level of appreciation in society. Humanism is life-affirming; it is positive and constructive. If applied, it would enable us to reform human culture by transcending the ancient religious, racial, ethnic, and ideological dogmas of the past that so adversely affect human civilization in the present. We thus call for a reaffirmation of the highest values of which humans are capable.

—Paul Kurtz, *Free Inquiry* (Summer 2003)

CONTENTS

Acknowledgments   9

Introduction. Up from Atheism, by Nathan Bupp   13

Chapter 1. Humanism as a Eupraxsophy   23

Chapter 2. Eupraxsophy and Naturalism   55

Chapter 3. Is a Naturalistic Alternative to Religion Possible?   75

Chapter 4. Conviction and Commitment   87

Chapter 5. The Practice of Reflective Ethical Inquiry   115

Chapter 6. The Valuational Base I: *The Common Moral Decencies*   145

Chapter 7. The Valuational Base II: *The Ethics of Excellence*   195

Chapter 8. Love and Friendship   237

Chapter 9. Caring   249

Chapter 10. Educating the Whole Person: The Liberating Arts   265

Chapter 11. Eupraxsophy: The Unification of Knowledge   277

Chapter 12. The Eupraxsophy of Hope   293

Chapter 13. Meaning and Transcendence   299

Chapter 14. The Human Condition   311

Afterword. From Philosophy to Eupraxsophy   333

Notes   355

ACKNOWLEDGMENTS

Chapter 1. **Humanism as a Eupraxsophy** is excerpted from *Eupraxsophy: Living without Religion* (Amherst, NY: Prometheus Books, 1989), pp. 13–48.

Chapter 2. **Eupraxsophy and Naturalism** was originally published in *The Future of Naturalism* (Amherst, NY: Humanity Books, 2009), pp. 179–96.

Chapter 3. **Is a Naturalistic Alternative to Religion Possible?** was originally published as "Afterthoughts" in *Science and Religion: Are They Compatible?* (Amherst, NY: Prometheus Books, 2003), pp. 351–59.

Chapter 4. **Conviction and Commitment** is excerpted from *Eupraxsophy: Living without Religion* (Amherst, NY: Prometheus Books, 1989), pp. 93–118.

Chapter 5. **The Practice of Reflective Ethical Inquiry** is excerpted from "Skepticism and Ethical Inquiry," originally published in *The New Skepticism: Inquiry and Reliable Knowledge* (Amherst, NY: Prometheus Books, 1992), pp. 277–301.

ACKNOWLEDGMENTS

Chapter 6. **The Valuational Base I:** *The Common Moral Decencies* was originally published in *Forbidden Fruit: The Ethics of Secularism* (Amherst, NY: Prometheus Books, 2008), pp. 93–131.

Chapter 7. **The Valuational Base II:** *The Ethics of Excellence* was originally published in *Forbidden Fruit: The Ethics of Secularism* (Amherst, NY: Prometheus Books, 2008), pp. 133–70.

Chapter 8. **Love and Friendship** is excerpted from *Exuberance: A Philosophy of Happiness* (Amherst, NY: Prometheus Books, 1977), pp. 119–31.

Chapter 9. **Caring** is excerpted from *The Courage to Become: The Virtues of Humanism* (Westport, CT: Praeger, 1997), pp. 79–107.

Chapter 10. **Educating the Whole Person: The Liberating Arts** was originally published in *The Philosophy of the Curriculum: The Need for General Education* (Amherst, NY: Prometheus Books, 1975).

Chapter 11. **Eupraxsophy: The Unification of Knowledge** was originally published in *The New Skepticism: Inquiry and Reliable Knowledge* (Amherst, NY: Prometheus Books, 1992), pp. 331–44.

Chapter 12. **The Eupraxsophy of Hope** was originally published in *Free Inquiry* 30, no. 2 (February/March 2010).

Chapter 13. **Meaning and Transcendence** was originally published in *The Transcendental Temptation: A Critique of Religion and the Paranormal* (Amherst, NY: Prometheus Books, 1986), pp. 17–26.

ACKNOWLEDGMENTS

Chapter 14. **The Human Condition** was originally published in *Decision and the Condition of Man* (Seattle: University of Washington Press, 1965), pp. 270–88.

Afterword. **From Philosophy to Eupraxsophy** is excerpted with modifications from "A Response to Critics and Commentators," published in *Promethean Love: Paul Kurtz and the Humanistic Perspective on Love*, edited by Timothy J. Madigan (Newcastle: Cambridge Scholars, 2006).

UP FROM ATHEISM

The main thrust of humanism is not to simply espouse the negative—
what we do *not* believe in—but what we *do*. We should not begin with
atheism or anti-supernaturalism but with humanism. I am a *secular*
humanist because I am not religious. I draw my inspiration not from
religion or spirituality but from science, ethics, philosophy, and the
arts. I call it *eupraxsophy*.

—Paul Kurtz, "The Convictions of a Secular Humanist,"
in *Multi-Secularism: A New Agenda* (2010)

I

The volume you hold in your hands is intended for the general reader. It
conveniently gathers together many of Paul Kurtz's key writings about
the theory and practice of *eupraxsophy* with a special concentration on
secular ethics. The concept of eupraxsophy was first introduced by Paul
Kurtz in 1988 to characterize a nonreligious (that is, humanistic and
naturalistic) approach to life. Derived from three Greek roots, *eu*
("good," "well"), *praxis* ("practice," "conduct"), and *sophia* ("wisdom"),
eupraxsophy (*yoo-PRAX-so-fee*) literally means "good practice and
wisdom." It is an authentic, comprehensive, *secular* outlook able to provide illumination, meaning, and direction to the art of living. Historically, the concept of eupraxsophy owes much to Aristotle's notion of

phronesis (practical deliberation and wisdom). Later, Schopenhauer would write about the importance of eudæmonology, an "art of ordering our lives so as to obtain the greatest amount of pleasure and success ... teach[ing] us how to live a happy existence." Eupraxsophy hearkens back to these precursors but, as we will see, moves beyond them in important ways. It draws out the implications of the scientific worldview—and specifically the scientific temper—for the individual and society. Its aim is distinctly *moral*; it addresses a paramount issue for those who have outgrown, or perhaps never had, belief in the supernatural. Namely, it asks, how do we set about the task of carving out for ourselves a meaningful and rich life in a natural world where, in the last analysis, each of us has only one chance to get it right?

The publication of this volume is especially timely. The influential Canadian philosopher Charles Taylor has written a much-discussed tome about our "secular age."[1] A group of authors known as "the new atheists" (most notably, Sam Harris, Richard Dawkins, Daniel Dennett, and Christopher Hitchens) have each published provocative and commercially successful books proffering an uncompromising critique of religion.[2] In September of 2010, physicist Stephen Hawking made international headlines when an excerpt from his new book *The Grand Design* (coauthored with Leonard Miodinow) appeared in the *Times of London*. In the excerpt, Hawking announced with aplomb that "the Big Bang was the result of the inevitable laws of physics and did not need God to spark the creation of the Universe," adding, "it is not necessary to invoke God to light the blue touch paper and set the Universe going."[3] It seems, as was recently reported by Religion News Service, that a significant number of women and men are expressing a "growing interest in secularism—the rejection of religion in public, and sometimes private, life—both in the U.S. and around the world."[4] This trend seems to be growing.[5]

Secularization, however, presents new challenges, for certain questions remain as absorbing and fundamental as ever. Individuals will continue to hunger for narratives of meaning, value, and purpose; they will continue to yearn for an overall sense of how things hang together—a broad interpretation of existence by which they can orient themselves in the world. These large-scale, existential issues demand a response. Being intrinsically *human* issues, they remain long after the God of theism has been dispatched by science and reason. Called "the things that matter most" by poets, theologians, and moralists since the foundation of human culture, these issues have been seen by many to be the exclusive domain of religion or a "higher" spirituality, yet, as we shall see, this need not be the case.

Philosopher of science Philip Kitcher (author of *Living with Darwin*) has written with great perspicacity:

> Each of us needs an account of ourselves and what is valuable, something towards which we can steer and by which we can live. . . . Secular thought shies away from the tradition question, raised by the Greeks at the dawn of philosophy, of what makes human lives, finite though they are, significant and worthwhile. . . . No advocacy of disbelief, however eloquent, will work the secular revolution until [certain] facts are acknowledged. The temporary eradication of superstition, unaccompanied by attention to the functions religion serves, creates a vacuum into which the crudest forms of literalist mythology can easily intrude themselves. . . . Secular humanism needs not only to be secular, but also to be humane. . . . To achieve this, we must go beyond disbelief.[6]

Eupraxsophy matters because it responds to these pressing challenges in a compelling way that resonates both with the findings of the sciences and the distinctly human aspiration to live with a sense of meaning and value. It offers a conceptual framework for thinking comprehensively about our lives in a secular, naturalistic way. Drawing from philosophy, science, and ethics, eupraxsophy provides a coherent picture of the world and the place of the human species within it. It represents a living, breathing set of convictions about the cosmos, the acquisition of reliable knowledge, and the construction (and maintenance) of human values in a natural world. In presenting a cohesive moral vision, it provides an indispensable resource—a North Star, if you will—by which we can steer as we live, act, and work. Hence, the function of eupraxsophy is essentially *liberative* and *life-enhancing*.

Written with eloquence and scope, the incisive essays in this book show how Kurtz's brand of eupraxsophic humanism moves above and beyond the new atheism by articulating a genuine and constructive ethical alternative to religion—one that is able to deal effectively with the complexities inherent in our increasingly fragmented secular age.

II

Chapter 1, "Humanism as a Eupraxsophy," provides an overview of the four essential components of eupraxsophy. These correspond with the traditional branches of philosophy; namely, epistemology (method of inquiry), metaphysics (cosmic worldview), ethics (life stance), and political theory (social polity). This chapter begins with its foundational commitment to scientific inquiry (or what Kurtz calls more generically "critical intelligence") as the preeminent technology that humans have to not only generate knowledge but to aid in practical problem solving, as well. This *method of inquiry* is the backbone of Kurtz's eupraxsophy.

It serves as a practical starting point, as it supplies the conceptual tool with which we investigate and interrogate nature with the aim of developing a systematic understanding of the fundamental structures of reality.[7] Second, the systematic organization and unification of scientific knowledge across disciplines yields an ever-expanding, ever-evolving *cosmic worldview*.[8] Third, the *application* of this stock of knowledge—along with the accumulated wisdom of long and edifying experience—informs the development of the humanist *life stance*, or set of principles and values, by which life may be guided. This leads to the fourth component of eupraxsophy, its *social polity*, or set of social values. This entails a stalwart commitment to the principal ideals of modernity—freedom, democracy, and social justice. Like a progressive series of steps, each component of eupraxsophy springs forth from, and builds on, the previous one. Hence, our *cosmic worldview* is a product of the most reliable knowledge drawn from previous scientific inquiries into the nature of nature—physical and human. This *scientific wisdom* is then consciously combined with the best *philosophical wisdom* in order to formulate concrete recommendations concerning the good life and the good society (our *life stance* and *social polity*). The cord binding all these components together is known as *naturalism*. This *synergistic relationship* between eupraxsophy and naturalism is examined in chapter 2. Chapter 3 is a meditation on a question of perennial significance: Can scientific naturalism, insofar as it undermines theism, provide an alternative dramatic, poetic rendering of the human condition, offering hope and promise? This is answered (and demonstrated) affirmatively in chapter 4, "Conviction and Commitment."

Chapters 5 through 7 constitute the centerpiece of Kurtz's normative ethical vision.[9] Central to Kurtz's form of ethical know-how is the practice of reflective *ethical inquiry* (chapter 5). Here we utilize reason and critical intelligence, in a way analogous to those methods found in the sciences, to negotiate the complexities inherent in life, while remaining especially sensitive to the consequences of our choices. This requires an educated and finely tuned moral imagination. While rejecting ethical systems based on religious absolutism, it is important to note that Kurtz has consistently been equally as critical of *ethical nihilism*, the idea that in the final analysis ethical choices are nothing more than the expression of subjective whim or taste. Accordingly, Kurtz has delineated a *valuational base*, a body of certain objective standards and principles that, in many ways, constitute the very bedrock on which civilization is built. These are the *common moral decencies* (chapter 6) and *ethical excellencies* (chapter 7), and they have been tested and vindicated in the crucible of human experience. Indeed, these touchstones may be called the *fruits* of refined and chastened experience. Now, these are not absolute; they are always open to revision and modification in the light of actual experience or circumstance. Still, they anchor ethical inquiry and fortify practical effort, equipping us with map and compass as we traverse the often rugged terrain of the moral life.

The discussion turns next in chapters 8 and 9 to the importance of an altruistic regard for others. This is achieved principally through love and friendship and caring and compassion.

Chapters 13 and 14, "Meaning and Transcendence" and "The Human Condition," take a distinctly existential turn as Kurtz grapples boldly, yet calmly, with those questions of great gravity and enduring significance that, for many, prompt the beginnings of the spiritual impulse, leading them to the altar of religion in search of satisfactory answers. This is Kurtz at his eupraxsophic best, elucidating a penetrating assessment of the human situation. Here we come face-to-face with those topics of profound import that concern what the philosopher George

Santayana has called the chief issue; namely, "the relation of man and of his spirit to the universe." The term "spirit" is taken here in its naturalistic sense to mean a moral stance toward life in the world that emanates from the innermost core of our being.[10] Kurtz's reflections in "The Human Condition" are especially kaleidoscopic, as he manages a vantage point from both inside and outside the sphere of human values, opening up shifting, yet equally valid, points of reference between the foreground and background of existence while plumbing the contradictions and uncertainties that confront us all in the game of life.

This volume's afterword, "From Philosophy to Eupraxsophy," is published here for a general audience for the first time. This special autobiographical essay is a summing up of Kurtz's own intellectual development as he considers the consequential ideas and events that have animated his lengthy career as a philosopher, public intellectual, and builder of humanist institutions. Beginning with an intense interest in metaethics (the concern with how to state ethical questions), Kurtz soon became disenchanted with the sterility and narrowness with which professional philosophy was being practiced in the academy, due largely to the hegemonic influence of analytic philosophy. For Kurtz, these trends ignored—and were often irrelevant to—the genuine intellectual problems pertaining to meaning and human practice. (Indeed, one can extend this criticism to atheism in the abstract, as it is being promulgated by some today.) Undeterred, Kurtz turned to the project of developing and enunciating normative ethical principles that could be applied artfully and wisely to live as lived. One must descend from the ivory tower and be prepared to defend normative propositions in the public square. Kurtz writes: "I was convinced that it was important to move from philosophy (the love of wisdom) to *eupraxsophy* (the practice of wisdom). . . . I have maintained that we can bring the best philosophical and ethical wisdom and scientific knowledge to deal with the problems of practice." Here, the influence of Kurtz's mentor Sidney Hook is especially felt. And like Hook, Kurtz has been a fierce defender of humanist values, institutionalizing ideas in a world where the winds of doctrine are constantly changing and one never knows when the forces of unreason will assert themselves anew, leading us to re-enter battles we thought had been won long ago. Kurtz's elegant conception of his role as a eupraxsopher in this afterword exemplifies the central thrust of his passionate commitments: "We need to 'minister to the soul.' . . . As an alternative to the medicine men of the past, gurus and spiritualists, soothsayers, rabbis, mullahs, and priests, we need to demonstrate that life can be lived and lived well without the illusions of religiosity, that it can be rich with significance and overflowing with joy, and that concrete choices can be made wisely and satisfactorily." Those of us fortunate enough to have worked side by side with Kurtz on this task can attest to his indefatigable spirit and drive. For Kurtz, ideas have consequences; but for him, more important *is what you do in the service of those ideas.*

Now in his eighth decade, Kurtz remains intellectually vital. In 2010, he drafted the *Neo-Humanist Statement of Secular Principles and Values*, a blueprint for "a way forward in the study and application of human values at a global level."[11] At around this same time, Kurtz founded the Institute for Science and Human Values, an organization committed to advancing (and preserving!) the vision articulated not only in the *Neo-Humanist Statement* but in this volume as well.

Ralph Waldo Emerson wrote that "the office of the scholar is to cheer, to raise, and to guide men by showing them the facts amid appearances." The Sage of Concord's epigrammatic brilliance is most appropriate here, as it captures the essential force and spirit of Kurtz's singular contribution to our ongoing need for wisdom in contingent life. For in articulating a vision that fuses head and heart, Kurtz has illuminated a path whereby we can summon our powers of critical and creative intelligence and, over time, aided by the appropriation of the best scientific and philosophical knowledge, come to carve out a personal destiny marked by the care, shape, and significance associated with a work of art. The writings of Paul Kurtz are a welcome companion in this quest.

—Nathan Bupp

Chapter 1

HUMANISM AS A EUPRAXSOPHY

Many friends and foes of humanism maintain that it is a religion. I think that they are mistaken, but if humanism is not a religion, what is it? Unfortunately, there is no word in the English language adequate to describe it fully—though there are words in other languages that do. Humanism combines, as I will argue, a method of inquiry, a cosmic world view, a life stance, and a set of social values. The Dutch, for example, have the word *levensbeschouwing*, which can be translated as "reflection on, consideration of, or view of life." Dutch also has the adjective *levensovertuiging*, which is stronger than *levensbeschouwing* because *overtuiging* means "conviction." Thus there are no religious overtones. *Religion* in Dutch is *godsdienst*, which means "service to God." English has no such terminology.

Accordingly, I think we will have to coin a new term in order to distinguish nontheistic beliefs and practices from other systems of beliefs and practices, a term that could be used in many languages. The best approach is to combine Greek roots. I have come up with the term *eupraxsophy*, which means "good practical wisdom." *Eupraxsophy* is derived from the following roots: *eu-*, *praxis-*, and *sophia*. *Eu-* is a prefix which means "good," "well," "advantageous." It is combined in words such as *eudæmonia*, which means "well-being" or "happiness"; it is also used in *euthanasia, eulogy, euphoria*, etc. *Praxis* (or *prassein*) refers to "action, doing, or practice." *Eupraxia* means "right action" or "good conduct." The suffix *sophia* is derived from *sophos* ("wise") and means "wisdom." This suffix appears in the term *philosophy*, combining *philos* ("loving") and *sophia* ("wisdom") to mean "love of wisdom."

In its original sense, philosophy, as metaphysics or "the science of being," investigated the general principles and categories by which we can understand nature and interpret reality. The classical philosophers attempted to work out a system of nature in which certain principles were considered to be basic. Metaphysics has been in considerable disrepute in modern times, particularly in the hands of skeptical critics. At the very least, metaphysics analyzes and interprets the basic concepts of the sciences, attempts to make some sense out of them, and, if possible, to unify them. This is a very complex task today because of the continuing proliferation of new fields of learning and the enormous difficulty of any one mind being able to master the expanding corpus of knowledge.

Philosophical inquiry also focuses on epistemology, the theory of knowledge. It is concerned with questions of meaning, truth, the principles of valid inference, inductive and deductive logic. There are many other branches of philosophy, including logic, æsthetics, ethics, the philosophy of science, political and social philosophy, and the philosophy of religion; indeed, almost any field can be approached philosophically.

Synthetic philosophy attempts to offer universal or general principles and to develop an overall view, a cosmic perspective or *Weltanschauung*. This is sometimes called synoptic or speculative philosophy, but since the development of modern science in the sixteenth and seventeenth centuries, this approach has been seriously questioned on methodological grounds, for it cannot be done independently of science but only in relation to it. Nonetheless, philosophy, in this sense, is thinking about generalities; it is concerned with root questions and cosmic coherence. Analytic and critical philosophy, on the other hand, are far more modest in scope. Analytic philosophy is concerned with understanding the nature of meaning and truth, and in defining and analyzing the key concepts within any particular field of inquiry. Critical philosophy is evaluative; it strives for clarity, but it also seeks to appraise the validity of truth claims.

These activities are primarily intellectual in purpose, and they are neutral in regard to their practical consequences. The Greeks distinguished contemplative from practical wisdom. Philosophy, as the love of wisdom, begins primarily in the theoretical or contemplative mode. There is another branch of normative philosophy, however, that strives for practical wisdom in ethics and politics. Here, classical philosophy sought to provide some guidance for the good life and the just society. Aristotle maintained in the *Nicomachean Ethics* that ethics has practical import and that we should study it in order to live well. He held that the development of character and virtue and the exercise of practical wisdom would contribute to the achievement of happiness. Many ethical philosophers, however, have focused primarily on the meta-analysis of concepts such as "good," "bad," "virtue," "value," "justice," etc. This was expanded in latter-day Kantian philosophy to the definitions of "right," "wrong," "obligation," "responsibility," etc. Whether or not these terms can be defined has been hotly debated down to the present;[1] objectivists believe that they can be defined, but there is a skeptical tradition which denies their definability. Be that as it may, classical ethics always had a normative purpose.

A basic distinction can be made between *customary morality*, which refers to the moral conceptions that already prevail in a given cultural group, and *ethics*, which involves a reflective and critical component. Today, many philosophers concerned with ethics emphasize the need for ethical rationality—but virtually for its own sake; and many eschew making any concrete recommendations beyond this in dealing with problems that arise in customary morality. This is particularly true in universities and colleges, where philosophy is taught as an academic discipline, where philosophers do philosophical research and publish their disquisitions in scholarly journals, and where philosophy teachers have no clearly identifiable positions. They consider their primary pedagogical method to be the presentation of alternative philosophical theories and do not attempt to inculcate a set of beliefs or values; that is, they do not seek to persuade their students or the general public to accept their philosophical outlook. Since their task is pure inquiry, similar to that of other disciplines, such as history and the natural and social sciences, they can safely retreat into splendid isolation in an ivory tower—philosophers *qua* philosophers—and do not have to vindicate their personal positions. The virtue of this form of philosophy is that the professor imparts a love of wisdom and the skills of critical thinking without imposing his or her own biases on the student. The professor does not wish to indoctrinate or propagandize for a particular cosmic outlook. He or she wants to be "objective"; he may even be fearful of reprisals from those who support the conventional wisdom of the day. Yet this kind of philosophy does not satisfy the deeper queries of students and ordinary men and women. It presents no world view; it does not defend a theory of meaning and truth; nor does it seek to persuade others of the comparative reasonableness of the philosopher's own considered normative or social ideology. Philosophy, as the love of wisdom, aside from being committed to fair-minded and objective critical analysis, must be *neutral*. It can take no position; it can draw no normative conclusions from its formal analyses. It is largely a cognitive enterprise; it involves no attitudinal or emotive component. Nor does it seek to arouse conviction or inspire commitment.

How far philosophy has come from the Socratic vision of the good life! For Socrates, philosophy had direct relevance to how we should live. The unexamined life is not worth living, he averred, and he was even willing to die for his convictions. Spinoza's *Ethics* seems to have expressed both a philosophy and a eupraxsophy, at least implicitly. We might even say that many or most philosophical systems implicitly had a pragmatic function and that their task was to provide an alternative to religion and a guide to ethics and politics. Contemplative wisdom was often a mask for deeper utilitarian purposes. Marx clearly marked a break with the contemplative mode of philosophy, particularly when he said that the task of philosophy was not simply to interpret the world but also to *change* it! Philosophy in this sense has momentous significance—as it did for Nietzsche, Schopenhauer, Russell, Sartre, Dewey, and others. Alas, today it has become wedded to the academy and corrupted by narrow specialization. Philosophy has lost out to religion and ideology, which in competition for the souls of men and women now rule the day. That is why we need to take new directions and to carve out a new approach.

Eupraxsophy differs from antiseptically neutral philosophy in that it enters consciously and forthrightly into the marketplace where ideas contend. Unlike pure philosophy, it is not simply the *love* of wisdom, though this is surely implied by it, but also the *practice* of wisdom. By that I do not mean that ethicists should not be interested in developing the capacity for critical ethical judgment or practical wisdom. That is an eminent goal. But eupraxsophy goes further than that, for it provides a coherent, ethical life stance. Moreover, it presents a cosmic theory of reality that seems reasonable at a particular point in history in the light of the best knowledge of the day. Humanist eupraxsophy defends a set of criteria governing the testing of truth claims. It also advocates an ethical posture. And it is committed implicitly or explicitly to a set of political ideals. Eupraxsophy combines both a *Weltanschauung* and a philosophy of living. But it takes us one step further by means of commitment; based upon cognition, it is fused with passion. It involves the application of wisdom to the conduct of life.

Non-eupraxsophic philosophies are unwilling to affirm this conviction. They examine all sides of a question, see the limits and pitfalls of each, but are unwilling to take a stand on any. As I have said, this has some merit; for the open mind must recognize that it may be mistaken and that views may have to be modified in the light of new arguments or evidence. Thus, one needs to be skeptical—but not at the price of forfeiting all convictions. The *eupraxsopher* does make a choice—the most reasonable one in light of the available evidence—and this enables one to act. After all, theologians, politicians, generals, engineers, businessmen, lawyers, doctors, artists, poets, and plain men and women have beliefs, and they act. Why deny this right to the informed philosopher-eupraxsopher? Surely, however, one's beliefs should be based upon reason, critical intelligence, and wisdom. This is what the suffix *sophy* refers to. Wisdom in the broad sense includes not only philosophical and practical judgment, but also scientific understanding.

Let us turn to *Webster's Dictionary* for a definition of *sophia* or *wisdom*:

> 1. The quality of being wise; ability to judge soundly and deal sagaciously with facts, especially as they relate to life and conduct; knowledge, with the capacity to make due use of it; perception of the best ends and the best means; discernment and judgment; discretion; sagacity. 2. Scientific or philosophical knowledge.

Explicit in this definition is a scientific component, for wisdom includes the best scientific knowledge drawn from research and scholarship in the various fields of inquiry. Unfortunately, the various scientific specialists often feel qualified to judge only matters within their own areas of competence, leaving out the broader questions that have a direct bearing on life. There is a crisis in modern science, for the specialties are growing exponentially, with many specialists feeling that they can talk only to those within their own disciplines. Science thus has become fragmented. Who is able to cross the boundary lines and draw meta-inferences about nature, the human species, society, or life in general? The eupraxsopher deems it his mission to do so.

Theoretical scientific research is morally neutral. The scientist is interested in developing causal hypotheses and theories that can be verified by the evidence. Scientists describe or explain how the subject under study behaves, without evaluating it normatively. There is, of course, a pragmatic element to science, particularly the applied sciences; for we constantly seek to apply our scientific know-how to practical technology. Moreover, the scientist presupposes epistemological criteria that govern his process of inquiry. He is committed to a set of values; truth, clarity, consistency, rationality, objectivity. But the scientist *qua* scientist does not go beyond that, and he restricts himself in the quest for knowledge to his specialized domain of inquiry.

Humanist eupraxsophy, on the other hand, attempts to draw philosophical implications of science to the life of man. It seeks to develop a cosmic perspective, based on the most reliable findings encountered on the frontiers of science. It recognizes the gaps in knowledge and the things we do not know that still need to be investigated. It is keenly aware of the need for fallibilism and agnosticism about what we do and do not know. Yet it boldly applies practical scientific wisdom to life.

Eupraxsophy, unlike philosophy or science, does not focus on one specialized field of knowledge; it seeks to understand the total impact of scientific knowledge on a person's life. Yet the areas of philosophy, science, and eupraxsophy are not rigid. Philosophers can assist scientists in interpreting their discoveries and relating them to other fields of inquiry, and in developing a broader point of view. Still, eupraxsophy moves beyond philosophy and science in seeking to present a coherent life view as the basis on which we are willing to act. It is the ground upon which we stand, the ultimate outlook that controls our view of reality.

Accordingly, the primary task of eupraxsophy is to understand nature and life and to draw concrete normative prescriptions from this knowledge. Eupraxsophy thus draws deeply from the wells of philosophy, ethics, and science. It involves at least a double focus: a cosmic perspective and a set of normative ideals by which we may live.

THE DEFINITION OF HUMANISM

Thus humanism is a eupraxsophy. But it is not unique; for there have been other eupraxsophies historically. In the Greek and Roman world, Epicureanism, Stoicism, and skepticism were eupraxsophies. Each had a metaphysical world view, each made concrete ethical recommendations about how to achieve the good life, and each had epistemological theories. There have been many other kinds of eupraxsophies: utilitarianism, Marxism, existentialism, pragmatism, perhaps even Confucianism and some forms of Buddhism; each contain various elements of eupraxsophy. Some of these schools, however, are concerned primarily with *eupraxia* (that is, with good practice) and they de-emphasize the *sophia*, the scientific and philosophic world view. Some, such as Marxism and utilitarianism, focus primarily on *social praxis*.

There are many variations of humanism: naturalistic, existential,

Marxist, pragmatic, and liberal. We may ask, what is distinctive about the eupraxsophy of modern-day secular humanism? I wish to propose a definition of humanism that is thoroughly secular. This definition is not arbitrary, since it classifies a set of propositions held by many scientists and philosophers who consider themselves to be humanists. Nonetheless, it involves a prescriptive recommendation about how to use the term *humanism*. Humanism includes at least four main characteristics: (1) it is a method of inquiry; (2) it presents a cosmic world view; (3) it contains a concrete set of ethical recommendations for the individual's life stance; and (4) it expresses a number of social and political ideals.

A METHOD OF INQUIRY

An essential characteristic of contemporary secular humanism is its commitment to a method of inquiry. This feature is so important that it may even be said to function as the basic principle of secular humanism. Questions concerning meaning and truth have been enduring ones in the history of philosophy, and they have come to the forefront since the growth of modern science. Epistemology is also pivotal to secular humanism.

Humanist epistemology may be defined first by what it opposes. It rejects the use of arbitrary authority to obfuscate meaning or to legislate truth. Throughout human history there have been persistent attempts by institutional authorities to do precisely that. The church and the state have been especially prone to define, codify, and enforce orthodoxy. The need for social order is such that humankind finds it useful or necessary to regulate conduct. Custom ensures some stability in social behavior and enables human beings to function with a clear understanding of expectations and of the acceptable parameters of civilized discourse and conduct. The rules of the game by which we live and work together are established—in constitutions, bylaws, contracts, laws, and regulations—and they enable us to fulfill our cooperative aims. It is one thing, however, to lay down the rules of conduct by law and to enforce them by sanction, leaving opportunities for them to be modified and revised in democratic societies. It is quite another to uphold unchanging orthodoxy of belief in the sciences, philosophy, literature, the arts, politics, morality, or religion and to seek to legislate acceptable modes of personal behavior. Here the appeal to authority is illegitimate, for it substitutes a conformist faith for intelligently grounded knowledge. Establishing orthodoxy in belief stifles discovery and blocks inquiry. Transmitting the fixed beliefs of an early age to future ones prevents bold new departures in thought. Even the most cherished beliefs so lovingly defended in time may become archaic; blatant falsehoods persist as prejudice encrusted by habits.

History is replete with pathetic attempts by past civilizations to enshrine their belief systems in perpetuity. Efforts to censor conflicting opinions have often led to violent social conflict. In worst-case scenarios such suppression degenerates into sheer tyranny over the human mind. Dictators, ecclesiastical princes, and vested oligarchs have tried to police the thoughts of everyone under their jurisdiction, using the Holy Inquisition, the Gestapo, or the NKVD to suppress dissent. In a weaker form, conformist pressures substitute public opinion or that of the leading authorities of the day for creative and independent inquiry. Abiding by conventional wisdom thus stifles new ideas. No one group can claim to have a monopoly on wisdom or virtue, and to proclaim one's fondest convictions as *obiter dicta* for everyone in the society is destined to fail. Even though power is the chief criterion for the perpetuation of a belief system, that is no guarantee of social stability, for the so-called authorities often disagree about truth. The reigning beliefs of one age may become the intransigent follies of the next. Thoughtless bigots wish to prevent any questioning of their revered articles of faith; they are fearful of change and challenge. Regrettably, all of the major religious orthodoxies historically have succumbed to the temptation to enforce their beliefs—when and where they had the power to do so—and to impose their practices upon the rest of society. Orthodoxies have allowed fanatic intolerance to prevail, and they have denied the right of those who disagree to voice their contrary faiths or dissenting opinions.

The same narrow mindset appears in powerful political and economic elites, who fear any challenge to their privileged positions and thus seek to enforce by law what they consider to be the only legitimate system of belief. They strain to exclude outsiders who threaten their hegemony by declaring them political heretics or religious infidels.

In religion, orthodox belief systems are rooted in ancient dogmas held to be so sacred that they are immune to objective examination. The claims made in the name of God are shrouded in privileged revelations received from on high. The claims to divine authority are shielded from critical scrutiny by popes, cardinals, bishops, rabbis, mullahs, gurus, and other defenders of the faith. In politics and economics dissident minorities are excluded from the corridors of power. There is no forum available for them, no opportunity to participate in open inquiry. Thus the so-called Higher Truth, so protected from investigation, lies beyond contest. A similar closed syndrome can be found in philosophy or science when it is held to be immune to free inquiry. Thomism, Calvinism, and Marxist-Leninism were considered official doctrines at various times in history by those who defended them in the name of an entrenched power elite. The same is true for Lysenkoism under Stalin or racist theories under the Nazis. In the battle for civil liberties in democratic societies political power has been wrested from repressive oligarchies. Unfortunately, the right to know has not been universally recognized as a basic human right in all societies, and there are wide areas—especially in religion and morality—that are still held to be immune to criticism.

The first principle of humanism is a commitment to free inquiry in every field of human endeavor. This means that any effort to prevent the free mind from exercising its right to pose questions and initiate inquiry is unwarranted.

But which methods of inquiry should be used? How do we evaluate truth claims? Philosophers have long debated the question "What is truth?" How we appraise knowledge claims depends on the subject matter under investigation, be it science, mathematics, philosophy, ethics, politics, economics, history, or the arts. Let it suffice for now to outline a minimal set of epistemological criteria that cuts across the various disciplines, without any lengthy explication in defense. I will focus on skepticism, the scientific method, and critical intelligence.

Skepticism is a vital methodological principle of inquiry. I refer not to negative or nihilistic skepticism, which rejects the very possibility of attaining reliable knowledge, but positive, selective skepticism. This principle of skepticism implies that the reliability of a hypothesis, theory, or belief is a function of the grounds, evidence, or reasons by which it is supported. If a claim is not justified by objective validation or verification, we ought to be cautious in holding fast to it. The amount of supporting evidence will vary with the subject under scrutiny.

Probabilism points to the degree of certainty by which we are willing to ascertain truth claims. We should not attribute to any belief absolute infallibility. We should be prepared to admit that we may be mistaken. Beliefs should be taken as hypotheses: they are tentative or hypothetical depending upon the degree of evidence or the validity of the arguments used to support them.

Fallibilism is a principle which indicates that even when a claim is thought to be well supported, we should nonetheless be prepared to modify our beliefs if new arguments or evidence arise in the future which show either that we were in error or that our truths were only partial and limited. This applies in fields of formal knowledge, such as mathematics, as much as to experimental domains of inquiry. The skeptic should have an open mind about all questions and not seek to close responsible inquiry in any field. If after investigation there is insufficient evidence, the skeptic may say that the claim is unlikely, improbable, or false, or if further investigation is possible, he may wish to suspend judgment and admit that he does not know. Agnosticism, in this respect, is a meaningful option. We should be prepared to exercise doubt about a wide range of belief claims which we have little expectation at present of resolving. Skepticism is thus an essential method used in science, technology, philosophy, religion, politics, morality, and ordinary life.

But the question may be asked: *Which* method should be used to warrant beliefs? What are the criteria of confirmation and validity? Without attempting to resolve this question fully here, let me suggest the following criteria:

First, we should appeal to *experience* in all areas in which it is pertinent to do so. By this I mean observation, evidence, facts, data—preferably involving some intersubjective grounds that can be replicated or certified. Purely subjective or private paths to truth need not be arbitrarily rejected, but, on the other hand, they are not admissible to the body of knowledge unless they can be reliably corroborated by others. This empirical test is fundamental. But if we are to draw any inferences from it then it must refer to experiential claims that are open to public scrutiny, not only in ascertaining whether they occurred but also in interpreting their likely causes.

Second, if an experience cannot be duplicated, there might be circumstantial evidence or at least *predictable* results by which we can evaluate its adequacy. In other words, our beliefs are forms of behavior, and they can be tested—at least in part—by their observed consequences. This is an experimental criterion used not only in laboratories but also in everyday life when we appraise beliefs not simply by what people say but by what they do.

Third, we use a *rational* test of deductive coherence, judging our theories or beliefs by relation to those we have already accepted as reliable. Hypotheses and theories cannot be viewed in isolation from other knowledge we believe to be true. They are logically consistent or inconsistent with it, and are judged by the criterion of validity. We can see this test at work not only in mathematical, logical, and formal systems but also in science and ordinary affairs when we test beliefs by their internal consistency.

The preceding criteria are used most explicitly in the sciences, where hypothetical-deductive methods prevail and where we formulate hypotheses and test them by their experimental adequacy and logical coherence. Science is not a method of knowing available only to an esoteric coterie of experts; similar standards of reasoning are employed in common everyday life when we are faced with problems and wish to resolve practical questions.

The terms *reason, rationality*, and *reasonableness* have sometimes been used to describe the general methodology that humanists have advocated: that is, we should test truth claims objectively as far as we can, and if claims cannot pass the tests of reason (broadly conceived to include experience and rationality), we should either reject them or suspend judgment. We face an epistemological crisis today, for with the increasing specialization of knowledge, experts often restrict the use of objective methods of inquiry to their own fields of competency and are unwilling to extend reason to other areas of human knowledge. What is at issue here is whether we can apply the powers of reason so that they will have some influence on the totality of beliefs.

Perhaps the best terminology to describe objectivity in testing truth claims is *critical intelligence*. This means that we must use our powers of critical analysis and observation to evaluate carefully questions of belief. We first need to define what is at stake. Here clarity in meaning is essential. We need to be clear about what we wish to know and what is at issue. We need to ask: What alternative explanations are offered? We formulate hypotheses and develop beliefs that help solve our puzzlement. The salient point is that only objective evidence and reasons will suffice to evaluate alternative hypotheses.

What is distinctive about humanism as a eupraxsophy is that *it wishes to extend the methods of objective inquiry to all areas of life, including religious, philosophical, ethical, and political concerns that are often left unexamined.* There has been extensive research into specialized areas of scientific knowledge, particularly since technological discoveries have provided an enormous boon to human welfare; however, powerful forces have often distrusted and indeed prevented free inquiry into the foundations of social, moral, and religious systems. The crux of the matter is whether objective methods of inquiry can be applied to these vital areas of human concern. If critical intelligence were to supplant blind appeals to authority, custom, faith, or subjectivity, it could radically transform society. Free thought can be threatening to the privileged bastions of the status quo.

No doubt a basic point of contention between humanism and

theism is precisely here: the application of scientific methods, rationalism, and critical intelligence to evaluate transcendental claims. The critics of humanism maintain that it excludes, almost by definition, claims to a transcendental realm. This, I submit, is not the case; for the humanist is willing to examine any responsible claim to truth. The burden of proof, however, rests with the believer to specify clearly the conditions under which such beliefs may be falsified. The humanist requests that whatever is under examination be carefully defined. God-talk is generally vague, ambiguous, even unintelligible. The humanist next wishes to know how the believer would justify its truth. If a meaningful claim is introduced, it needs to be corroborated. This means that private, mystical, or subjective claims to revelation or divine presence or mere declarations by ecclesiastical authorities that something is true are inadmissible unless they can be intersubjectively confirmed. We cannot exclude on *a priori* grounds any insights derived from literature, poetry, or the arts. These express enduring human interests. We only ask that they be analyzed carefully and tested objectively. Æsthetic experience is a rich part of human experience, and it may provide a wealth of insight and inspiration. Any knowledge about the world drawn from these sources, however, requires careful evaluation.

The humanist is open to the subtle nuances of human experience, but he insists that we use our powers of critical judgment to appraise the claims to truth. In this sense, he draws upon the tested knowledge and the best available wisdom of the day. He will accept the claims of others—even if he has not personally scrutinized each of these claims—but only if he is assured that those claims have been warranted by objective methods, and that if he or someone else had the time, energy, and training he could scrutinize the procedures used to corroborate the findings. The methods of critical intelligence apply not only to descriptive truth claims, where we seek to describe and explain natural processes, but also to normative judgments, where we formulate eupraxic recommendations in the various domains of human action.

A COSMIC WORLD VIEW

Humanist eupraxsophy does not simply assert a method of inquiry based upon the methods of science; it also seeks to use the sciences to interpret the cosmos and the place of the human species within it. The humanist thus attempts to make some kind of generalized sense of reality. Speculative metaphysics is in disrepute today, and rightly so if it seeks to derive universal principles about reality from purely intuitive or metaphorical methods. The primary source for obtaining knowledge about nature should be human experience. It is within the various disciplines of scientific research and scholarship that reliable hypotheses and theories are elaborated and tested. If this is the case, then any comprehensive view of nature must draw heavily upon the scientific understanding of the day. Since science is a rapidly expanding body of knowledge, there are ongoing modifications of principles, hypotheses, and theories. There may at times be fundamental shifts in outlook, in which long-standing paradigms are altered, as for example, the fundamental transformation of Newtonian science by relativity theory and quantum mechanics. We note also the basic changes that have occurred in genetics, biology, psychology, the social sciences, and other fields of research in the twentieth century. There are times when we build up and elaborate a body of knowledge by a process of accumulation and addition. At other times there may be radical disruptions: novel theories may be introduced and tested, and they may fundamentally alter the prevailing outlook. One must be prepared to change a cosmic perspective in the light of new data and theories. We must be tentative in our formulations and prepared to revise theories in the light of new discoveries.

Unfortunately, scientists in specialized disciplines are often unaware of developments in other fields, and they may be unwilling or unable to relate their findings to domains of knowledge outside their competence or to develop a cosmic view. This is where philosophy enters: the philosopher should interpret the knowledge of one discipline and relate it to other fields. Philosophy, by definition, is general, for it is concerned with finding common methods, principles, postulates, axioms, assumptions, concepts, and generalizations used in a wide range of fields. Here I refer to the philosophy of science and to the methods of analysis and generalization by which it interprets the various sciences.

The great philosophers have always attempted to do this. Aristotle's *Metaphysics* provided a critical interpretation of the key concepts and categories underlying our knowledge of nature. Similarly, Descartes, Leibniz, Hume, Kant, Russell, Dewey, Whitehead, and others reflected upon and attempted to interpret the sciences of their day. We need to do the same today, though it may be far more difficult than in previous ages because of the immense proliferation of the sciences; it is difficult for any one mind to sum up the enormous bodies of specialties in some sort of interrelated whole. If we cannot as yet succeed in this ambitious venture, at the very least we can try in a more modest way. Using physics, astronomy, and the natural sciences, we can develop some cosmologies that explain the expanding universe. Using biology and genetics we can try to interpret the evolution of life. We can use psychology to understand human behavior, and we can draw upon anthropology, sociology, and the other social sciences to develop appropriate theories about socio-cultural phenomena. This is an ongoing quest. We do not have a comprehensive theory of the universe at present. Nonetheless we do have integrated pictures of nature that are based on the sciences.[2]

What does humanist eupraxsophy tell us about the cosmos? Let us approach the question at first by negative definition, by indicating what is unlikely. There is insufficient evidence for the claim that there is a divine creator who has brought the universe into being by an act of will. The invoking of God as a cause of everything that is, is mere *postulation*, without sufficient evidence or proof. It is a leap outside nature. The concept of a transcendent supernatural being is unintelligible; the idea of a First Cause, itself uncaused, is contradictory. Even if the Big Bang theory in astronomy is useful in explaining the rapidly receding and expanding universe, this does not provide support for the claim that there was a Being who existed coterminous or antecedent to this explosion. The Big Bang may be the result of a random quantum fluctuation, not an intelligent plan.

To read into such a cosmological principle selective human qualities—intelligence, perfection, or personhood—is unwarranted. The universe does not manifest design; there is apparent regularity and order, but chance and conflict, chaos and disorder are also present. To describe the entire universe as good is an anthropomorphic rendering of nature to fit one's moral bias. If there is apparent good in the universe, there would also have to be apparent evil, at least from the standpoint of sentient beings, who at times devour one another in the struggle for survival or who encounter natural disasters that destroy them. If so, how can we reconcile evil with a provident deity? Theists are so overcome by the tragic character of human finitude that they are willing to project their deepest longings into a divine mind, and this enables them to transcend nothingness. For the theist the universe involves some teleological conception of salvation. Man, in some way, is at the center of creation;

for God is endowed by man with human qualities, especially with a compassionate concern for our plight. God will save us if only we will devote ourselves completely to adoring Him, accept on the basis of faith that which passeth all human understanding, and obey His moral commandments as interpreted by His self-proclaimed emissaries on earth.

Much of the anthropomorphic character of the deity is derived from ancient texts held to be sacred and to have been revealed by God to specially appointed individuals. The Bible predicates the intervention of the Holy Ghost in history. Yet scientific and scholarly biblical criticism has made it abundantly clear that the Bible is a human document, a thousand-year-old record of the experiences of primitive nomadic and agricultural tribes living on the eastern shore of the Mediterranean. There is no evidence that Yahweh spoke to Abraham, Moses, Joseph, or any of the Old Testament prophets. The biblical accounts of their experiences are the records of Hebrew national existence, seeking to sustain itself by the myth of the "chosen people." These books have not been empirically validated; they express an ancient world view and the moral conceptions of a prescientific culture that invoked deities to sanctify its ideological aspirations.

The New Testament presents the incredible tale of Jesus, a man of whom we have very little historical knowledge. Obviously this is not an objective historical account. The "divinity" of Jesus has never been adequately demonstrated. Yet powerful churches have sought to inculcate the mythic story and to suppress dissent. The tales of Jesus' life and ministry expressed in the Four Gospels and the letters of Paul were written twenty to seventy years after his death. They are riddled with the contradictions implicit in an oral tradition. Defended by propagandists for a new mystery religion, the biblical accounts are hardly to be taken as dispassionate historical evidence for Jesus' divine origin. The tales of the so-called miracles and faith healings of Jesus are based on uncorroborated testimony by an unsophisticated people who were easily deceived. That the Jesus myth was elaborated by later generations and was eventually promulgated by powerful church institutions that dominated Europe for almost two millennia and still have inordinate influence on large sectors of the globe is evidence for the presence of a transcendental temptation within the human heart, which is ever ready to seize upon any shred of hope for an afterlife.

Similar skeptical criticism may be leveled against other supernatural religions. Islam is a religion based on the alleged revelations to Muhammad, received from on high through the archangel Gabriel, at first in caves north of Mecca and later in various other places. Careful reading of the literature about the origins of the Koran enables us to give alternative naturalistic explanations of Muhammad's ministry. He may have suffered from some form of epilepsy, which explains his trance states or swoons. He was able to convince others of his divine calling, and he used this ploy to achieve power. All of this is testimony to the gullibility of human beings and their willingness to abandon acceptable standards of rationality when they are confronted with claims to a Higher Truth. The same thing can be noted of the legions of saints, prophets, gurus, and shamans throughout history who have proclaimed divine revelations and have used their claims to delude and influence their followers.

Basic to the monotheistic approach is the belief in an afterlife. Is it possible for a "soul" to survive the death of the body? Jewish, Christian, and Muslim adherents fervently believe in the immortality of the soul, and Hindus, in its reincarnation from previous existences.

Unfortunately, the most resolute and objective investigations of claims of survival have shown them to be without empirical corroboration. Psychical researchers, parapsychologists, and paranormal investigators, for over a century, have produced reports of ghosts, spirits, apparitions, and poltergeists, but there is insufficient data to support the reality of discarnate existence, despite the legions of spiritualists, trance channelers, and past-life regressors who claim to be in touch with an unseen realm of spiritual reality. Although our fondest hopes and desires may *demand* life before birth or after death, the evidence points in the other direction. Even if it could be proved that something briefly survives the death of the biological body, there is no evidence of an eternal state of existence or of a blessed union with God. The evidence for survival is based on wishful thinking and is totally inconclusive. Death seems to be the natural state of all life forms, even though modern medical science and technology are able to ward off disease and prolong life. Humanism is thus skeptical about the entire drama of the theistic universe: that God exists and that we can achieve salvation in an afterlife.

But what picture of the universe does humanism provide as a substitute? Perhaps not one that slakes the existential yearnings of the desperate soul, but one that is more in accordance with the world as uncovered by science. What we have today is an open-ended universe, perhaps ragged at the edges with many gaps in our knowledge, but it is a picture supported by the best available evidence. At the present stage of human knowledge, the following general propositions seem true:

Objects or events within the universe have material explanations. All objects or events encountered have a physical character. Matter, mass, and energy may, however, be organized on various levels, ranging from the minutest microparticles on the subatomic level in fields of energy to gigantic objects such as planets, moons, comets, stars, quasars, and galaxies.

We encounter within the universe order and regularity on the one hand and chaos and random fluctuations on the other. Objects and events within the universe seem to be evolving. Change is an enduring trait of existing things. The cosmos as we presently understand it is something on the order of ten to twenty billion years old; it is expanding from what seems to have been a huge explosion. In any case, our planet is only one satellite of a minor star in the Milky Way, which is merely one galaxy among billions in the vast universe. What preceded the Big Bang, the physicists are not yet able to explain, and what will be the end of the universe—a whimper or a big crunch as matter implodes—is also difficult to say.

The universe is not, however, inanimate. There is some likelihood that organic life exists in other parts of the universe. The earliest known fossils uncovered on the earth are more than three billion years old. The most useful hypothesis to explain the diverse forms of life on our planet is that they evolved from common genetic material and split into diverse species. Evolution is a product of chance mutations, differential repro- duction, and adaptation. The human species most likely evolved over a period of several million years, exhibiting processes that follow similar patterns in other species. Distinctive to human primates is the large cere- bral cortex and the development of highly complex social systems in which tools are manipulated and signs and symbols function to enable linguistic communication. Genetics, biology, and psychology explain the emergence of human behavior and how and why we function the way we do. The social sciences are able to account for the development of the complex social institutions that help to satisfy basic human needs.

The study of culture demonstrates that individual members of the human species are physiochemical biological systems genetically predis- posed to certain forms of behavior, yet able to learn; they are influenced by environmental factors and capable of adaptive behavior. There seems to be a creative component to all forms of organic life—this is especially true of the human species. The human organism is able to respond to stimuli not only by conditioned behavior but by expressing creative impulses and demonstrating cognitive awareness. Humans, as products of nature, are able to understand the causes and conditions of their behavior, and they are able to intervene in the processes of nature and change them by discovery and invention. Formerly, the course of human evolution was largely unconscious and blind. We can now redirect to some extent by conscious effort the evolution of the species. Human behavior may be modified by imaginative effort and ingenuity. Human beings manifest rational choice. They are able to solve the problems encountered in living and thus, in part, to determine their futures. This is the message of the humanist outlook.

A LIFE STANCE

Men and women are capable of free choice. How much and to what extent has been hotly debated by philosophers, theologians, and scientists. Clearly, our behavior is limited or determined by the conditions under which we act. There are physiochemical, genetic, sociological, and psychological causes at work. Yet, in spite of these causal factors, we are consciously aware and we are capable of some teleonomic and preferential choice. Cognition can selectively direct our behavior.

"What ought I to choose?" and "How ought I to live?" are questions constantly raised. Are there any norms that humanism can offer to guide our conduct? Can we discover any enduring ends or goals? Is there a good which we ought to seek? Are there ethical standards of right and wrong? Is there a distinct set of ethical values and principles that may be said to be humanistic?

These are large questions, and I will only sketch in outline form what I consider to be the ethics of humanism. Its critics maintain that humanism lacks proper moral standards, that it is permissive, and that it allows subjective taste and caprice to prevail. Without belief in God, these critics assert, an ethic of responsibility is impossible.

These charges are unfounded. They emanate from an abysmal ignorance of the history of philosophical ethics, for philosophers have demonstrated the possibility of an autonomous ethic in which moral obligations emerge.

By arguing that ethics is autonomous, I simply mean that it is possible to make moral judgments of good, bad, right and wrong independently of one's ultimate foundations; i.e., there is a fund of common moral decencies that can be developed in human experience. Yet humanist ethics does have foundations, and these are its eupraxsophy, which in the last analysis completes it; for when questions of "ultimate" obligation or moral purpose arise the theist falls back on God, whereas the humanist is skeptical of that claim and places his ethics in a naturalistic evolutionary universe that is devoid of purpose. The humanist life stance thus has its grounding in nature and human nature.[3]

What are the essential ingredients of the ethics of humanism? The humanist life stance has a clearly developed conception of what "good practice" and "right conduct" are. The ethics of humanism may be said to begin when men and women eat of the "god-forbidden fruit" of the tree of knowledge of good and evil. Critical ethical inquiry enables us to transcend unquestioned customs, blind faith, or doctrinaire authority and to discover ethical values and principles. Humanists maintain that a higher state of moral development is reached when we go beyond unthinking habits to ethical wisdom. This includes an appreciation of the standards of excellence and an awareness of ethical principles and one's moral responsibilities to others.

Here is the humanist life stance: humanists do not look upward to a heaven for a promise of divine deliverance. They have their feet planted squarely on Mother Earth, yet they have the Promethean fortitude to employ art, science, sympathy, reason, and education to create a better world for themselves and their fellow human beings.

From the standpoint of the individual, the *summum bonum* is worthwhile happiness. This is not a passive quest for release from the world, but the pursuit of an active life of adventure and fulfillment. There are so many opportunities for creative enjoyment that every moment can be viewed as precious; all fit together to make up a full and exuberant life which makes the world a better place.

The ethics of humanism stands in sharp contrast to theistic doctrines. The end of the good life is to realize the worthiness of life itself, to fulfill our dreams and aspirations, plans and projects here and now. It involves not only a concern for one's own life (some self-interest is not wicked but essential) and the fulfillment of one's own desires, needs, and interests, but also a concern for the well-being of others, an altruistic regard for the communities where one interacts. And it extends eventually to all within the planetary society.

Humanist ethics does not rest on arbitrary caprice but on reflective choice. Ethical principles and values are rational: they are relative to human interests and needs. But this does not mean that they are subjective, nor are they beyond the domain of skeptical critical inquiry. Our principles and values can be tested by their consequences in action.

What is vital in humanist eupraxsophy is that humanists are not overwhelmed by the "tragic" character of the human condition; they must face death, sorrow, and suffering with courage. They have confidence in the ability of human beings to overcome alienation, solve the problems of living, and develop the capacity to share the goods of life and empathize with others. The theist has a degraded view of man, who, beset with original sin, is incapable of solving life's problems by himself and needs to look outside of the human realm for divine succor. The humanist accepts the fact that the human species has imperfections and limitations and that some things encountered in existence are beyond repair or redress. Yet even so, he believes the best posture is not to retreat into fear and trembling before injustice or the unknown forces of nature, but to exert his intelligence and courage to deal with these matters. It is only by a resolute appraisal of the human condition, based on reason and a cosmic world view, that the humanist's life stance seems most appropriate. He is unwilling to fall to his knees before the forces of nature but will stand on his own feet to battle evil and build a better life for himself and his fellow human beings. In other words, he expresses the highest heroic virtues of the Promethean spirit: audacity and nobility! And he has also developed moral sensibilities about the needs of others.

SOCIAL POLITY

Humanism is not concerned only with the life stance of the individual—however basic this is as an alternative to theism; it is also concerned with the achievement of the good society. The early Greek philosophers had discussed the nature of justice. For Plato justice can best be seen writ large in the state, but it is also seen in the life of the individual soul. Justice involves the principles of harmony, order, and reason. For Aristotle ethics and politics are related. He is concerned with the happiness of the individual, but the more comprehensive art is politics, for it deals with questions about the polity of governments and good constitutions. Historically the philosophers Machiavelli, Hobbes, Spinoza, Locke, Hume,

Rousseau, Comte, Hegel, Dewey, and Russell have been vitally concerned with the nature of the just society.

Does humanism today have concrete recommendations for the social polity? Surely humanist eupraxsophy must deal with the well-being of humanity on the larger scale, for if the ultimate good is life here and now, then this cannot be achieved by the solitary individual alone but only in concert with others within a larger socio-cultural context. It is clear that eupraxsophy does not simply delineate a theoretical intellectual position but also has something to say about social practice.

An indelible feature of humanism is its emphasis on *freedom*. The good society must seek to maximize freedom of choice and the autonomy of the individual as a basic value, and this cannot be sacrificed at the altar of the collective. This has been the first principle of classical liberalism—as expressed by Locke, Mill, and the Utilitarians—and it cannot be compromised. The pragmatic political philosophers John Dewey and Sidney Hook have attempted to accommodate both the individualism of liberalism and the sociality of Hegelian philosophy. The individual cannot live in isolation, for he interacts with others in society and culture. But what are the appropriate dimensions of individual freedom?

For the liberal democratic humanist it is first and foremost freedom of thought and conscience—philosophical, religious, intellectual, scientific, political, and moral freedom. This includes free speech, freedom of the press, the freedom to form voluntary associations and to pursue one's life style as one sees fit so long as one does not harm or limit the freedom of others. In specific terms, this means that the full range of civil liberties must be recognized by the just society, including the right to dissent and the legal right to oppose the policies of the government. This entails a commitment to political democracy: the right of the people to form political parties, to elect the officials of government, to determine the policies and programs of the state, to have some means to redress grievances, to be immune from arbitrary arrest and punishment, to be entitled to a fair trial and due process. Representative democracy bases its decisions on majority rule with the full protection of minority rights. Democracy also cherishes as basic values diversity, pluralism, creativity, and the uniqueness of individual citizens and groups in society.

Humanists can disagree about many things in the political and social sphere. Humanism is not a dogmatic creed. We cannot identify humanism with specific candidates or party platforms, in a particular period. Honest men and women often differ about what ought to be done. We can dispute about policies in the economic and political sphere: "Should there be high or low interest rates or none?" "Should taxes be on consumption or income?" "How can we increase productivity and not despoil the environment?" and so on. Humanists share with orthodox Christians and Jews any number of social ideals, and they may support common programs of political reform or stability. Humanists may differ among themselves on any number of concrete proposals. Such disagreement may be healthy, for there is not only one road to truth or virtue. We are all fallible. Humanism thus does not have a doctrinaire political platform on which it stands. Any effort to politicize humanism in a narrow sectarian way is unfortunate; one should not read political or economic conservatives out of the humanist fold. Nor should one ally humanism simply with socialism or free-market economic systems; the policies and programs that seem wise in one generation may give way to the experience of the next. The earlier identification of many idealistic humanists with left-wing socialism has been broken by the recognition that one should not compromise democratic freedoms or abandon incentive, which is so essential to expanding production. Many libertarians today, interested in defending freedom in the economic sphere, claim to be humanistic. Others believe that the wisest course of social polity is a mixture of welfare (socialist) and free-market (capitalist) policies.

Humanist eupraxia in regard to social polity thus should focus on the *basic values and principles* that all humanists share. What are some of the basic principles of humanist eupraxis as we enter the twenty-first century? The first commitment of the humanist, I submit, must be to the *method of intelligence* (as John Dewey argues in his definition of liberalism) as the most reliable way of solving social problems.[4] This means that social policies should be considered hypotheses based on the findings of the best empirical research of the day and tested by their consequences in action. The wisest and most sensible method of political governance and social change is by *democratic methods of persuasion*. Our ultimate reliance in a democracy must be on a fully informed citizenry as the chief source of power and decision making. The broader ideal here is the need to encourage widespread participation by the people in all the institutions of society in which they live, work together, and function. How this works out depends on the specific institutions. Here we are talking about political, economic, and social democracy.

If the methods of intelligence and democratic participation are to succeed, we need a well-educated and intelligent public. Thus, *opportunity for education* must be made available to all individuals in society; the right to knowledge is not only a basic human right but is also the key instrument by which society can best solve its problems. By expanding the ranges of cultural appreciation of all citizens, we contribute to our own moral, intellectual, and æsthetic development.

A central value for humanism and democracy is *tolerance*; a just society will allow alternative points of view and a plurality of life styles, beliefs, and moral values, all existing side by side. The chief method of resolving differences should be wherever possible the *peaceful negotiation of differences and compromise*, not force or violence.

A democratic society is one that recognizes the obligation to provide the opportunity and means for all individuals to *satisfy their basic economic and cultural needs*. Thus, an open democratic society will attempt to redress gross inequities in income and provide for the satisfaction of the basic minimal needs for those who are unable, through no fault of their own, to do so. I am referring here to policies of social welfare, unemployment and social security insurance, and aid to the handicapped and disadvantaged. This involves providing both economic and cultural opportunities so that individuals can participate in the democratic society and develop as self-reliant, autonomous, and productive citizens.

The just society will seek *to end discrimination* based on race, gender, creed, sexual orientation, physical handicap, ethnicity, or economic background and accord all of its citizens equal rights. It will provide women with full equality under the law. It will recognize the rights of children.

The preceding is only a thumbnail sketch of some of the principles of humanist social eupraxia. Heretofore, this has been interpreted as applying only to local communities or nation-states, and efforts have been made to democratize these from within. The world has reached such a level of economic and political interdependence today that it is no longer possible to resolve many problems concerning humanity on the local or national level alone. Thus, we need to develop an appreciation for universal (or general) human rights and apply them to all corners of the globe and all members of the human family. We need to build an *ethical commitment to the world community as our highest moral devotion*.[5] There are conservative and reactionary nationalistic, separationist, and ethnic forces throughout the world that oppose this development. Yet it is central to the next stage of human civilization.

Chapter 2

EUPRAXSOPHY AND NATURALISM

Naturalism has been an influential outlook in American philosophy in the twentieth and twenty-first centuries; though today there are powerful forces attempting to undermine it. In this chapter I wish to reflect on the impact of naturalism—past and present—on the broader culture and on the possible directions that might be taken in the future to clarify its meaning and extend its influence.

In one sense, naturalism is synonymous with modernism. Beginning with the Renaissance there was a new emphasis on humanistic values. The scientific revolution of the modern world and the quest for a method of inquiry by scientists and philosophers has had a profound impact on modern consciousness. Insofar as science uses objective standards for testing truth claims, it assumes at the very least *methodological naturalism*: that is, it abandons the quest for "occult" causes and seeks natural explanations of phenomena. Notwithstanding the enormous influence of science and technology on modern life, recalcitrant antinaturalistic and antihumanistic forces seek to counter naturalism. Witness the recrudescence of fundamentalist religions in the United States and worldwide, religions that question the very foundations of the scientific outlook, as in the defense of intelligent design by right-wing evangelicals against the theory of evolution. "It is only a *theory*," they insist; but when we ask, "Is the theory of gravity *only* a theory?" we receive no response.

No doubt it was the Enlightenment of the eighteenth century that was pivotal in the application of naturalism to sociocultural institutions. Especially noteworthy were the Industrial Revolution; the democratic revolutions in France and the United States; and the progressive ideals expressed by Condorcet and *les philosophes*, who declared that science, education, democracy, human rights, and the secularization of values would emancipate human beings from *les anciens régimes* and religious intolerance. Today, strident voices in opposition to the Enlightenment continue to bleat, among them the postmodernist disciples of Heidegger, who denigrate the role of science and technology and the optimistic agenda of liberation humanism. Some critics have proclaimed that we are already in a postsecular era and that naturalism is being supplanted by a new religiosity.[1] They point to the fact that a renascent Islam will in time outbreed secular cultures in Europe, that orthodox religions are recovering ground in Eastern Europe and gaining converts in Asia and Africa, and that spirituality is capturing the younger generation.

I wish to focus in this chapter on the continuing relevance of naturalism to civilization and the need for a New Enlightenment appropriate to contemporary conditions. For one who has spent a lifetime *engagé* on the barricades, so to speak, defending naturalism, humanism, and secularism against their detractors, the question is not simply academic but has real practical consequences.

I have entitled my chapter "Eupraxsophy and Naturalism," for I wish to focus on the direct relevance of naturalism to social values and institutions. We can debate analytic issues—important as they are. But we should, I submit, also appraise the relevance of naturalism to individual persons, social institutions, and the planetary civilization that is emerging.

I wish to defend pragmatic naturalism: that is, I wish to focus on the wisdom of *practice*, not simply the practice of wisdom. In my view, *praxis* should have equal standing with *sophia*; often, those concerned primarily with *sophia* never get the opportunity to influence the course of affairs. I consider myself a pragmatic pragmatist in the tradition of Sidney Hook, who dealt directly with practical moral and social issues. I wish to *institutionalize* naturalism and transform it from abstract concepts to concrete applications. Indeed, I have at times said "*Au revoir philosophia, Bonjour eupraxsophia*."

I have coined the term *eupraxsophy* by combining the Greek roots *eu* (good), *praxis* (practice), and *sophia* (wisdom); this is not the love of wisdom, but the practice of wisdom. Eupraxsophy differs from antiseptically neutral philosophy in that it enters consciously and forthrightly into the marketplace of human affairs. By saying this, I do not mean that we should not develop the capacity for critical ethical judgment, but that we should go further and provide a coherent life stance based on the naturalistic outlook and we should endeavor to deal with concrete decisions encountered in daily life.

At this point I should express the premise of this endeavor: to create alternatives to religion, new programs and agendas to cultivate inquiry and human enrichment, focusing on the meaning of life and providing passional-rational guides, instead of the cathedrals, temples, and mosques that have dominated the cultural landscape for so long. These ancient parables need to be replaced by new institutions based upon naturalistic science and ethics.

Unfortunately, naturalism is often identified by friend and foe alike as antisupernaturalism, simply equivalent to atheism. Naturalists find insufficient evidence or reasons for a transcendental realm, and least of all for divinely inspired knowledge of God, by means of revelation or mysticism. Naturalism rejects command-morality, the implication that one can deduce from the Fatherhood of God the moral obligation of human beings.

Naturalism is skeptical of God language, finding it unintelligible. To say "God exists" is not comprehensible, because *exists* is not a predicate; we do not know in what sense God exists. I'm not talking about the imminent God of historical revelation, which claims that God manifests himself in human history. This form of theism is meaningful, though *false*, for there are clearly identifiable prophets, or in the case of Jesus, a divine person. This is different from the transcendental God of the philosophers. The case against God is of course familiar to naturalists: the burden of proof rests with the theists; and we find the deductive arguments either fallacious or inconclusive. This applies to the classical cosmological, ontological, and teleological arguments, but it also applies to recent arguments such as "intelligent design" and "fine tuning," neither of which account for the widespread extinction of species or the deal-breaker problem of evil.

I think it important that we apply the tools of methodological naturalism to examine the Hebrew Bible, the New Testament, the Koran, and the Hadith. The range of phenomena examined is natural, or at the very least *paranatural*; it is amenable to empirical research. Carbon 14 has been employed to date the historical artifacts of archeology, and the linguistic examination of ancient documents has been applied with devastating results. Today the scientific investigation of miracles, stigmata, relics, and shrouds provides naturalistic explanations. I agree with Daniel Dennett that we need to press into service our knowledge of the brain and consciousness, biology, and genetics; I would add that we should draw upon all the sciences, including the social sciences, to provide naturalistic explanations for the persistence of religious beliefs and practices.[2]

The term *naturalism* has been used primarily as a weapon in the battle against religion: the existence of God, the existence of a nonmaterial spiritual realm, or the postulation of separable souls that survive death.

Much has been made lately of "the new atheism." There is intense public interest in books by authors Richard Dawkins, Sam Harris, Daniel Dennett, Christopher Hitchens, and Victor Stenger.[3] This "new atheism" connotes only a *negative* definition of naturalism, in terms of what it is *against*. I think that we should put our best foot forward and start with the *positive* case for naturalism. We should begin not with God, a myth to be debunked or refuted, left over from the prescientific age, but with *nature itself*, directly experienced, and with our efforts to explain *the primordial world of diversity and plentitude that we encounter in living and interacting*.

Supernaturalism at first represented the attempt by the primitive mind to account for the mysteries and tragedies of existence. God was postulated as a hidden cause of inexplicable events. The human response to them was to supplicate hidden deities by prayer and sacrifice in the pious hope that God would rescue human beings from the world of sorrow and weltschmerz.

Supernaturalism dug such deep roots in human culture because it had been institutionalized; beliefs were ingrained by indoctrination, enshrined by law, and made virtually compulsory. Heretics were exiled, excommunicated, or burned at the stake. Richard Dawkins and Daniel Dennett attribute the persistence of religious beliefs and practices to *memes*, patterns of culture conditioned and transmitted from generation to generation. The classical religions derived from the so-called Books of Abraham—Christianity, Islam, and Judaism—were enshrined before the emergence of modern science (as were the historic traditions of Hinduism, Confucianism, Buddhism, and other Asian religions).

These are the questions that we need to address: Can naturalism provide a genuine alternative to theism? Can it create new institutions to promote this alternative? This is already happening in the modern world with the development of secular economic, social, legal, and political institutions, the growth of democracy, the emergence of consumer cultures that enable ordinary people to enjoy the goods of this life, and the opportunities for education at all levels. But we need to further develop other aspects of the secular naturalistic outlook—particularly an appreciation for the role of science and the introduction of thoroughly humanistic ethical values.

There are three key normative principles of naturalism that can provide an effective alternative to religion.

The first is *methodological naturalism*, which recommends the use of scientific methods as broadly conceived as the most effective way of justifying beliefs, hypotheses, and theories. Hence, every effort is made to be impartial in evaluating, testing, and validating claims to knowledge. This entails theoretical and mathematical coherence, an appeal to evidence, the use of experimental prediction. What are the grounds for accepting a claim to knowledge?—that it must be corroborated (or replicated) by competent inquirers in the field under study. It does not depend on subjective caprice or arbitrary authority. Unlike religious claims, scientific knowledge is open to revision in the light of new discoveries or theories. It is fallible, according to Peirce. Thus some skepticism is intrinsic to the very process of scientific inquiry.

Many naturalists take the natural sciences as the only area where reliable knowledge has been achieved; this presupposes that only natural entities or processes exist and/or are dependent on physical causal processes. Here the physicalist reductive model reigns supreme. My caveat is that the methods of justification should not be narrowly construed, for the strategies of investigation and confirmation may vary from field to field, depending on the context under inquiry. The natural sciences—physics, astronomy, chemistry, geology, and so forth—surely stand as an ideal model, using a physicalist framework. The biological sciences, however, introduce new concepts and theories not reducible entirely to their physical-chemical substrata. Similarly, the behavioral sciences of psychology and the social sciences, such as economics, political science, and sociology, introduce new constructs and theories, and their modes of confirmation may not be as precise as those in the natural sciences. I share the general hypothesis that all "mental" processes are dependent on physical processes and that knowledge of the underlying physical causes is a necessary condition for full understanding; but it may not be sufficient. At this stage of human knowledge, we cannot hope to understand how the economy functions by monitoring the micro-nerve patterns of billions of brains; rather, we need to correlate market forces with the rise or fall of interest rates or earnings, and supply-and-demand on the macro level. The need is similar for other fields of inquiry.

What is especially important is the practical need to educate students and the general public to think critically, and this is an extended sense of the application of scientific methods. In my view, scientific methods grow out of the practical ways in which people cope with the world and solve problems: as Dewey pointed out, it is continuous with common sense. Methodological naturalism in the final analysis is a prescriptive principle tested by its pragmatic consequences.

It is a normative recommendation based upon effective methods of inquiry; though the corroboration of claims to knowledge may vary from field to field. We should strive for physicalist explanations wherever we can, but these surely need to be supplemented by others at various levels of inquiry. I will illustrate the need for a plurality of strategies of research by reference to the projects pursued by researchers at the Center for Inquiry.

I am here referring to efforts we have expended in our three decades of investigating anomalous phenomena, paranormal claims, parapsychology, and cognate fields. Following in the tradition of philosophers such as William James, Henry Sidgwick, H. H. Price, C. D. Broad, and Curt Ducasse, and the Society for Psychical Research in England and Cambridge, Massachusetts, we have continued the scientific investigation of the evidence for ESP, telepathy, clairvoyance, precognition, and psychokinesis (PSI)—which, according to its proponents, such as J. B. Rhine, could not be explained by reference to natural scientific causes, and may open us up to a realm of non-natural phenomena. To his credit, J. B. Rhine (whom I debated at the Smithsonian Institution three decades ago) wished to use the experimental methods of the psychological laboratory to test PSI. CSICOP (now CSI, the Committee for Skeptical Inquiry) has investigated anomalous phenomena in cooperation with (and criticism of) parapsychologists, and we've tested mediums and psychics, examined communication with the dead, ghostly apparitions, near-death experiences, and other alleged evidence for survival. We've gone even further and dealt with extraterrestrial visitations, the newest form of space-age religion that has become popular in the contemporary world. Although we've approached this area with an open mind, we are largely skeptical of the claims of paranormal investigators who are convinced that something strange is intruding in our universe. We have found a good deal of the data unreliable, based on anecdotal information and uncritical eyewitness accounts. Other difficulties that we uncovered were faulty protocols, experimental bias, the leakage of data to the experimenters, and errors in grading "hits."

The first question that we raised was whether such anomalous phenomena even exist. One cannot decide a priori that this phenomenon is impossible because it contradicts naturalism, as C. E. M. Hansel, the noted skeptical psychologist, assumed. He surmised that since it contradicted our understanding of the natural world, fraud was involved, which he attempted to uncover.[4] I dissented. We cannot prejudge. Thus I was interested in examining the empirical data. The first criterion that we used was a demand for reliable evidence, not merely hearsay testimony that cannot be substantiated by impartial investigators or replicated in the laboratory. Most often we did not find that the anomalous phenomenon existed. Insofar as people insisted that it did, we sought causal explanations to fit the alleged observed data. These turned out to be perfectly explicable in prosaic normal terms! I have spent more years of my life than I intended in examining the claims of mediums, faith healers, astrologers, palm readers, dowsers, and UFOlogists that strange phenomena were occurring. Those involved in our work were able to evaluate the claims by using powerful investigative techniques, not necessarily reducible to a physicalist model. We detected psychological and sociological processes of deception and self-deception. We could not find a physical mechanism for telepathy or clairvoyance; these were attributed to elusive "extrasensory" perceptions, so we drew upon *both* psychology and physics.

Another vital area where scientific methodology has been used with effectiveness is the examination of sacred religious texts—in opposition to the general view that science cannot deal with matters of faith or revelation. Historically, revealed theology was supposed to be accepted on the basis of faith.[5] We, however, examined the evidence for the virgin birth, exorcisms, and the Resurrection, all pivotal to Christianity, in the light of their historical or scientific credibility—was there an original body of reliable empirical evidence? I doubt it. The utter speciousness of the evidence for Revelation has by and large been ignored by philosophers, yet the contemporary reexamination of Biblical claims demonstrates the factual inadequacy of the sources, and demonstrates that it involves "news from nowhere," transmitted by unreliable sources. None of the writers of the Gospels in the New Testament, for example, were eyewitnesses. Their accounts were based on hearsay, derived from a second- or third-hand oral tradition, and hence are highly suspect. The criterion here is the need for corroboration of extraordinary claims of divine origin by impeccable eyewitness testimony, and/or the careful drawing upon circumstantial evidence that provides inductive evidence that is independently verifiable. The results of this painstaking research now over two centuries old have thrown doubt on the birth, ministry, and resurrection of Jesus, let alone his existence. None of the four Gospels—Matthew, Mark, Luke, John—were written by those who witnessed the miraculous events. They were most likely written by propagandists for a new faith; hence they are Gospels of fiction, not reliable historical accounts. Yet a powerful religion is based on these claims.

Similar considerations apply to the accounts of the life of Muhammad in the Koran and the stories of his life by his alleged companions, as related in the Hadith. Meticulous historical research demonstrates that there were many Korans, that we do not know whether the received doctrines about the life of Muhammad are accurate. Thus we are able to cast skeptical doubt on the traditional accounts of his divine calling. Similar considerations also apply to the Hebrew Bible. We at the Center for Inquiry have spent almost thirty years in this area of Biblical and Koranic research. Such historical research is impartial; it is a form of *Wissenschaften*, though it does not strictly reduce to the natural sciences. Hence the need for various strategies of research to establish whether claims made are credible. We have again found that the psychology of deception is very important in reconstructing the readiness to believe.

I move on to a second form of naturalism, which I call *scientific* rather than philosophical naturalism. This form of naturalism entails another normative recommendation, the importance of describing and interpreting the body of scientific knowledge at any one time in history. This requires generalists who are skilled in uncovering overlapping interdisciplinary generalizations, common concepts and theories, and shared assumptions and presuppositions. I think that philosophers working closely with scientists are well qualified to participate in this important task. The eventual goal of scientific inquiry is to achieve, if possible, the "unity of the sciences"; that is, to develop comprehensive theories from which all subdisciplines can be deduced. This might entail, as Ernest Nagel said, "bridge hypotheses" between various disciplines. An ambitious goal, no doubt, and perhaps never achievable. We are well aware that philosophers today have some trepidation about spinning out metaphysical systems encompassing everything in the universe. The metaphysical conjectures of the past often turn out to be untested speculative ontologies, which are discarded as new discoveries are made or when radical paradigm shifts occur.

What should concern us is that today there is an abysmal lack of information among members of the general public and indeed among scientific specialists themselves about scientific discoveries. Botanists may not be familiar with what astronomers have discovered, mathematicians of what is going on in crystallography, neurologists of what is going on in economics or genetics. Indeed, it is especially unfortunate that our political and corporate leaders display abysmal ignorance about the basic sciences, and all too often they turn to religion, or literature, or the arts to develop an understanding of nature or human life. Scientific illiteracy is rampant. That is why we need to provide general outlines of our knowledge of the universe as far as we can. Most often it is scientists rather than philosophers—for example, Carl Sagan, or Isaac Asimov, or

E. O. Wilson—who make contributions to the public understanding of science. E. O. Wilson, in *Consilience: The Unity of Knowledge*,[6] draws upon the nineteenth-century English philosopher of science, William Whewell, who recommends that we seek "consilience instead of coherence." This means a "jumping together of knowledge, by linking of facts and fact-based theory across disciplines to create common groundwork of explanation."

According to Whewell, consilience occurs "when an induction obtained from one class of facts coincides with an induction . . . from a different class."[7] All of this is an extrapolation; yet I submit that it is important to develop a kind of synoptic view of the universe at any one time in history. This is sometimes described as the quest for the "generic traits of nature" (to use the words of John Herman Randall Jr.) or the "general categories" or "presuppositions of science." I prefer, myself, to label it as the quest for *empirical descriptive accounts* of what has been discovered across the sciences.

In this venture we draw from physics and chemistry first, in order to provide the bedrock of a wide range of systems. I quote from the famous physicist, Richard Feynman, in one of his famous lectures at Cal Tech. Feynman asked, "If, in some cataclysm, all of scientific knowledge were to be destroyed, and only one sentence passed on to the next generation of creatures, what statement would contain the most information in the fewest words?" His response to this was, "I believe it is the atomic hypothesis, or the atomic fact, or whatever you wish to call it, that all things are made of atoms. Little particles that move around in perpetual motion, attracting each other when a little distance apart but repelling upon being squeezed into one another."[8] Feynman is alleged to have said that if we take that one sentence and throw in imagination and thinking, we have the history of physics. In other words, physics uses reductionism, understanding complex things in terms of their constituent parts, and it has been extraordinarily successful in that inquiry. Physicalist explanations apply on the macro as well as micro levels. Physicists and astronomers observe the behavior of large bodies in our solar system, calculating precisely the orbits of the planets around our sun. They have extrapolated this theory, using the principles of mechanics and gravitation, to other planetary systems. The question of scale is crucial, as we go from the micro to the macro level, yet the basic principles of physics still seem to apply, though they are adapted to very large physical systems, including galaxies.

The biological sciences depend upon physics and chemistry, but a high-level law, the Darwinian principle of natural selection, has been formulated to explain the evolution of species. Many think that physics and chemistry are the primary sources of the basic laws of nature; yet there are other fundamental regularities that have emerged in the life-sciences—for example, the theory of evolution. Of course, micro level explanations are relevant—such as the discovery of DNA and the genetic determinants of behavior. But there are principles that have emerged on the macro level that are not simply reducible to micro causality.

I have called the interaction of explanations *coduction*, where we draw upon many factors or causes to explain phenomena. The logic of coduction recognizes that to understand a living system we need to use *both* physics and chemistry, in which the atomic, molecular, and cellular functions of organisms are observed, but also on macro-like laws as in natural selection, where chance mutations, differential reproduction, and adaptation are essential in our understanding of biological systems. Both provide us with sets of explanation that are extremely useful. In some species we find that social behavior emerges—as in a beehive, an ant colony, or human society—and here other higher-level principles are relevant in explanations of behavior.

Does our understanding of human consciousness reduce experience entirely to the micro structures and functions of the brain, or do we not at the same time seek to understand intentional behavior, the role of cognition, the psychology of motivation? Many find the concept of *emergence* relevant here, for there are systems in which new properties and qualia manifest themselves. Explanations drawn from sociology and the social sciences also help us to comprehend sociocultural institutions.

Many naturalists have assumed that hard determinism is the ultimate presupposition of all scientific inquiry. The classical thesis was that if you knew the exact state of the physical universe at any one moment, you could predict the future course of all events. This presupposes that all things in the universe are interconnected. This I submit is an oversimplification, which does not apply if we view the universe as an open, pluralistic scene in which order and disorder, contingency and regularity, determinism and indeterminism, chaos and stability, accidents and catastrophes are observed. I hope that I am not dealing in metaphorical language by saying that contingencies are real: I think that they reflect the evidential facts of nature. Are they contingent because we are ignorant of the causes, or does brute facticity include chance and indeterminacy? I submit that contingency is not only found in human affairs, where calamity and distress may suddenly engulf a tribe or nation-state, or in the struggle of competing species to adapt and survive or be vanquished by forces beyond their control—like the dinosaurs, the saber-toothed tigers, the mammoths, or the intricate, exquisite forms of life uncovered in the Burgess shale in Canada, which became extinct some 500 million years ago. Is contingency manifested in the crash of meteors, comets, and asteroids into our solar system, the birth and collapse of planets and stars, and the collision and explosion of galaxies in the universe at large, as viewed through telescopes, where we also observe a receding universe expanding at terrific speeds, black holes, and dark matter? The earlier conviction of scientists that nature was perfectly ordered in terms of deterministic laws hardly seems to accord with nature as we find it, in which the polarities of order and disorder seem manifest.

Scientific explanations are contrived by human beings in order to make sense of the world. The great ongoing adventure of scientific discoveries both advances our knowledge and introduces new puzzles, such as the discovery of over 250 planets outside of our solar system (in 2007) and the understanding that there most likely are billions and billions of planets and billions of galaxies, many of them involved in humongous collisions in outer space. So the notion of a fixed universe or the idea "that God would not roll dice in outer space" is perhaps a bias of the human mind, which demands order and perfection, whereas the evidence points to chance and contingency as facts of the universe at large.

In view of this, I wish to pose a series of questions for naturalists: Our age is the time when the human species confronts absolute death—not only death in terms of our own mortal existence as individuals, but the likely death of our own species and solar system at some remote time in the future. Arthur Toynbee has graphically dramatized for us the rise and fall of past civilizations, with the clear implication that this likewise applies to our own. We have dethroned God and the planet Earth from the center of creation. The point is that science has shattered the anthropocentric religions of our forebears, but skepticism destroys any lingering conceit that our ideals will prevail throughout eternity. If God is dead because we killed him, so is the Human Prospect(s) in the long run bound to fail. In view of this, is the picture of reality presented by the sciences too bitter a pill to swallow, and will this lead to despair and hopelessness in the general public? This is the question that William L. Craig, the theistic theologian, hurled at me when I debated him recently.[9] He said that secular humanism led to nihilism. I denied that accusation.

What are the implications of methodological and scientific naturalism for life as lived? Both involve normative recommendations. The first requires a vigorous code of epistemological austerity, skeptical about speculative flights of faith and fancy. It wishes to extend the rigorous methods of corroboration to all claims to truth. This applies to secular ideals no less than to theistic; it admonishes us to be careful. We should not leap in with unfounded wishful thinking. Continuous peer review of ideals and values may kill off any humanistic agendas of liberation and undermine the audacity of hope.

The second form of naturalism presents us with a universe in which the God delusion is whacked to death (we cheer!) and religion is exposed as poison (hear! hear!), a universe that is without purpose, rhyme, or reason, indifferent to human ideals and values. It just *is*.

The response of secular humanists is that although nature has no intrinsic purpose or meaning, life presents us with opportunities (within limits) to create our own meanings, plans, and projects for ourselves and our fellow human beings. Countless generations have found life intrinsically worthwhile for its own sake; they have lived their lives full of satisfaction and happiness unmindful of the ultimate nature of an evolving biosphere, without any worry that humans do not have a privileged place in a vast mysterious universe of expanding galaxies, devoid of any illusions of immortality. The good life is achievable, we insist. But we are the only species apparently aware of its own death and the eventual degradation of our lovely habitat, the planet Earth. What is the meaning of life, we ask, as viewed from the galaxariums of the future?

This leads to the third form of naturalism, *ethical naturalism*, which focuses on human values. Naturalistic ethics came under heavy criticism in the early part of the twentieth century—from G. E. Moore onward. This criticism is now widely accepted. We cannot deduce what we *ought* to do from what *is* the case; we cannot derive our values from the facts. For example, if it is the case that the human male is prone to aggression in competition for females, it surely does not follow that it is morally permissible to act aggressively. If the universe has no special place for humans, how shall we assert our own significance? Human life is an audacious expression of how we choose to become what we want. What is the relevance of nature to our decisions?

May I present a *modified form of ethical naturalism* that survives the critique of naturalistic ethics: I submit simply that the facts of the case are relevant to our moral values and principles, and that we need to take them into account in decision making. We need to understand the limits and constraints, opportunities and openings, in the environments in which we live, the circumstances and facts within the contexts of choice. The consequences of our choices may persuade us to modify them, and the relevance of the means at our disposal help us to evaluate our ends. These considerations are value neutral; yet they are relevant to the things we hold dear, cherish, and esteem, a form of objective relativism. I have called this the *valuation base* and I submit that we can make reasonable value judgments in the light of it.[10] Hence, there is an intermediary relationship between values and facts, an *act-ductive*, if not deductive or inductive, relationship of facts and values to actions. Accordingly, naturalism has direct relevance to the decisions we make and the values we select.

Theists complain that a person cannot be good without God; that secular ethics is groundless, hence unreliable. I deny that. I maintain that both methodological and scientific naturalism have profound implications for a meaningful life. However, this depends on the flexible application of the naturalistic method and outlook to life. I submit that philosophy is a stepping stone to normative morality, but it needs to be transformed directly into *eupraxsophy*. As I view it, eupraxsophers are skilled in the art of living and their recommendations have behavioral implications for the practical life.

Unfortunately, there has been considerable opposition to this agenda from philosophers and scientists. First, the lion's share of philosophical ethics—I call it formalistic or abstract ethics—has been focused on meta-ethics, in two senses: first the definition of normative terms and concepts, such as *good* or *bad*, *right* or *wrong*, *valuable* or *worthless*. There is a philosophical prejudice against redefining normative terms. This is a kind of definition-mongering, we are admonished. Why should I accept your definition? Is that not a form of *persuasive* definition, and is that not largely *subjective*? Philosophy, we are told, needs to be neutral and not engage in rhetorical definitional games. There is no rational ground for arbitrary fiat, they say. Second, there is another fallacious move, we are told, in proposing criteria, standards and norms, to be appealed to in order to justify valuational judgments. It is surely one thing to carefully analyze the logic of formulating practical judgments on the meta level, pointing out the pitfalls and/or advantages of one or more over others; it is another to seek to actually make judgments and recommend them to others as worthy. To do so, we are cautioned, is to descend into the battleground of moral disputes, to get entangled in the passionate, indeed often bloody, moral battles in the well-trafficked public square.

I concede that point, but I insist that it is important that we define our moral concepts, and also defend our moral principles and values in the process. In other words, naturalists need to advocate ethical positions in the *agora* of life as lived, and to *intellectually and passionately propose and defend them.*

Does this betray the philosophical position of neutrality and objectivity?—possibly; yet it is necessary to do so to satisfy the demand for meaning, the hunger for ideals, the quest for principles that deserve our devotion, the beloved causes that are worthy of our energy.

My response here is that "Everyone is doing it, doing it, doing it—why not us?" If we do not defend the naturalistic outlook, try to apply it concretely, and seek to persuade others to accept it, then we have abandoned the melee and turmoil of controversy in order to seek refuge on higher ground—for fear of offending those in power who may disagree. The point is that the bishop and soldier, corporate president and senator, lawyer and rock star, teacher and nurse, worker and student *have* moral convictions upon which they act; so the *eupraxsopher*, if not the philosopher, needs to concentrate on real practical problems in an effort to help solve them; he or she will need to take moral and political positions; will speak out about abortion or same-sex marriage, war or peace, poverty or privilege, plutocracy or democracy, love or hate, joy or despair, the sense of the tragic or the promise of exuberance.

The reason why naturalistic philosophy has failed is that it has not ministered to the passionate needs of students, colleagues, co-workers, citizens in the communities in which we live, and to strangers in the broader community of humankind. We need, if I can borrow the metaphor, *eupraxsopher ministers of the soul, practitioners in the art and science and poetry of living.*

Ranged against naturalism, dealing in illusion and delusion, fantasy and nonsense are the priests and mullahs, rabbis and ministers, who seek to intrude, cajole, persuade, convert, and have no qualms about it. We also need to be forthright and bold about our deeply held convictions, which we need to vindicate.

The posture of the philosopher who is a professor in the university classroom is "Let's look at all sides of a question. We must never advocate, only analyze and explicate!"

That is why I have proposed *eupraxsophy* as a new branch of the applied sciences, which has broken off of the main trunk of philosophy to develop skilled expertise in the arena of valuation and action.

Bertrand Russell once said: "The good life is one that is inspired by love and guided by reason." To this I add that we need to be inspired by a *passionate commitment* to naturalistic humanism, as well as our devotion to reason.

IS A NATURALISTIC ALTERNATIVE TO RELIGION POSSIBLE?

Does contemporary scientific cosmology demonstrate the existence of God? Do the big bang, the anthropic principle, or the design argument justify the claims of theists? Skeptic inquirers deny that they do. The so-called singularity of the big bang does not tell us what happened before the initial bang, how or why it was caused. To infer a divine being as the cause of the universe, only pushes our ignorance back one step; for one can always ask, Who or what caused God? This is an illegitimate question we are told by believers, but then is it not likewise illegitimate to seek a single cause or ground of being for the entire universe—to take a leap of faith outside of nature? If the existence of God is postulated to explain the physical universe, then what is the justification for the claim that He, She, or It is a *Person*, as theists assume; indeed, that God responds to our prayers?

Similarly the attempt by theists to invoke "intelligent design" has insufficient evidential support. Natural selection, genetic mutations, differential reproduction, and other natural causes are sufficient to explain the evolution of species without the interposition of design in the universe. The anthropic principle maintains that some form of "fine-tuning" is responsible for the existence of life, particularly human life, on this planet. But how does this accord with the extinction of millions of species as discovered in fossil remains? If one assumes a designer, what about conflict, malfunctioning, and evil in the universe? Why is this not evidence for unintelligent or bad design? It is the height of anthro-

75

pocentric chutzpah to assert that the purpose of the fine-tuning of the universe is for the emergence of the human species!

Heidegger posed the question: "Why should there be something rather than nothing?" Skeptics doubt that this question is meaningful. How would one go about confirming the theistic answer that is proposed? Why not accept the *brute facticity* encountered in the world as the given: matter and energy, the variety and forms of things, events, qualities, and properties that we experience in nature, from electrons and atoms to planets and galaxies, from single-cell paramecia to dinosaurs, from daffodils to human beings, from social institutions to cultural expressions? Why not treat these in pluralistic rather than unicausal terms in the contexts in which we encounter them? A nonreductive naturalistic account of nature is open to the richness and diversity that is uncovered. Perhaps the appropriate response to these questions is that of the *agnostic*, who admits that he does not know the ultimate ground of reality (whatever that means). In any case, the skeptic finds insufficient evidence or reasons for the classical theist position, and in that sense he is a *nontheist* or *atheist*.

Those who defend the existence of the supernatural believe that a transcendent God is also immanent in the universe. If this is the case then his presence may be judged experientially. Skeptical inquirers have investigated the alleged paranatural evidence adduced for the existence of "discarnate souls," "near-death experiences," or "communication with the dead"; similarly for the "efficacy of prayer," the Shroud of Turin, and other alleged anomalous phenomena—which have been found evidentially lacking.

The presumption that religion offers a special kind of higher spiritual truth is thus unwarranted, as is the claim that there are *two* truths: those of science, justified on experimental and rational grounds; *and* those of religion, which transcend any empirical/rational confirmation.

IS A NATURALISTIC ALTERNATIVE TO RELIGION POSSIBLE?

The most reliable methods of inquiry attempt to satisfy objective standards of justification. The historic claims of revelation in the ancient sacred literature are insufficiently corroborated by impartial eyewitnesses and/or are based upon questionable oral traditions. These were compiled many decades, even centuries, after the alleged death of the prophets. Many miraculous claims found in the Bible and the Koran—for example, the claims of healings and exorcisms, within the New Testament or the creationist account in the Old Testament—are totally unreliable. They depend upon the primitive science of ancient nomadic and agricultural peoples, and cannot withstand scientific scrutiny.

Unfortunately, some proponents of these historic religions appeal to them in order to block scientific research. Freedom of inquiry is essential for human progress; any effort to limit science is counter-productive; for example, attempts to restrict embryonic stem-cell research on alleged moral-religious grounds. Opponents of such research argue that once a cell begins to divide (even if it grows to a small number of cells—a blastocyst), the soul of a person is implanted, and that any effort to experiment with this is "immoral." The postulation of the soul to prohibit scientific inquiry is reminiscent of the opposition of the findings of Galileo and Darwin. Insofar as religionists insist that they can issue an imprimatur or *fatwah* against the kinds of scientific research the first conclusion that can be drawn is that there is a need for the strict *separation of religion and science*.

A second inference that may be drawn concerns the relationship between religion and morality. Stephen Jay Gould proposed that there are two *magisteria*, which he says do not compete and do not contradict each other. The domain of science, deals with truth, he says, but that of religion deals appropriately with ethics. I think that this position is profoundly mistaken. Indeed I submit that there ought to be *a separation between ethics and religion.* I do not deny that religious believers have often espoused and supported moral behavior, including charitable and beneficent acts, love, sympathy, and peace. But many believers have also invoked commandments from On High, which they sought to impose on society. Moreover, religions have often disagreed about what are the basic moral commandments; and they have waged warfare against other religious or secular moral systems. Religions often ground their moral commandments on faith and tradition and many have sought to oppose constructive social change. One needs to open ethical values and principles to examination in the light of rational and empirical considerations. Religionists have demonstrated that they have no special competence in framing or evaluating such moral judgments.

I say this because there is a vast literature in the field of secular ethics—from Aristotle to Spinoza, Kant, John Stuart Mill, John Dewey, and John Rawls. These thinkers seek to demonstrate that ethics can be autonomous and that it is possible to frame ethical judgments on the basis of rational inquiry. There is a logic of judgments of practice and valuation that we can develop quite independently of a religious framework. Moreover, science has a role to play in decision making, for it can expand the means at our disposal (technology), and it can modify value judgments in the light of the facts of the case and their consequences. The applied and policy sciences are normative insofar as they frame prescriptive judgments. Yet many people today mistakenly suppose that you cannot be moral without religious foundations. This is a false supposition; for ever since the Renaissance, the secularization of morality and the realization of naturalistic values continue quite independently of religious commandments.

A third area which has been hotly debated in the modern world is the relationship between religion and the state. Democrats vigorously defend the open secular society and *the separation of religion and the state*. Although religionists have every right to express their point of view in the public square, religion should be primarily a private matter. Religions should not seek to impose their fundamental moral-theological principles on the entire society. This would be tantamount to a theocracy. A democratic state is neutral, not seeking to favor one religion over any other or none. It does not seek to establish a religion; it does not legislate religious principles into law. In particular, it seeks to avoid the censorship of scientific inquiry.

II

What then is the proper domain of religion? Is anything left? My answer is in the *affirmative*. In a minimal sense, I think that religion and science are compatible, depending of course on what is meant by religion. Religions have performed important functions that cannot be easily dismissed. Religions will continue with us in the foreseeable future and will not simply wither away.

No doubt my thesis is controversial: religious language, I submit, is not primarily descriptive; nor is it prescriptive. The descriptive and explanatory functions of language are within the domain of science; the prescriptive and normative, are the function of ethics. Both of these domains, science and ethics, have a kind of autonomy. Certainly within the political domain, religious believers *per se* do not have any special competence, similarly for the moral domain. It should be left to every citizen of a democracy to express his or her political views. Likewise, for the developing moral personality who is able to render moral judgments.

If this is the case, what is appropriate for the religious realm? The domain of the religious, I submit, is expressive and emotive. It presents moral poetry, æsthetic inspiration, performative ceremonial rituals, which act out and *dramatize* the human condition and human interests, and seek to slake the thirst for meaning and purpose. Religion—at least the classical religions of revelation—deal in parables, narratives, metaphors, stories, myths; and they frame the divine in anthropomorphic form. They express the existential yearnings of individuals endeavoring to cope with the world that they encounter and seek to wrestle some meaning in the face of death. Religious language in this sense is eschatological. Its primary function is to express *hope*. If science gives us truth, morality the good and the right, and politics justice, religion is in the realm of promise and expectation. Its main function is to overcome despair and hopelessness in response to human tragedy, adversity, and conflict, the brute, inexplicable, contingent, and fragile aspects of the human condition. Under this interpretation religions are not primarily true, nor are they primarily good or right or even just; they are, if you will, *evocative*, attempting to transcend contrition, fear, anxiety, and remorse, providing balm for the aching heart—at least for a significant number of people, but surely not all.

I would add to this the fact that religious systems of thought and belief are products of the creative human imagination. They traffic in fantasy and fiction, taking the promises of long-forgotten historical figures and endowing them with eternal cosmic significance.

The role of creative imagination, fantasy, and fiction cannot be easily dismissed. These are among the most powerful expressions of human dreams and hopes, ideals and longings. Who can deny that so many humans are be entranced by fictionalized novels, movies, and plays? The creative religious imagination analogously weaves tales of consolation and of expectation. They are dramatic expressions of human longing, enabling humans to overcome grief and depression.

In the above interpretation of religion as dramatic existentialist poetry, science and religion are not necessarily incompatible, for they address different human interests and needs. My interpretation of the function of religion is on the meta-level: classical religions are attempts to transcend the tragic dimensions of human experience, even though, in my judgment, they are false in what they claim or promise.

III

A special challenge to naturalism emerges at this point. *Methodological naturalism* is the basic principle of the sciences—we should seek natural causal explanations for phenomena, testing these by the rigorous methods of science. *Scientific naturalism*, on the other hand, goes beyond this, because it rejects as nonevidential the postulation of occult metaphors, the invoking of divine spirits, ghosts, or souls to explain the universe; and it tries to deal in materialistic, physical-chemical, or non-reductive naturalistic explanations. It is the second form of naturalism that especially worries theists, for it rejects their basic cosmic view. The frenzied opposition to Darwinism which persists today is clearly rooted in the gnawing fear that scientific naturalism undermines religious faith.

If this is the case, the great challenge to scientific naturalism is not simply in the area of truth but of *hope*, not of the good but of *promise*, not of the just but of *expectation*—in the light of the tragic character of the human condition. Darwinian evolutionists recognize that death is final, not simply the death of each individual but the possible extinction some day in the remote future of the human species itself. Evolutionists have discovered that millions of species have become extinct. Does not the same fate await the human species? Cosmological scientists indicate that at some point it seems likely that our sun will cool down, or indeed, looking into the future, that a deep freeze or big crunch may eventually overtake the entire universe. Some star trekkers, inspired by science fiction, romanticize that one day the human species will be able to leave the earth, and inhabit other planets and perhaps other galaxies. Nonetheless at some point the death of the individual, the human species, even our planet and solar system seem likely.

What does this portend for the ultimate human condition? We live in an epoch where the scale of the universe has expanded enormously. It is billions of light years in dimension. Much of this no doubt is based on mathematical and astronomical extrapolations, which may be altered by future science. Nonetheless, the role of the human species pales in insignificance in the vast cosmic scene. Clearly science enables us to explain much about our universe; and this knowledge is truly a marvel to behold. Yet the universe that we have uncovered far outstrips our small effects upon it. It was not made *for us*, as theists presuppose. Nor did God create us in his image; rather we etched him in ours. Does this naturalistic perspective of the universe and our place or lack of it within it forever extinguish any grandiose aspirations that humans harbor? Does it destroy and undermine hope? Does it provide sufficient consolation for the human spirit? The central issue for naturalists is the question of human *courage*. Can we live a full life in the face of our ultimate extinction?

These are large-scale questions, yet they are central for the religious consciousness. Can scientific naturalism, insofar as it undermines theism, provide an alternative dramatic, poetic rendering of the human condition, offering hope, and promise? Countless numbers of brave individuals have lived significant lives and even thrived, aware of the possible future extinction of our species and our solar system. Many other humans apparently cannot bear that thought. They crave immortality; and theistic religion responds to their need. Others do not stay awake nights worrying what will happen five, ten, or fifteen billion years from now. They find life worthwhile for its own sake here and now.

There is another dimension of the human condition in the twenty-first century that we need to consider—the expanding immensity of the universe and the mystery of the unknown. The dazzling reality of human imagination today is that our conceptions of the size of the universe are continually being revised and enlarged. This process has been going on at least since the sixteenth century. The Copernican revolution dislodged our terrestrial home as the center of the universe and replaced it by the heliocentric perspective. The twentieth century has seen several revolutions in cosmology: the theory of relativity, quantum mechanics, and the uncertainty principles that have altered our views of reality. But it is the Hubblean revolution that is of special relevance today because it has extended our perspective exponentially. It has taken us beyond our solar system and our own galaxy, the Milky Way, into the vast outer reaches of space—to other galaxies, nebulae, and black holes, where the birth and death of star systems and galaxies can be observed. The telescope named after the astronomer Hubble has left the density of the earth's atmosphere and enables us to penetrate still deeper into the recesses of the universe. The idea of a constantly evolving and changing universe, not a static eternal one, now dominates the outlook of scientific cosmologists. In this we are like mere specks of dust on a minor planet at the edge of one galaxy hurtling through space. Perhaps there are other universes or multiverses, which from our perspective are virtually infinite in number. If one traverses in reverse from the macro realm to the micro realm, one contemplates a similar virtually infinite number of subatomic particles. Thus our view of the universe is breathtakingly endless in either direction!

Many theories in contemporary cosmology are no doubt based on theoretical conjectures; these need to be verified before they are accepted. Nonetheless our present cosmic perspective heightens awe, astonishment, amazement. We are confronted by resplendent, elegant, and majestic scenes. Bertrand Russell once observed that insofar as the human mind is able to contemplate the vastness of the universe, it enlarges its horizons by becoming a citizen of the universe.

Recent discoveries of new planets in nearby star systems lead us to infer the probability that there are not only billions of stars and galaxies, but billions of planets. If we add to these discoveries the possibility, indeed likelihood that other forms of life may exist in other parts of the universe, then we may not be alone. One might ask: Are not these reflections not a form of religious contemplation? No, they need not be. They are rather forms of æsthetic exaltation at the beauty and scale of the cosmic scene, which Carl Sagan so admirably expressed in his television series *Cosmos*.

There are other attitudinal reactions that these speculations no doubt inspire. First, there is some appreciation of our own finitude and limitations. From this awesome perspective many human beings develop fear and trembling, dread and anxiety, perhaps even horror. No doubt a recognition of the limits of human power leads to a desire to supplicate the vast forces beyond and even to deify them. The familiar human tendency to develop anthropomorphic conceptions of the universe or to relate everything within it to human aspirations and hope is to give way to the transcendental temptation. In our dreams and reverie we are tempted to repeople the universe with Titans engaged in star wars. The universe of science today far outstrips the imaginative scenes of the science-fiction literature of the past.

There is, however, another possible attitude in response: the recognition of our power in our own sphere of action on our own planet and solar system and our need to develop the courage to realize our plans and projects and to resolve to live fully. We can and do enjoy life, pursue science and reason, love and be loved, share our aspirations and hopes with other individuals, build a better global community, and prosper and exult as human beings.

Religious narratives in the last analysis are like other great works of art, Shakespeare's *Macbeth* or Verdi's *Requiem*, Michelangelo's *David* or Picasso's *Guernica*, Beethoven's Ninth or Mahler's Third symphonies. They dramatize various aspects of the human condition—though religious mythologies provide fanciful remedies that should not be taken as literally true. The question nonetheless remains, Can or should we seek to replace the mythological response of the monotheist with more realistic appraisals and proposals for coping with the human condition? Perhaps the beginning of wisdom is implicitly suggested: science has catapulted the human species into outer space, both in imagination and exploration; and it reveals a marvelous structure far more stunning than anything contrived by the ancient theistic religions. Can we as a species evidence in a naturalistic universe, recognizing the elements of mystery that still remains and the vast fringes of the unknown? Can we at the same time each find life worthwhile, live with reason and courage, compassion and exuberance? That is the challenge facing scientific naturalists in the future, as science continues to enlarge our understanding of the cosmos and our place within it.

Chapter 4

CONVICTION AND COMMITMENT

Is humanist eupraxsophy able to develop beliefs that can be held with conviction and values that can inspire us? Can it present a reliable cosmic view of the universe and the place of the human species within it? Can it provide some meaningful guidelines for how to live the good life and achieve the just society?

There are many contending approaches to knowledge. On one end of the scale lies extreme skepticism, a state of being unwilling or unable to make judgments or to take a stand about the nature of reality or the best values to pursue in life. Its natural state is neutrality and indecision. On the other end of the scale is dogmatic religion and ideology, fanatically certain about the truth of its claims and seeking to impose them on all. It will harbor no doubts, nor brook any opposition to its articles of faith.

Some forms of scientific and philosophical inquiry veer naturally toward the neutral pole, and not without reason. For it is essential that we be objective in appraising knowledge claims and cautious about those that are as yet untested.

THE ROLE OF SCIENCE

Let us examine the scientific frame of reference first. The scientist qua scientist is committed to a set of methodological criteria which he needs to follow scrupulously if his inquiry is to succeed. The scientist must be open-minded about all questions. He must not allow his bias to color his judgment. He usually begins with a problem or puzzle that arouses him or others within the community of scientific inquirers. There are facts, perhaps anomalies, that need to be described, accounted for, explained. He asks: "What is occurring and why?" He formulates hypotheses and seeks to test them by observing the evidence. He develops theories which need to be internally consistent with other hypotheses that have already been confirmed and are considered more or less reliable. His theories are tested under controlled experimental conditions. He asks: "What is the cause of this strange disease? Can we isolate the virus?" "How do you explain the perturbations observed in the orbit of the planet Neptune? Is there still another planetary body exerting a gravitational influence on it?" "Why should price inflation suddenly occur? What are its causes?"

Each of these questions is asked in a specialized field of knowledge: biology, astronomy, economics. The hypotheses offered as solutions to the queries may be judged objectively only by reference to the evidence, and the scientist must deduce reasons to support them. Presumably other competent authorities inquiring in the same field can examine his grounds and evaluate the adequacy of his hypotheses. The scientist must not allow his bias to intervene. He may have preconceived hunches about what is happening and why, and these may guide his research. But he must not become the overzealous advocate, allowing his speculative theories to color his data. The court of last resort is a body of his peers, who can appraise the data and methods of verification and corroborate whether or not they support his claims. Granted that scientists are all too human and that they often allow their predilections to get the best of them. Especially when novel theories are introduced, inquirers have had to contend against strong opposition. It may be an uphill battle to convince the scientific establishment that new claims are reliably supported by the evidence. This has been true of many great scientists who devoted years of unending struggle to vindicate their research projects.

Science is a *human* affair, and it depends in the last analysis upon the energy and efforts that human beings are willing to devote to its success. Cultural fashions also shape attitudes within the community and tend to favor one paradigm over another. Still, if science is to succeed in its ongoing quest for reliable knowledge, scientists must be impartial about their hypotheses and in the evaluation of the evidence. The scientist must ask questions about nature, but he must listen carefully without allowing his preferences or personal convictions to influence the facts he records. The methodological rules governing inquiry and research must be fairly applied. Thus, there is an objective ideal that applies to scientific inquiry, one which members of the community of inquirers share: the appeal to clarity, parsimony, evidence, experimental results, and logical consistency. The scientist qua scientist cannot be an advocate or propagandist. He cannot turn the dispassionate quest for truth into a passionate defense of one theory over another. He must be the disinterested spectator, doing his research and allowing his findings to speak for themselves. This does not mean that he is uninterested—he may be intensely aroused by his project—but only that he does not allow his interests to shift the balance of evidence in favor of one hypothesis. He is not a passive bystander; for science demands an active posing of questions, an ingenious thinking up of solutions, and a creative devising of methods to test hunches. He is only passive in observing and recording the data. To say that the scientist must be neutral within his own field means that he is aware of the evidence in favor of the current theories but also knows the gaps in the evidence and the ragged edges still not resolved.

The field of parapsychology is one that immediately comes to mind by way of illustration. Many researchers have invested years of effort to investigate paranormal phenomena, and they have attempted to devise experimental laboratory conditions to test the claims. Some parapsychologists act as true believers, for they are convinced of the reality of extrasensory perception. But there are also committed skeptics, who, in spite of intensive efforts, have not been able to replicate their results or demonstrate the reality of the phenomena. One must, however, continue to look, and here the only appropriate scientific posture is the persistent fair-minded examination of new hypotheses and data. Science depends on honest inquiry, not advocacy pro or con. All of this needs to be reiterated. Science is among the most important of human endeavors, but it can only be furthered by the open mind and the impartial quest for truth.

There are problems with this dispassionate scientific program, however, for as science moves ahead, it becomes enormously complicated and compartmentalized. If one is to succeed in research, one needs to specialize in a subfield and devote intensive efforts to unraveling the intricacies of that discipline. Within the field of expertise the only effective tools to be used are the rigorous criteria of objective inquiry.

Although it is convenient to divide a subject matter into parts, the specialization that develops may be based on arbitrary divisions, for the objects under study may be continuous and non-discrete. For example, social scientists focus on political, economic, psychological, or sociological processes, drawing upon the literature and the techniques used within their own specialties; but society is an integrated whole, and the divisions of labor need to be synthesized at some time in the future. Medicine deals with the patient as a whole, yet specializations focus on one or more parts—cardiologists on the heart, ophthalmologists on the eyes, orthopedists on the skeletal system. Who will tie the detailed discoveries into integrated theories about how society or a human being functions? Here there is competition between specialists; but we need generalists who can integrate the body of knowledge derived from these separate disciplines into an overall framework.

This becomes all the more important when one recognizes that, although scientists are interested in expanding basic theoretical research, scientific knowledge has some kind of pragmatic application. Economists wish to understand how the economy functions, but they also wish to apply this knowledge normatively: to lower the inflation rate, stimulate production, or cure a recession. Political scientists wish to understand the nature of political behavior—for example, the role of power in human institutions—but this has implications for the policy sciences; for we wish to know so that we can do. Similar considerations apply to natural scientists. Much of the research conducted in the laboratory is done for the technological applications that may result. With rapid scientific advance, new industries are spawned overnight to put new discoveries to concrete uses: biogenetic research and superconductivity, to mention only two recent trends. This being the case, questions of normative value are at the core of science. There is a give and take between theoretical and practical interests. Social needs and interest at any one time direct theoretical research along specified lines. Often funds are expended because of political considerations. Some kinds of scientific research are given strong impetus during wartime. Enormous military expenditures pay for basic research because of its application to new weapons systems. For example, the progress of nuclear physics was accelerated because of the possible military use of the atom bomb. Related to pure research is the role of invention. Scientific technologies are constantly finding applications for new products. Theoretical discoveries in electromagnetics led to the application of electricity to a wide range of products. Discoveries in theoretical nuclear research led to the nuclear-power industry.

Thus questions are raised constantly: What areas ought we to study? Are there some things that we should not seek to know? Some people, for example, have called for restrictions on biogenetic-engineering research, for they fear that we will open a Pandora's box, whose discoveries an authoritarian regime may be tempted to use; or they worry that we may inadvertently damage the gene pool. If cloning becomes possible, it might lead to positive, as well as negative, results. Many today are fearful of further research into the Strategic Defense Initiative, or Star Wars, as it is popularly called. Such research might be dangerous to the future of humankind on this planet and might accidentally provoke a nuclear winter. There have been calls for the restriction of scientific research into the relationship between IQ and race, because it might be used by racists to deny equal rights to some racial minorities. After all, we know that the Nazis designated some races as "superior" and others as "inferior." Some people are so frightened about the possible misuses of science that the scientist is viewed as a Frankenstein figure. There has been some retreat from earlier confidence in the ability of science to contribute to human progress.

It is thus difficult to conduct pure scientific research anywhere without taking into account the possible uses and abuses of the knowledge gained. Here questions of value are central to the very doing of science. Ought we to engage in free research in every field of interest? Should we in every case apply the knowledge that we have learned? Questions of right and wrong, good and bad thus become highly relevant.

Virtually every prospective advance in science has been met with doubt and fear. In the past there have been constant efforts to thwart free scientific inquiry. Civil libertarians, on the other hand, insist that we should not censor scientific research but should allow free reign to the inquiring mind. Humans wish to augment knowledge both for its own sake and for the possible long-range benefits for humanity. The right to know is one thing; the application of this knowledge is something else. We have a right to object to the misuses of science, especially where there are noxious consequences. Understanding the nature of heat and the combustion of gas led to the invention of the gas oven. Gas ovens can be used to cook food or heat homes, but they can also be used to murder people, as during the Holocaust. Freedom of research does not entail freedom of application. The dynamic factor in social change in the modern world is the application of the methods of science to nature and society. How are we to evaluate the uses of science? What is the relationship of research to practice, knowledge to action, science to eupraxia?

Science has enormously expanded our understanding of the universe. It has converted the unknown into the known. It has unraveled formerly unintelligible mysteries by discovering the causes of natural phenomena. Thus science has contributed to our comprehension of the nature of the cosmos and our place within it. This runs into direct conflict with religious metaphors and a wide range of cultural beliefs of the past that are in need of revision. Regrettably, many intransigent believers find this aspect of science even more threatening than its impact on technology and industry. For it is unsettling to ancient conceptions of man as a discarnate soul capable of immortality and of a universe where divinity is working out an inscrutable plan.

Is the scientist able to resolve questions concerning the application of his discoveries? In technology he can point out possible consequences of various choices. He can calculate the cost-effectiveness of different courses of action, and he can provide alternative technical means to achieve ends, but is the scientist the best-qualified person to make decisions about what is to be done and why? Can he make wise value judgments?

Unfortunately, scientific specialization, so essential to its advance, is often the chief obstacle to interpreting or evaluating the applications of its findings. The problem is that a scientist who is a specialist in one field may not be competent to judge questions that go beyond his field of expertise. Scientists are citizens like everyone else, and they may be no better equipped than the next person to engage in moral deliberations. For ethical wisdom requires skills that he may not possess. When it comes to judging questions concerning the impact of this knowledge on other domains of knowledge, the problems are compounded, for science is fragmented.

Does this not suggest that there is a need to develop over and beyond scientific specialization the *eupraxsophic frame of mind*, one that can interpret and evaluate the findings of the sciences and critically judge their uses? The techniques used in scientific research are not necessarily the same as those used in ethical decision-making. For example, a man or woman may be deeply involved on the frontiers of astronomical research, yet unable to make a wise decision about family, personal life, or his or her role in the university or society.

Eupraxsophy concerns good conduct and wisdom: how we should use the findings of science, not simply how nature operates. The fact that we can do something does not mean that we ought to do it. One cannot simply derive a normative judgment from a description of the world. Here we enter into the field of individual and social action; and here all of the members of the community, particularly in a democratic society, have some stake in what is undertaken.

Problems of choice thus transform cognitive scientific questions into practical discussions. Corporate executives not scientists, political leaders not pure researchers, most often are those who decide what should be produced or which policy ought to be adopted—hopefully after consulting scientific experts about the consequences and costs of alternative means.

Some people have encouraged the development of the policy sciences—decision-making theory, game theory, value science, even politics and economics—to help in making wise decisions. Undoubtedly, these fields can provide enormously useful tools to facilitate effective choices. But we still have the problem of how to integrate the detailed knowledge derived from specialized fields.

Another serious challenge we face is how to interpret the various sciences and relate them in a cosmic perspective. How do we interrelate the separate sciences into a broader framework? Is it possible to develop a more comprehensive view of humankind, society, life, or nature, a synthesis of the sciences? Heroic figures in the history of thought have attempted to unify the sciences of the day. Sir Isaac Newton's masterly work seemed to integrate the natural and physical sciences at a crucial moment in history. Ignaz Semmelweis's germ theory of disease provided a powerful tool in medical research. Marx offered a comprehensive theory of historical development, Arnold Toynbee a historical account of the rise and fall of civilizations, and Freud an integrating psychoanalytic theory of human motives. Are all of these theories within the domain of science, or are some of them inherently nonfalsifiable?

The need for integrating theories to tie together the disparate and often fragmented elements of our knowledge is clear. At present the rapidity of scientific progress is such that no one mind seems capable of doing so. A chemist can be an expert in his field, yet may believe deeply in Christianity; a computer scientist can engage in transcendental meditation after work; a mathematician may be a mystic.

It is not inconceivable—and indeed it is likely—that the sciences will ultimately develop their own integrating theories. What would be more appropriate than to have testable scientific theories to unify the principles of political and economic theory, or the laws of biology and psychology, with physics and chemistry? It is important that we attempt to find integrative principles, and it is unfortunate that most scientists are reluctant to venture a cosmic perspective. Since such speculation takes them out of their fields of competence, they suffer the risk of being called dilettantes or popularizers.

THE ROLE OF PHILOSOPHY

Historically, it has been the role of philosophy to support general interpretations of the universe. The pre-Socratics sought to uncover the underlying principles of the universe. Plato postulated the theory of ideas. Aristotle developed concepts and categories that helped interpret and unify the sciences of his day. The classical philosophers have each attempted systematic theories of metaphysics: Aquinas, Spinoza, Descartes, Leibnitz, Hegel, and Whitehead, among others. Thus philosophy has attempted to develop a *Weltanschauung*, a general perspective of reality. As we have seen, this task is exceedingly difficult because of the sheer complexity and accelerating size of the body of knowledge. Philosophers today are generally reluctant to try to fit so many pieces of the puzzle together, and they even deem philosophy to be merely one specialty among others. They eschew the broader questions, such as the meaning of life or the nature of the cosmos. Philosophy today, unlike science, is primarily an *intellectual* affair. The philosopher is concerned with knowledge on the meta-level. The primary task of analytic philosophy is to achieve clarity, to get rid of ambiguity, to attain clear meaning, to define terms and concepts, to bring to light hidden presuppositions, and to analyze whether they are internally consistent or contradictory. Philosophy thus hones our tools; it deals with questions about foundations. It does not engage in empirical research nor does it seek to substitute philosophical knowledge for knowledge derived in any scientific field. Critical philosophy is concerned with evaluating the concepts of others in separate fields of knowledge: the sciences, religion, the arts, history, politics, ethics. By so doing these philosophers believe they can best help researchers in their progressive quest for knowledge.

William James observed that philosophy in its earliest stages sought to encompass the entire body of the tree of knowledge. As newer intellectual fields developed, separate branches of the tree of knowledge broke away from the main trunk. Thus, in the seventeenth and eighteenth centuries natural philosophy became natural science. In the nineteenth century, chemistry and biology developed as autonomous fields of inquiry. The social sciences, originally part of social philosophy, became separate disciplines. In the late nineteenth century, the philosophy of mind was transformed into psychology and neurobiology; in the twentieth century, logic became an integral part of computer science. It is as if philosophy proposes and science disposes, by breaking away into distinct fields of scientific specialization once empirical solutions seem available. What remains to philosophy is a "residue of questions left unanswered." Many of these perennial questions have never been fully resolved to everyone's satisfaction: What is the nature of ultimate reality? Does free will exist? Is man determined? Does God exist? Is the soul immortal? What is truth, beauty, justice? Can we define the good? And then there are new questions thrown into the hopper of unresolved questions of any age, questions that are spun off by the rapid development of the sciences. And so we ask today: Is there intelligent life in the universe? If so, what would this mean to the human species? Does precognition exist? How would it change our perceptions of time? What does neurobiology tell us about the relationship of mind to brain functions? What import does sociobiology have for our understanding of morality? Is moral altruism found in other species?

By dealing with such questions, philosophy thus seeks to clarify meanings, to examine implications, to expose contradictions. It tidies up, so to speak, the conceptual framework of others.

Now this surely is a vital role to play. In any university a department of philosophy can have an important function, and students can be intellectually stimulated by reading great philosophical works. But—and this is a large but—what about the original quest for *sophia*? Can philosophy give us wisdom, that is, some kind of general theoretical understanding of the universe and our place within it? Philosophy historically and almost by definition deals in generalities. Is the philosopher still the wise man able to take the cosmic view? Is he aware of the history of thought and culture, on the one hand, yet attuned to the frontiers of research? Is it the fate of the philosopher to man the rearguard, cleaning up the conceptual debris left by past scientific breakthroughs? Is philosophy ever on the cutting edge, advancing beyond the present, helping to get glimpses of exciting new possibilities? The future of humankind depends in part on our creative audacity, whether we dare to dream of new ideas and to bring these visions into reality. Can philosophy help us in the adventuresome, innovative voyage into the unknown? Or is philosophy simply condemned to tidy up after scientific researchers who have already forged ahead and are far out into uncharted realms? Perhaps it is the science-fiction writer who is the true philosophical harbinger of the future—speculating about the possible, which at some future moment may become the actual. Alas, philosophy cannot do this very well, and thus we must move on into the domain of eupraxsophy.

THE ROLE OF EUPRAXSOPHY

Philosophy presumably involves the love of wisdom, and wisdom can mean many things. It involves some comprehension of what is known and some ability to interpret or relate this knowledge into a meaningful whole, and thus achieve *sophia*. The wise man can sum up what is known and synthesize this into a coherent picture. This is the philosopher-at-large dealing with the broader picture; and the philosopher can provide a valuable service—if only he will undertake this task today as he has in the past. But still he is dealing primarily with the love of wisdom, and this is largely an intellectual affair. Ideas are vital to the life of the mind, and intellectuality is among the highest qualities that we can attain. But man is not simply a passive spectator, beholding in contemplation the majestic scheme of things. He is an actor on the stage of life; he is not only a knower but a doer. The nub of the question concerns not the love but the *practice* of wisdom (*eupraxia*). It is the difference between the stance of the scholar and that of the doer, the passive spectator and the active participant. Thus, we ask, how does one apply wisdom to life as lived? How do we enter into the fray? How do we concretely use our knowledge in the process of living? Here we come directly to *eupraxsophy*.

The Greeks had the ideal of contemplative wisdom: the task of the metaphysician was to understand reality in an abstract way and to make nature intelligible. Knowledge was worthwhile for its own sake, to be enjoyed intrinsically. Man was a curious animal; he found great pleasure in learning about the past, discovering new facts, solving puzzles. All of this is granted. But knowledge also has an instrumental function, as we have learned from Francis Bacon. Knowledge is power. We wish to know so that we may do. Knowledge is a tool of action. It is not simply an internal set of ideas within someone's mind; it spills out into the real world in the form of behavior. Knowledge is not locked within the brain cells of an isolated individual but is expressed on the cultural scale through language. It involves transactions, not only between the individual and nature but also between culture and nature.

The Greek philosophers were interested in practical wisdom, particularly in ethics and politics. This involved the art of living well in the light of reason and of wisely governing states and societies. This is normative wisdom, not merely contemplative but moral wisdom. It begins first with clarifying questions about the meaning of *good*, *bad*, *right*, *wrong*, *justice*, and *injustice*, on the meta-level; but then it goes on, presumably to recommend paths to take. Aristotle offered recipes that the man of practical wisdom should use if he were to be happy. Later, during the Roman era, philosophical schools, such as Epicureanism, Stoicism, and skepticism, provided guidelines on how to live and how to find peace of mind. They were more or less naturalistic efforts to improve life here and now.

The fact that these Hellenistic-Roman schools of ethical wisdom were overthrown by Christianity is one of the great tragedies in human history. Pagan civilization was conquered by a new mystery religion of the East, and naturalistic ethical philosophy was virtually destroyed by a spiritual quest derived from biblical sources. Although impressive efforts were made by theologians, such as Augustine and Aquinas, to use philosophy, the picture they drew was that of a divine universe, in which the supreme duty of man was to know and love God. Religion and theology had conquered philosophy. One reason for the defeat was the fact that Christianity, and later Islam, offered definite faith and commitment, whereas philosophy seemed to provide only indecision and doubt. It has taken Western culture a long time to wrestle free of the stranglehold that successive waves of Christian-Islamic fervor have had on the free mind. It was only during the Renaissance that a new humanistic morality could emerge independently of religion. The humanism of the period was inspired by rediscovering the classics. It attempted to secularize much of life and to substitute a humanistic rather than a spiritual version of reality. Since that time, science has been liberated from a repressive, authoritarian church, and it enabled modern man to examine the book of nature directly, without benefit of clergy.

Let us return to our original question. Can we develop *sophia*— wisdom in practical life where choices are made by individuals and societies on the basis of rational inquiry *and* wisdom in a sense not emphasized by classical philosophy, wisdom as it relates to living (eupraxsophy), that is, theoretical wisdom that is not simply intellectual *but is itself transformed into the practical*? In short, can we develop a cosmic view (*sophia*) that would enable us to live wisely in the world (*eupraxia*)?

In dealing with this task we need to draw upon (1) the methods of scientific inquiry to enable us to understand nature; (2) philosophical analysis in interpreting and integrating scientific knowledge; and (3) ethical philosophy in developing ethical principles and values on the basis of which we can live. We need to tie these strands together into a *philosophy of life*—but more than that, *into a posture of life*, namely, a *eupraxsophy*. Science, philosophy, and ethics can all contribute to this unity, but eupraxsophy involves another element, namely, a *life stance*. It provides us with both a cosmic outlook and a focus or direction within our life-world. In this sense, eupraxsophy can compete with religion in a way that scientists qua scientists or philosophers qua philosophers are unable to do. Can the philosopher compete with the theologian for the souls of men and women? Can the philosopher seek to deconvert true believers and convince them that their conceptions of reality are mistaken? Can the philosopher debate with the fundamentalist Christian, Jehovah's Witness, Mormon, devout Catholic, Orthodox Jew, Muslim, the committed Buddhist or Hindu? Can the philosopher demonstrate how and why he is skeptical and can he offer a positive alternative?

Time and again my colleagues in philosophy say no, that it is not their mission to descend into the marketplace of ideas. Thus they will not debate theologians, Marxists, conservatives, liberals, radicals, or reactionaries. But if not they, then who will do so? Is the role of philosophers to remain in their ivory towers, secluded from the world, analyzing ideas and debating one another, but never seeking to persuade the public? There have been exceptions to this view of the philosophic mission: Marx and Dewey believed that philosophy had a definite role to play in civilization, that it could help transform blind prejudice and habit by means of rational criticism. Nietzsche was an oracle who derided Christianity and socialism and defended the heroic virtues. So did Jean-Paul Sartre, Sidney Hook, and Bertrand Russell. Sartre not only developed a phenomenological existential theory of the human condition but later in life entered into the public political arena. Sidney Hook constantly attempts to use pragmatic intelligence to criticize ideological, religious, and social viewpoints, and he has been forthright in making his views known in the arena of ideas and action. He justifies his beliefs, as did Dewey, on philosophical grounds: philosophers have a role to play in society, and objective judgments about normative matters can be made. Bertrand Russell combined two qualities: He was a skeptical philosopher whose contributions to logic, the theory of meaning, and epistemology were very important; yet he had his own strong convictions upon which he lived and acted. Paradoxically, Russell thought that ethics was not amenable to rational or scientific proof but expressed emotive feelings, for he was aware of the skeptical critiques of the emotionists in ethics. Nevertheless, he was a staunch pacifist who was arrested for breaking the law. He was also throughout his life a resolute defender of sexual freedom, and was fired from the City College of New York for his views. How can we reconcile Russell the philosopher with Russell the activist? He was, I submit, not only a philosopher but a *eupraxsopher* in his public declarations.

By and large, eupraxsophy has not prevailed in the mainstream of the philosophical life, because philosophers deal primarily with *thought*, and to seek to persuade, to the contrary, is to engage in "persuasive definition," perhaps to enter the realm of rhetoric rather than philosophy. Heretofore eupraxsophy has not been enunciated, nor its rationale explained.

If the philosopher qua philosopher will not view philosophy as a way of life, the eupraxsopher will explicitly do so. For the eupraxsopher is not concerned simply with the quest for truth in the world of ideas, as vital as this is to his life, but with life also. In order to live he needs *convictions* upon which he can act and *commitments* to which he can devote his energies. The philosopher may raise objections to any theory—he sees all sides of a question and often cannot make up his mind about any. Philosophy thus never gets beyond the intellectual quest. In this sense, its task is to pose questions, albeit sometimes at the wrong time and in the wrong place. Socrates was a gadfly, and so he was sentenced to death by the Athenians for raising unsettling questions. The philosophic mind deals with questions; it does not provide answers. For even when a solution is proposed, the philosopher sees the difficulties with it and the possible arguments against it. How can the philosopher enter into the fray qua philosopher? Does he not belie his craft as an analytic philosopher? Philosophers lead perilous lives, for when they go outside their craft they can be accused of converting ideas into doctrines, beliefs into dogmas, and betraying their true mission.

RELIGION AND IDEOLOGY

But if the philosopher fears to tread untested waters, others do so with impunity, most especially religionists and ideologues. Let us examine the other end of the scale of human knowledge, religion, where faith is exalted as the preeminent virtue. If we view faith in its extreme sense, it is the willingness to accept as true or real that which is unsupported by evidence or rational proof. Some theologians have exalted the faith-state: "It is the door to things unseen that must first be opened to be understood," declared Augustine. "I believe because it is absurd," asserted Tertullian and Kierkegaard. Belief in Christianity is held to be the most eloquent affirmation of the believer, in spite of obvious con-tradictions. Although the true believer may find such faith morally worthy, the skeptic deplores the betrayal of the standards of logic and evidence and the self-deception involved. Granted that many religion-ists wish to use evidence and to be rational to some extent. Modern bib-lical scholarship has demythologized the Bible, and what survives for some believers is a metaphorical view of God. There are, however, lin-gering forms of religiosity that persist and involve the willful commit-ment to doctrines in *spite of evidence to the contrary*.

Such religiosity is an abandonment of all the standards of objective science and philosophy. Passion dominates critical intelligence. Is not one reason for this sorry state the fact that scientists and philosophers are unwilling or unable to respond to questions or to provide answers to the hunger for meaning? "Does the universe have any purpose?" "What is the meaning of life?" Such questions are rarely answered by the cautious intellectual who will not demean himself to deal with the pleas of ordinary persons. But if the scientist and the philosopher will not respond to these questions, the eupraxsopher will. He has a role to play: for he consciously criticizes the pretentious follies of true believers; he debunks untested tales; and he offers constructive alternatives.

Competing for the souls of men and women in the public arena are ideology and politics, especially the latter, for many have replaced religious faith with a new social dogma, and sometimes even skeptical minds have embraced an ideological-political stance with a vengeance. A good illustration of this, of course, is the devoted Marxist, for whom ideology becomes virtually a holy cause. With the collapse of religious beliefs, new secular messianic ideals fill the void. For many liberal reformers, the chief inspiration for their political views is their indictment of the social order and the desire to transform it into a more just system. Conservatives are likewise determined to defend existing society against it detractors, whom they consider to be immoral. At loggerheads are conflicting moral principles, which are upheld with intense passion by either side, the party of stability versus the party of reform. Stalwart proponents of liberty will view any erosion of it as a threat to the entire moral framework. Some will defend equality, and still others peace, law, and order. A good illustration is the intensity of the abortion debate, where the putative rights of the fetus are pitted against free choice by women.

Political and moral passions may be held as strongly as religious faiths. But often they are held because of class, race, or ethnic background. Here unexamined habits of belief and conduct persist. One may defend a royalist regime because of one's background and breeding; someone else will go to the ramparts because he identifies with the masses. There are free-floating intellectuals who become enthralled with a political ideology; they may even be born-again socialists or libertarians. They may be as firmly committed to their belief as those who hold them as mere habit and prejudice.

Such political and ideological beliefs may not be grounded primarily in *cognitive* states; they are inflamed by feelings and emotions. Once a basic belief system is in place, it may be difficult by argument or persuasion to change it; rationalizations can always be made for faults committed by *our* party candidate or cause, which when committed by the other side are considered egregious moral defects.

An American political convention vividly demonstrates the powerful emotive forces at play. These are not unlike Stalin's Red Square on May Day or Hitler's finely tuned and choreographed rallies at Nuremburg, where the crowds were worked into a frenzy during torchlight parades and were overwhelmed by charismatic orators. A candidate for the American presidency similarly may arouse intense feelings. There is excited cheering on his behalf in halls bedecked with flags. Patriotism is the underlying theme. For many their candidate unquestionably has the *best* policies for the future. The opposing candidate is frowned upon and booed. Such political antics are like football games, where two teams are pitted against each other and where highly excited crowds egg on the home team and jeer the opponents. Seated on either side are the rooters and the cheerleaders; the sports champions are heroic defenders of the home team.

It is one thing to vent one's feelings in an overflowing sports stadium, where mass psychology holds sway and good clean fun is expressed; it is quite another in the political arena. At the far end of the scale there are ideological belief systems that are based on blind faith in party programs and candidates and that are intolerant of dissent. Certainly such political naiveté warrants criticism. The support of the policies, programs, or candidates of political parties should be chastened by some kind of reflective inquiry. One should recognize that everyone makes mistakes, that policies may have to be modified, and that laws may have to be rescinded in the light of empirical consequences. No one candidate is perfect; no one party has a monopoly on sagacity or virtue. Blind allegiance is no substitute for intelligent political wisdom. Would that we could ground political programs in a study of the facts, a comparative analysis of alternatives, and the testing of their consequences in practice. If any field of human endeavor needs a strong dose of skepticism, it is the political; but a candidate is told that such an attitude will not win voters or enlist voluntary support, and that it would be a dull campaign with no fervor or glamour. But do people need outrageous, simplistic emotional appeals in order to participate in the democratic process? These problems are only compounded by the introduction of television into the selling of candidates.

Similar considerations apply to the economic sphere. The ideal economic model is one in which producers and consumers make intelligent choices based upon cost/price considerations, always calculating self-interest and profit. The rational consumer foregoes expenditures today in order to save for tomorrow, investing his capital in productive enterprises that will provide a return. Under this model, the consumer's choice of products is a function of cost, need, and quality.

Alas, the realities of the marketplace are such that decisions are not based on cognitive considerations alone but on taste, fancy, and caprice. There is a disparity between needs and wants, between rational interests and felt desires; and the passionate feelings of a person will intrude in his cognitive estimations of worth. Advertisers have found that there are subliminal and emotive appeals that will sell their products more effectively than consideration of price or quality. Economic value thus is a function of need-want, cognition-feeling. It involves not simply an intellectual belief-state but attitudinal motivation, the so-called subjective factor that stimulates people to produce or consume. In deciding whether to buy something—say a house or an automobile—one can point out the objective properties of the object. One can compare alternative products, but advertisers say that unless a consumer is dazzled in his heart or titillated by his taste buds to want it, unless he really likes the house or the car, he probably will not buy it. Do not similar considerations apply to being in love? If a man loves a woman, there are no doubt objective properties that she possesses. He finds her to be beautiful; she may have a compatible personality; they may share similar values. On the other hand, a woman may be a perfect mate on a computer scale, but love may be absent because there is no *magnetism*.

MAGNETISM

We need to raise similar questions concerning fundamental beliefs, especially in regard to eupraxsophy. The quandary we face is this: Is it possible for those committed to the use of critical intelligence and scientific methods of inquiry *to arouse sufficient conviction and stimulate enough commitment* so that eupraxsophy can compete with the promises of religion and ideology?

We have seen the two extremes: on the one hand, unthinking faith and frenzied dogma, whether in religion or politics; and on the other hand, neutrality and skepticism, the cognitive mind-set in which a person has no strong beliefs or values, but adopts a purely reflective mode. The latter is a highly commendable approach, but it may arouse no convictions and may not be able to compete very well against powerful, antirational belief systems that promise everything.

Surely there is a middle way; surely we can develop convictions based upon the best available evidence, beliefs for which we can give reasons and which yet are of sufficient force to stimulate passionate commitment. By this I mean that at some point what at first is taken as pure hypothesis can be converted into intelligent conviction. This, I submit, is the distinctive role of eupraxsophy; that is, it expresses a cosmic outlook and a life stance, but it also arouses convictions. It appeals to both our intellect and our feelings, and it moves us to action. The eupraxsopher does not betray his objectivity in so moving, since to have passionate convictions is as essential to life as bread. Convictions cannot be disowned as alien to what we are as humans. Though philosophers may reject them as mere "persuasive definitions," the blood and guts of living require that we have some deep convictions. To have convictions is to fuse our beliefs with our attitudes, our cognitions with our feelings, our thoughts with our actions. I am using *conviction* here to refer primarily to root hypotheses or beliefs that are basic to our make-up and frame of reference, those things that we are willing to defend against attack, live and perhaps even die for, the beliefs and values we cherish most. If these beliefs are to motivate us profoundly and to hold our imagination, they must become rooted in our very being; they must give us direction, for they express our life stance. They act as a magnet upon us, drawing us back time and again to our convictions.

To say that we have convictions means that we are convinced of the truth or merits of the beliefs and values we cherish *and* that they are based on evidence, reason, or proof. To be convinced of something means that we give assent because of arguments in its favor. Doubt recedes into the background. We are willing to affirm our beliefs. We are impressed by the logic and persuaded by the evidence. We find the justification conclusive, the proof telling, the facts unmistakable. Thus the beliefs that pass these tests have enduring strength within our belief-structure, and they become convictions. But to be convinced means more than purely intellectual assent—though at a minimum it must mean that—it involves emotive magnetism as well.

Every person has a large number of beliefs that he asserts as being more or less true as part of the body of knowledge. He may feel indifferent about many or most of these beliefs in the sense that he would not care if the opposite were the case. I say that the Amazon River cuts across Brazil, that Iraq has large oil deposits which it is rapidly depleting, or that there is no evidence of intelligent life on Mars or Venus. I may be convinced of the probabilities of these truth claims, but none may have much urgency for me unless I live in Brazil, Iraq, or am involved in space research. I may believe that they are true because of evidential grounds, but they are not *convictions* because convictions involve a moral dimension and an affective force. My convictions point to the basic beliefs and principles within my belief system: my cosmic outlook, my method of inquiry, my life stance, and the social polity to which I am committed. A conviction is a deep belief within my eupraxsophy.

To say that someone is a person of conviction means that he or she is truly committed to beliefs and ideals and that these operate with compelling force. A scientist qua scientist has no convictions per se, only hypotheses and theories, which he can dispense with as the evidence dictates. A philosopher qua philosopher has no convictions, only intellectual concepts, postulates, and presuppositions that are amenable to critical argument. Both the scientist and the philosopher are human beings

and as such surely have their convictions, but not within their disciplines—except possibly in the decision to adopt their professions as a
life stance and to use certain objective methods of inquiry. The reli-
gionist, on the contrary, has more than convictions; he has a creed and a
faith, and for him, evidence or reasons receded into the background.
What is vital to him is the passionate devotion and psychological need
which the faith-state satisfies, often in spite of evidence to the contrary.
The eupraxsopher, on the other hand, has convictions, and these are
double-edged: cognitive beliefs based on evidence rationally coherent
and tested by their consequences *and* attitudinal dispositions that move
him to action. Convictions have cognitive form, but they also express
emotive content and imperative force.

By this I do not mean to imply that a person can never change his
convictions, particularly if he is committed to scientific methods in
inquiry. Presumably the principle of fallibilism applies, and he may need
to revise his views, however difficult this may be. Beliefs are hypothetical, and the probabilities of their truth are a function of the grounds by
which they are supported. Thus we are not *bound* (*religare*) to them,
because they grow out of intelligent processes of critical analysis and verification. They are reflectively grounded, but they are not simply items
of intellectual assent. For once our cognitive hypotheses are transformed
into convictions, they have emotional and motivational power. They are
magnetic and have persuasive force.

Thus one can believe, for example, in democracy as the best form of
government, and one's whole being will be prepared to die for it if it is
threatened; or one can believe in the integrity of science or the importance of human rights. All of these express our convictions as humanists.
But they will be empty beliefs unless they are acted upon. Thus we see
that closely related to convictions are the commitments that flow from

them; once we are persuaded of the truth of our beliefs and of the worth of our values, we are motivated to do what we can to implement and defend them and even to try to convince others of their truth. We are prepared to dedicate our time, efforts, and honor to see that they are implemented. We are ready to act upon them, to put them into *praxis*. In other words, our *sophic* convictions have a *eupraxic* role; they directly affect our conduct. Convictions are not simply internalized belief-states; insofar as they lead to commitments they spill out into the practical world in concrete terms; they guide and direct our choices and our behavior, for they express our deepest beliefs.

INSPIRATION AND ASPIRATION

Can a humanist eupraxsophy sufficiently inspire human beings to develop lofty aspirations? Religionists seize the imagination by denying human finitude, thereby overcoming the fear of mortality. They postulate unseen forces, which allegedly control our destiny and offer us salvation. Religious myths soothe the aching soul and provide an uplift. Can eupraxsophy do the same?

Millions of secularists and atheists have found life ennobling, overflowing with manifold opportunities and excitement. If a person cannot find a divine purpose to human existence, he or she can face the world with courage, accept his or her own finitude, and endure. It is not the "courage to be" that we must develop as much as the "courage to become." We are responsible for our destiny. The meaning of life is not located in some hidden crevice in the womb of nature but is created by free persons, who are aware that they are responsible for their own futures and have the courage to take this project into their own hands.

The choices that are made in life depend upon the socio-cultural context in which we live, and there is a wide constellation of forces at work, including chance and luck. We were cast into the world by our parents without our consent. At some point, as we mature in life, we realize that we are responsible for our choices. Perhaps only in terms of tragedy and profound soul-searching do we raise the questions: Why am I here? What does it mean? How shall I live?

The reply of the theist is untrustworthy, for he offers spurious fairy tales spun out in the infancy of the race and has perpetuated them in continued self-deception. An objective mind cannot easily swallow the myths. But where shall skeptics turn for meaning? It is here that humanist eupraxsophy has something to say. For humanism is an effort to plumb the depths of existence, using science and philosophy, and to commit us to a life stance.

To the question "What do I want?" the humanist replies, "Why not happiness and the full life?"

To "How can I face death?" he answers, "Why not with resolute courage?"

And to "How shall I live fully?" he responds, "By sharing the creative joys and sorrows of life with others."

The tools of the eupraxsopher are not dogma or creed preached to credulous souls, but critical intelligence; not fiction, but truth. Are the responses given to a person in existential despair sufficiently eloquent so that he can be sustained in times of adversity? Can they raise the levels of aspiration to exalted heights? Can they evoke within us strenuous endeavour? Can they motivate us to achieve excellence? Do they have sufficient grandeur?

I respond: They can if they are based on *conviction* and if they can arouse *commitment* and if they call forth our *creative impulses*. Can the nonbeliever live intensely? Can he affirm his life with vigor? I do not see why not. Indeed, the pagan civilizations of the past and the humanist civilizations of the present have done so with vitality and gusto. It is possible to live exuberantly once we shed the illusions that bind us, once we overcome the corroding sense of guilt, once we enter into the world as thinking but passionate beings. Can we overcome pathological belief systems that seek to cripple us? Can we release our natural tendencies to live for ourselves and others in this life without the vain hope of immortality? Can we express the highest ideals? Can we affirm them in the act of living? Can we adopt a Promethean stance, shatter the gods and goddesses of the past, yet live fully as creative beings? Can we share our joys with others and have robust personal lives rich with meaning? Can we create our own plans and projects, and in fulfilling them find them intrinsically rewarding?

These are the questions that the eupraxsopher who has finally given up religion needs to consider and respond to. In the last analysis, the authentic resonance of humanist eupraxsophy is its ability not only to explain the world in the light of the best scientific evidence but also to stimulate within us passionate intensity and the will-to-live, the courage to dream of new goals and to bring them to fruition. The ultimate test of eupraxsophy is whether it helps us to lead joyous full lives and to embark upon new adventures in living.

THE PRACTICE OF
REFLECTIVE ETHICAL INQUIRY

Is it possible to apply reason to conduct? Can we formulate objectives judgments? Is there such a thing as "ethical truth"?

There is a long historical tradition, from Protagoras and the Sophists down to Hume and the emotivists, that denies the possibility of a rational or a scientific ethics, and that reduces ethical judgments to subjective sentiment. These skeptics deny that values are amenable to cognitive criticism, or that standards of objectivity can be discovered. I think that they are profoundly mistaken and that a modified naturalistic and situational theory can provide some basis for rationality and objectivity in ethics.

In what follows, I wish to review the key arguments brought by classical skepticism against the possibility of ethical knowledge, and my responses to them. We may distinguish three types of ethical skepticism.

ETHICAL NIHILISM

The first kind of skepticism is that of *ethical nihilism*, i.e., total negative skepticism. This is the claim that it is not possible to test ethical judgments empirically or by an appeal to reason. This argument assumes various forms. Let us begin with the critique of ontological value. Ethical skeptics, I submit, correctly observe that it is impossible to discover any framework for morality in the universe at large, independent of human experience. The converse is more likely the case; namely, human beings are disposed to read into nature their fondest hopes and to attribute moral qualities to the universe, but these represent the expression of their own yearnings to find an eternal place for their values in the scheme of things.

The most common illustration of fallacious moral extrapolation is the postulation of a divine being (or beings) and the attribution to him or her (or them) of the highest good. For Aristotle, the unmoved movers were engaged in *nous*, or pure thought; they were thinking about thinking. This was considered the noblest form of excellence that Man could attain, and it was what Aristotle himself prized as the highest good. The Old Testament had man created in the image of God, though in reality God is fashioned out of the human imagination and assumes human form, possessed of all of the qualities that we cherish, but in extended form: power, omniscience, immortality. Yahweh is prone to anger and is vindictive and unremitting in his demands for obedience to the moral rules. He is a lawgiver, who issues commandments (through his emissaries, the priests and prophets) that men and women are required to submit to if they are to escape punishment; but these rules in actuality reflect the social structure of the times. The New Testament continues the same kind of moral deception, for it deifies certain moral imperatives found desirable: for example, to love one another as God loves us. In the case of Jesus, this divine form of morality is embodied in human flesh at some point in history. Mohammed has given the Muslim moral code endurance and strength by claiming that it was Allah who defined and proclaimed the code.

Thus theistic creeds that attempt to ground the moral life in ultimate theological truths simply mask the tendencies of humans to attribute their own moral purposes to the universe at large, and to use this postulation to insist that those divine commandments ought to be obeyed. Skeptics have identified the implicit self-deception intrinsic to theological foundationalism. They have pointed out that mutually contradictory injunctions have been derived from the same deity. God has been used to defend both slavery and freedom, monogamy and polygamy, abortion and laws against abortion, war and peace, depending on the religious tradition and the social context in which it was revealed or interpreted. The divine commandments are made to fulfill eminently practical purposes, and the universe is endowed with moral qualities. These ultimately have their source in existential despair, which is transferred into hope by means of religious faith. God is invoked to enable people to endure death and tragedy, to provide some consolation and resolution of the human condition and to guarantee a future existence *in saecula, saeculorum.*

Skeptics have rightly demonstrated that all human values and ethical principles are intrinsically related to the human condition. "Man is the measure of all things, of things that are that they are, and of things that are not that they are not," observed Protagoras, the great Sophist who denied the reality of moral ideas independent of human existence. Theological moral systems do not depart from this, for their moral beliefs and Gods are drenched in human significance and relative to human concerns, although believers may deny that this is the case. Indeed, theism holds that God is a person much like a human being, which only emphasizes the anthropomorphic basis of theistic morality.

A similar indictment can be brought against any kind of Platonic moral realism, i.e., the notion that eternal moral ideas are implicit in a realm of being, and that the task of human reason is to discover and apply these essences to life. Socrates attempted to define "justice" and "the good," hoping that his definitions of absolute ideas would provide a beacon for both the individual soul and the *polis*. For Plato, nature is interpreted as the basis for "the good" over and beyond convention. Skeptics have rightly rejected this theory as pure postulate, without reasonable justification or proof. The reification of essences makes an unwarranted epistemological leap. According to Protagoras, ethics has a relativistic basis: "Whatever is seen just to a city is just for that city so long as it seems so."

A similar critique has been brought against naturalistic theories, that is, any effort to find an ultimate ground for ethics in "human nature," "natural law," "the march of history," or "evolutionary progress." Surely these naturalistic forces are not without human content, for they are related to human institutions. Accordingly, relativism would seem to be necessary as a starting point for any conception of value.

An important distinction must be made, however, between relativism and subjectivism, for to say that morality is related to human beings does not necessarily mean that it is irreducibly subjective. Relativism and subjectivism are not the same, and the former does not imply the latter. One can be a relativist and objectivist. Total negative skeptics argue that there are no standards that can be used to appraise what the individual city deems to be just or good. They maintain that to say something is good or right means simply that we feel this to be the case, and that our sentiments are disposed either to like or dislike it. Some forms of subjectivism reduce to nihilism. For if moral beliefs in the last analysis are nothing but an expression of tastes, feelings, and sentiments—*de gustibus non disputanem est*—then we cannot really demonstrate the moral excellence of one belief over another. If, from the standpoint of the state, whatever is just is relative to convention, custom, or power, then there are no normative criteria for adjudicating differences. "Justice is the interest of the stronger," affirmed the nihilist Thrasymachus in the *Republic*; therefore "might makes right." It is the strongest faction of society that defines moral rectitude and lays down laws to adjudicate conflicting interests. Ethics is nothing more or nothing less than that.

The emotive theory, introduced in the twentieth century by the logical positivists, also expresses a strong form of ethical skepticism. The emotivists distinguish between three kinds of sentences: (1) descriptive statements, which they said could be verified directly or indirectly by factual observations or experiment; (2) analytic statements, which are tautological and established as formally true by deductive inferences; and (3) emotive utterances, which have no cognitive or literal significance, but are expressive and imperative in force. To say that "rape is wrong," for the emotivists, merely means that I (or we) are repulsed by it, and that I (or we) condemn it and command others to do so as well. These sentences cannot be verified in any objective manner, for they violate the principles of verifiability and analyticity.

Extreme subjectivity thus leads us to an impasse, because we need to get on with the business of living with others in the community. Nihilism is a posture that we can hardly afford to adopt in practical life. There is therefore a serious question as to whether or not the reduction of ethics to subjectivity is true to our ethical experiences. For to maintain that there are no cognitive criteria that can be brought to bear in ethical questions, and that in the last analysis it is simply a question of feeling or force, seems to impose a tremendous strain on credulity. For example, if there are no objective standards of ethical value, is the statement that "the policies of Hitler and Stalin were evil" without any basis other than that I or we do not like them? Is the ethical principle "Mothers ought not to torture their children" similarly without any merit? If so, subjectivity reduces human morality either to the toleration of barbarism, for there is no meaningful ground to oppose it, or utter absurdity, in which anything is as good as anything else, and right and wrong have no signification. Under this theory, monsters may be equivalent to martyrs, sinners to saints, egoists to altruists. But if no ethical distinctions are allowed, social life would become impossible. Why doesn't a person steal, murder, torture, or rape? Is it simply a question of sentiment or the fear one will be punished by the police (or God)? This position is contradicted by the evidence of the ethical life: We *do* make ethical judgments, and some are considered warranted. We criticize moral monsters and tyrants and applaud altruists and humanitarians, and with some justification. Ethical nihilism is infantile, and those who vehemently proclaim it in all ethical situations have not fully developed their moral sensibilities. They are concealing their own moral ignorance, and by their total negative skepticism reveal that they have not achieved mature moral growth.

To argue the position of the ethical neutralist—that is, one must be "morally neutral" about *all* moral questions—is similarly mistaken. I would agree that *some* moral quandaries are difficult to resolve, particularly where there are conflicts between rights and goods, both of which we cannot have, or the choice between the lesser of two evils, one of which we must choose. To urge the *universal* suspension of ethical judgment, as the ethical nihilist advocates, however, does not follow. If a skeptic cannot decide between two sides of *any* moral issue, and refuses to choose or to act, is he or she not confessing a similar blind spot concerning the phenomenological character of moral experience and reflection? Or, if one does act, but only from feeling, or because one thinks that following conventional custom is the safest course, is one not insensitive to the deeper nuances of the moral life? Such a position, if consistently defended, reduces to a perverse kind of moral dogmatism.

Agnostic skepticism is not without some redeeming virtues, however. For in opposing moral absolutism or fanaticism, and in seeing through the sham of self-righteous claims that one's moral theories are the ultimate truth, skepticism may be a useful antidote for paternalistic or authoritarian claptrap. Moral absolutists assume that their views are intrinsic to reality, and they all too readily are prepared to suppress those who dissent. Some will seek to apply Reason or Progress or Virtue or God to impose views that simply mask their own preferences. As such, they have substituted dogmatism for inquiry. On the other hand, the persistent denial that there are *any* moral truths at all, if it is consistently asserted, belies its own form of moral intransigence, based largely upon epistemological error, for to deny that there is any kind of moral truth or reliable knowledge is to flout the considerable body of reliable ethical knowledge that we have as a product of the collective wisdom of the race.

MITIGATED ETHICAL SKEPTICISM

A second kind of skeptical theory is less extreme than the first. This we may call *mitigated ethical skepticism*. It assumes various forms. In particular, it states that although sentiment is at the root of all human values, this still leaves some room for rational criticism and control.

One can see this position again first presented by the Sophists. Glaucon, in the *Republic*, outlines the social contract theory, which is later elaborated by modern political philosophers like Thomas Hobbes: All men seek to satisfy their own desires, and self-interest dominates their choices. But they soon see that if individuals had carte blanche to do whatever they wished, there would be "a war of all against all," in which case life would become "solitary, poor, nasty, brutish, and short."

Rational persons thus are willing to limit their liberties, and abide by the rule of law. Here the criterion is the social good, and this is justified because it is to the self-interest of every person to establish a framework of peace, law, and order, in which common guarantees and protections are provided by the civil society and the state. One variation of this is the utilitarian theory; namely, we agree to adhere to the moral rules of society because they provide the conditions of happiness for all. This theory does not attempt to ground justice in God, the Absolute, or Nature writ large. Ethical principles are related to human interests, and they have a conventional basis. But they also provide a consequential and experimental test. Although they are relative to the individual, it is not subjectivity alone that rules, for ethical judgments are still open to rational criticism and may be justified in terms of their instrumental effectiveness.

Hume was critical of certain assumptions implicit in classical ethical theory; for he argued that a moral judgment intrinsically involves feelings: When we judge an act or trait of character as good or bad, we are saying that we approve or disapprove; and we do so because we have sentiments of pleasure or displeasure, and/or we consider it to be useful or harmful. Hume argued that there were basic differences between judgments of fact and judgments of value. Judgments of fact can be ascertained to be true or false. Judgments of morality, on the contrary, like judgments of taste, cannot. Hume inferred from this that reason by itself cannot decide moral judgments, nor can it alone make distinctions or resolve moral quandaries. It is "moral sentiment" that is the wellspring of action, not rationality. What we consider good or bad is dependent on whether moral sentiment is attached to it, and by this he meant the feeling that something is pleasant or useful. Hume was thus a skeptic in ethics, for he held that reason by itself cannot resolve moral questions.

His statement that "Reason is, and ought to be, the slave of passions," is both provocative and controversial. The point that he wished to make was that moral judgments are neither like factual statements, tested by observation, nor like logical inferences, concerned with the relationships of ideas.

In his *Treatise on Human Nature*,[1] Hume observed that in all "systems of morality" that have been enunciated, the proponent would begin with "ordinary ways of reasoning." For example, he might attempt to prove that God exists, or he might describe human society; but at one point he makes a leap, going from what "is" or "is not" the case, to suddenly introducing what "ought" or "ought not" to be the case. Here something not contained in the premise is suddenly introduced into the conclusion. There is an unwarranted gap in the argument. The "ought" is not deduced from the "is," but is arrived at by the surreptitious introduction of the author's sentiment or feeling. The conclusion that Hume drew from his analysis is that we cannot deduce the "ought" from the "is" and that any effort to do so is fallacious. Interestingly, given his skepticism, Hume ended up a conservative; for if there are no ultimate guides or moral truths, then we ought to abide by the customary rules of conduct.

In the twentieth century, a great deal of effort has been expended by philosophers, from G. E. Moore to the emotivists and analysts, to analyze moral language. Moore used the term *naturalistic fallacy* to describe all efforts to define "the good." The naturalistic fallacy is similar to Hume's theory of the "is-ought" dualism.[2] Moore thought that any definition of "good" was vulnerable to the open question argument and that it applied to theological as well as naturalistic systems, to John Stuart Mill as well as Thomas Aquinas. He asked, "*Why* should we accept your definition of 'good'?" and he ended up doubtful of any and all attempts to define "good." Moore's own epistemological theory assumed a form of Platonic realism. "Good" was an "indefinable, non-natural property" by definition, and that was why it could not be defined.

Other twentieth-century neo-Kantians (H. A. Prichard, Henry Sidgwick, and W. D. Ross) agreed that ethical predicates could not be derived from nonethical ones.[3] They thought that the basic ethical terms were deontological ("right," "wrong," "obligation," and "duty") not teleological ("good" and "bad," "value" and "disvalue") and that these were indefinable because they contain an implicit *obligatoriness*. Even though they could not define ethical terms, neither Moore nor the intuitionists considered themselves to be ethical skeptics. Prichard thought that classical ethical inquiry rested on a mistake, for it attempted to prove its first principles, whereas one's moral obligations could be known intuitively and directly within moral situations.

It was the emotivists, whom we have already referred to, especially Charles L. Stevenson, who were ethical skeptics, though some were mitigated.[4] They maintained that the reason *why* we could not define ethical terms was that they were not descriptive, like "hard" or "brittle," but emotive in character. Ethical words were expressive or evocative, much like "ugh" or "whew," and imperative such as "drop dead" or "kiss me." These terms give vent to our emotional attitudes and they express our desires that people agree with us and/or do our bidding. Efforts to define such terms are at best "persuasive definitions," they said, for they simply express our own moral sentiments.

Of special significance is the belief of the emotivists that disagreements in the moral domain often degenerate into disputes between contending parties that could not, even in principle, be resolved. This was due to the fact that the disagreements were "disagreements in attitude," as distinct from "disagreements in belief." As mitigated ethical skeptics, they said that the latter agreements could be resolved by empirical, rational methods, where two or more parties to a dispute differed about factual claims. These controversies at least in principle could be overcome—that is, if the moral dispute was based upon the facts. In some cases the disputes may be purely analytical and concern the meaning of a term, and these could be overcome. For example, C maintains that a fetus weighs 8 ounces, and D claims that it weighs 6. Presumably they could weigh the fetus and decide the factual issue. Or again, if C and D disagree about the definition of "euthanasia" and whether or not it is voluntary or involuntary, then presumably by clearly defining what they mean, they can possibly overcome some forms of disagreement. However, if the dispute is distinctively *moral*, according to Stevenson, then it is attitudinal, and we may not be able to resolve the differences. For example, if D says that "abortion is *wrong*" because the fetus is a person, and E declares that "abortion is *right*" because it is based upon the principle of freedom of choice for women, then we may not be able to resolve the dispute; for the disagreement is not purely factual, but an attitudinal difference about which principle to accept. Hence, an impasse may be reached.

Such moral disputes may not in principle be resolvable. F may think that euthanasia is wrong, because we ought never to take the life of another, and suffering is not necessarily evil; and G may think that euthanasia is right if it is voluntary, because unnecessary pain and suffering in terminal cases is evil. Unless both parties can agree in their basic attitudes about suffering and pain, or voluntary and involuntary death, then they may never be able to resolve their moral controversy.

This second form of ethical skepticism is *mitigated*, because in spite of the ultimate subjective differences in sentiment, feeling, or emotion, the moral life is not entirely bereft of rational considerations, and some moral disagreement may be grounded in belief, not attitude. If, for example, H says that she is in favor of capital punishment because it is a deterrent to future murders, since that belief is contingent on the deterrence issue presumably we can do a factual study to resolve the disagreement. Similarly, if J is against the death penalty because she doesn't think it deters murder, we could again perhaps resolve this by doing a sociological study, examining murder rates in those states or countries that have the death penalty and those that do not, to see if there is any statistical difference. Similarly, we can study those states or countries before and after the imposition or repeal of the death penalty to see whether there is any significant difference. If these moral judgments pro or con were truly a function of the facts, then if they were mistaken about the factual truth, the persons involved might change their beliefs regarding the death penalty.

There are other arguments that mitigated skeptics can introduce in disagreements in an effort to persuade other persons to modify their judgments. They can appeal to the *consistency* criterion. If some persons hold a particular moral principle, and yet make exceptions to it, they are contradicting themselves. For example, they may say they believe in democracy as the best form of government, yet they may exclude one portion of society from exercising the franchise. Presumably, if we show them that they have disenfranchised blacks, we would have an argument against apartheid in South Africa; or if they disenfranchise women, we could make the case for universal suffrage. And if our moralists believe in consistency, they will change their views, for they would want to order their values in some coherent form.

The same considerations apply to the test of *consequences*; that is, persons who hold a principle, even with intensity, may not appreciate all of the consequences that may ensue from it. They may, for example, be committed to equal legal rights for all adults above the age of eighteen, the age at which an individual can vote or be conscripted into the armed services. Yet they might be willing to make an exception to this general principle and prohibit the serving of alcohol in bars to individuals under the age of twenty-one. They may have changed their views because the dangerous consequences—in the form of high rates of fatal automobile accidents—have been pointed out to them. Here consistency may give way to considerations of consequences, and in weighing the latter they may be willing to override the former.

Therefore, even though values may at root be attitudinal, they may be restructured by rational considerations. We have to live and function in the world and to modify our attitudes of these considerations.

The subjectivistic skeptical rejoinder to this, however, is that the reason that some individuals believe in deterrence is that they find murder emotionally repulsive. The reason they find drunk driving abhorrent is that accidental death due to negligence is likewise repugnant to their feelings. Likewise, they believe that universal suffrage is right because they approve of it attitudinally. Even the mitigated skeptic agrees that rational criticisms are accepted ultimately only because they rest on nonrational grounds. These moral postulates, they insist, are without any cognitive justification beyond our sentiment.

Aware of the epistemological pitfalls inherent in morality, some skeptics have urged a return to custom, and they have adopted a conservative bias. If no sentiment is ultimately better than any other, we had best choose those that are less dangerous to society and/or those that do not impede individual liberty. Even this stance is mitigated in its justification. Other skeptics, in agreeing that there are no rational foundations for ethics or politics, may choose to be liberals or radicals. But this stance, in the final analysis, say the skeptics, is likewise based on taste, and no rational proof is possible.

ETHICAL INQUIRY

This leads to our third form of skepticism, that which is related to inquiry. This position involves a skeptical component that is never fully abandoned: cognition in the course of skeptical inquiry. Our search for ethical judgments is thus continuous with our quest for reliable knowledge in all fields of human endeavor. At the very least, our choices are based upon our knowledge of the world and ourselves. The relationship between knowledge and value is central to the concept of *ethical inquiry*.

If we say that ethical choices may be related to rationality, the question that is immediately raised is whether there are any *ultimate* principles that are foundational to our ethical decisions and to which we must be committed if we are to make sense of ethical rationality. I must confess an extreme reluctance to assert that there are; at least all such efforts heretofore to find such first principles *a priori* seem to have failed.

The salient point is that ethics is relative to life as lived by specific persons or societies, and it is rooted in historical-social conditions and concrete behavior. Ethical principles are thus in the mid-range; they are proximate, not ultimate. We do not reason about the moral life *in abstracto* and hope to make sense of it; we always begin *here* and *now*, with *this* individual in *this* society faced with *these* choices. The basic subject matter of ethics is action and conduct. It is not concerned essentially with *propositions* about practice, as some analytic philosophers thought, but with *praxis* itself. The knowledge that we seek is practical: what to choose, how to act, and how to evaluate the courses of action that confront us. We are interested in formulating wise, prudential, effective judgments of practice. This does not deny that we can generalize about human practice, and indeed formulate rules of conduct applicable to similar situations or values that have a wider appeal. Still, the contents of our judgments have concrete referents.

Rarely when we engage in ethical inquiry do we begin at the beginning—except perhaps in crisis/existential situations where we are forced to examine our root values. Rather, we find ourselves in the midst of practical demands and conflicts, trying to make sense of the web of decisions and behavior in which we are entangled. And included in our nexus is the considerable fund of normative data that we bring with us: the things we cherish or esteem, or conversely detest or reject, and the principles to which we are committed. Ethical inquiry is initiated when there is some puzzle about what we should do or some conflict between competing values and norms. It is here that skeptical inquiry is vital: for it is the open mind in operation that is willing to examine our values and principles, and to select those that seem appropriate. The ethical inquirer in the best sense is committed to the use of reflective intelligence in which he is able to define and clarify his values and principles and to search for alternative courses of action that seem most fitting within the context of inquiry.

The ethical inquirer, like the scientist, seeks knowledge, but he does not simply describe what is factually the case or explain events by means of causal theories. Nor is he interested in arriving at analytic or formal truths. His goal is eminently practical: to choose something that will guide behavior and affect the world. This knowledge is similar to the kinds of knowledge sought in the applied practical sciences and arts. It is similar in one sense to the use of technological know-how in such fields as medicine, pedagogy, engineering, and architecture, where we are concerned with doing something, changing events, or creating, making, or manufacturing things. These require some skill and expertise, the prudential adaptation of means to ends. The doctor, lawyer, or teacher wishes to achieve certain goals: to cure patients, protect clients' rights, or educate students. And there are reliable procedures by means of which these purposes can be achieved. An engineer wishes to build a bridge or construct a space station. There is a considerable body of technological knowledge to guide him or her in doing so. Ancient Greece and Rome had not developed the technological arts to the extent that they have been developed since; if they had, they would have recognized their tremendous impact, and the skeptical schools of philosophy would perhaps have made less headway. Nihilistic and neutralistic skepticism about technological knowledge makes no sense today, since technology presupposes causal theories about how nature operates, and its principles are tested experimentally. However, all such technological fields, replies the ethical skeptic, presuppose their ends—for example, the desire to improve health, to achieve rapid travel, and so on. Where do we get our ends from, if not sentiment? asks the ethical skeptic.

VALUATIONAL BASE

My answer is that cognition has a role in formulating our ends. But we begin again *in the middle*; there is already a body of ethical principles that we possess concerning our ends. The evaluation of ends in each case is a function of tested procedures. In any context of ethical inquiry, it is best to consider ethical beliefs—including those inherited from the past—as *hypotheses*. They should be tested each time by reference to the relevant facts, the *valuational base*. What do I mean by this?

Common Moral Decencies

First, there are, as I will show in chapter 6 the common moral decencies, that is, the ethical wisdom that we have inherited from human civilization. I am here drawing on the abundant evidence that humans, no matter what their culture, have similar needs and face similar problems—such as the need to survive, maintain health, and find adequate food and shelter; to engage in sexual intercourse and reproduction; to nurture, protect, and educate children; and so on. In spite of cultural relativity, there are similar responses to life's problems. In order to satisfy human needs and guide human interactions, a set of common moral decencies have developed. I have listed the basic moral decencies as follows: (1) *Integrity*: truthfulness, promise-keeping, sincerity, honesty. (2) *Trustworthiness*: fidelity and dependability. (3) *Benevolence*: good will, nonmalfeasance, sexual consent, and beneficence. (4) *Fairness*: gratitude, accountability, justice, tolerance, and cooperation.

To illustrate: The principles that we ought to tell the truth and that we ought to keep our promises are prima facie rules that in general apply to all civilized societies, notwithstanding that in some situations there may be conflicts between them and that exceptions may be made. Our *actual* duties in practical situations are not the same as our *prima facie* general duties. These principles, I submit, are transcultural, and they are as meaningful to the Christian and the Hindu as to the Confucian and the Muslim, the atheist and the unbeliever. Those who violate the common moral decencies challenge the basic body of ethical truths governing moral conduct that has been transmitted to us as the collective learned wisdom of humanity. I recognize that there is still considerable cultural diversity, and that not all societies recognize all of these principles. Moreover, there are many disputes about values and principles that are virtually irreconcilable. But I submit that humankind has reached the stage where the fundamental decencies are now generally accepted by the reflective person, and they are even endowed by some with "sacred" significance or legal sanction and support. The term *civilized* is virtually identical to the recognition of the common moral decencies; and *uncivilized* or barbarous behavior means that they have been grossly violated.

Basic Human Needs

Similarly, we discover a set of basic and invariant human needs that are essential to all members of the species. These require some satisfaction if human beings are to survive and function in a meaningful way.

First are the biogenic needs: (1) *Survival needs*: the need to be protected from dangers or death from natural disasters, wild animals, or threatening human beings. (2) *Homeostatic needs*: sufficient food, clothing, and shelter. The organism needs to maintain some equilibrium against threats to its health and, when it is disturbed, to restore homeostasis. (3) *Growth needs*: the normal patterns of growth and development of the infant, child, and adult, including standing, walking, talking, reading, sexual development, and maturation. These are intrinsic to the biology of the species and have some genetic basis, though they also have a socio-cultural dimension. (4) *Reproduction* is essential to the survival of the species, though it is not necessary for each individual to reproduce. (5) The need to *discharge surplus energy* is also an organic requirement for healthy functioning.

Second are the *psycho-sociogenic needs*: (6) *Love needs*: the ability to relate to others intimately and to achieve orgasmic satisfaction. Love entails affectionate regard for other persons on many different levels, not only the ability to receive love, but to bestow it upon other persons. This implies not simply sexual love but parenting care and other forms of tender attachment to the well-being of others. (7) *Belonging to some community*: the ability to identify on a face-to-face basis with others, both in friendship and collegiality, and this involves a relationship of charity and some altruistic concern. (8) *Self-respect*: some self-confidence in one's own abilities is essential for normal growth and development. Self-love may be in part a reflection of how a society evaluates a person, but is also depends on a person's own self-validation. (9) *Creativity*: the ability to adapt to problems, work creatively to do so, to reorganize the varieties of materials in the world, and to introduce changes in the environment.

Related to these needs are a concomitant set of excellences, or virtues, which I explore in chapter 7. There are comparative standards by which we may evaluate whether or not a person has achieved a good life. These are normative criteria that we may use to appraise moral excellence. These are qualitative standards of nobility that apply to moral character and behavior and they express the ethics of humanism. Thus we may ask of a person, Has he or she (1) developed some *autonomy* and power, the ability to control his or her own life, (2) has some capacity for cognitive *intelligence* and critical thinking, (3) maintains some measure of *self-discipline* and self-control, (4) has developed some *self-respect* for oneself, (5) has reached some level of *creative actualization*, (6) is sufficiently *motivated* to live and function; (7) has an *affirmative* attitude that life is worth living; (8) has achieved some degree of *health*; (9) is able to find pleasure in living and some *joie de vivre*; and has developed some *æsthetic appreciation*.

Now I realize that a skeptical challenge may be brought against elements within the valuational base as outlined above. Someone may ask: Why accept the common moral decencies? Why have integrity or be trustworthy, benevolent, or fair? To which I respond that some reflective inquiry can be made about the application of each of these principles to a given situation. These are only *prima facie*, general rules that provide us with some general guidelines, not absolute norms. Yet a nihilist may seek to deny them all. "Why not kill or rape if I want to?" he asks.

A skeptical critic may raise similar doubts about the concept of "basic human needs" I refer to above or they may reject the ethical excellences I have enumerated. "Why actualize my potentialities, or seek to grow, or be intelligent?" A drug addict or alcoholic may throw caution to the winds and abandon health for the sake of pleasure. "Can you prove or demonstrate *why* I cannot overthrow all of these norms?" he may plead. My response is that there are processes of growth intrinsic to the ethical person and that we are potentially moral beings, both in relation to others and to ourselves. Individuals, however, need to go through the stages of development in order to appreciate the authentic ring of ethical excellence. I am thus presupposing a level of ethical awareness, or conscience, that individuals at certain periods of life need to understand and realize. Human beings have some means of freedom, and they may choose to abandon the call of the ethical life in a mad quest for power or pleasure. Or they may wish to tempt fate by a determined effort to think the unthinkable and perform the grotesque or bestial. There are moral monsters who will lie, steal, cheat, torture, and maim others for the hell of it, or because they are self-destructive. What are we to say of them?

I submit that such individuals are grossly underdeveloped; they are moral cripples. Their ethical understanding has been thwarted or is impaired; they are impervious to ethical truths and unsuited for ethical conduct. Some individuals are unable to do mathematical computations; some lack technological know-how or musical proficiency; some are unable to change a fuse or fix a flat tire. Ethical actions likewise depend upon some degree of ethical knowledge, and some individuals may be sadly deficient in this regard. They may need ethical education in order to develop general habits of responsibility, to have an authentic regard or a loving concern for another person. They may lack self-discipline and self-restraint, temperance, moderation, prudence, or practical ethical wisdom. I am prepared, of course, to admit that some individuals may be psychopaths (such as serial killers), though this may be due to some genetic defect and some distortion in their psycho-sexual development. They may have lacked proper moral training as youngsters, such that they never developed a mature ethical appreciation. But this says more about their personal disorientation than it does about the existence or nonexistence of a body of ethical truths as the repository of civilized conduct.

PLURALISM IN VALUES

Now I have referred to the "common moral decencies," "basic human needs," and "ethical excellences" as data within the valuational base to which we may appeal. But this no doubt is too general to tell us what to do in specific cases. Moreover, human wants and needs, values and norms, and principles and standards, are infinitely multifarious. They differ as human personalities differ, and they change as society changes. There is a wide range of tastes in food, wine, sports, art, dress, and mannerisms, and there is pluralistic diversity in cultural values. Many different kinds of idiosyncratic wants become virtual needs and are linked with our basic biogenic and psycho-sociogenic needs. Ethical choices are always functions of the unique, deeply private tastes and desires, wishes and preferences, of each person. The choices we make are also relative to the concrete socio-cultural-historical framework in which we live, and this includes the particular laws and social customs of our society. Life in ancient Egypt, Israel, Greece, or Mesopotamia, differs from that lived in medieval China, modern Japan, the Middle East, Western Europe, or the Americas.

All of these differences must be packed into the valuational base, and they influence the choices we make. The decision whether something is good or bad, right or wrong, is accordingly a function of the actual *de facto* prizings and valuations, customs and mores, laws and institutional demands of the times in which we live. What was a wise choice for Pericles in ancient Athens may not be the same for the Roman statesman Seneca, or for Abelard's Heloise, or for Sir Walter Raleigh, Mary Wollstonecraft, or Admiral Peary. Hence, there is an intrinsic *relativity* and *contextuality* of all choice, for it is always related to specific individuals and cultures. Yet, although the relativity of choice is *endemic* to the ethical life, there are still ethical qualities that are generalizable to the human condition. This is why we can empathize with a Hamlet or an Othello or a Lady Macbeth as they wrestle with their moral dilemmas. They have a kind of universal message, and can speak to each and every one of us.

The point that I am making is that there is a phenomenological structure to ethical experience, and some objective considerations are relevant to choices. Our individual values and principles may be tested on a *comparative* scale, in terms of the alternatives and options facing us. They may be *evaluated* by their *effectiveness*. They may be appraised by their *consistency* with the norms that we hold. In judging, we can estimate the real consequences of our decisions in the world, the effects upon us and others within the range of interaction. Insofar as we take into account these factors, then a reflective component has intervened in the process of judgment. John Dewey has distinguished between a *prizing*, where we value something and an element of immediacy, feeling, and pleasure is involved, and an *appraisal*, where a cognitive element intervenes.[5] It is the difference, he says, between a *de facto* acceptance of the given and a *de jure* warrant that it is fitting within the situation. The difference between prizing and appraisal is that the latter involves a *transformative* aspect; that is, in the process of inquiry the reflective judgment can become constituent of the valuation and may modify the prizing.

For example, I may be in the market for a new car. The infantile approach would be to buy the automobile with the most appealing lines and color. An adolescent's response would be to purchase the sports model simply because he or she *likes* it. But an adult would say that he or she needs to appraise the value of the automobile. In a process of valuation, the adult weighs merit on a comparative scale: "Can I afford this car?" "How much will I receive for my trade-in?" "Does it get good mileage?" "How safe is it?" "How does it compare with other models of other manufacturers?" In the process, this person may end up by purchasing a different model after having calculated the comparative costs, effectiveness, and consequences. Although one's feelings are relevant in the valuing process, the final decision is also related to one's cognitive beliefs. An estimate of the value of the car is a function of the objective qualities of the object. One's prizings are dependent upon one's appraisals. Ralph Barton Perry[6] defined a value as "the object of any interest." I would modify this definition as follows: "A value is an interest in an object in which I have both prized and appraised its worth."

A normative belief is not the same as a descriptive belief. The first entails an evaluation and prescription of a course of conduct, the second describes or explains a factual state of affairs. Formulating a normative belief is not dissimilar, however, to testing a descriptive belief. In both cases we seek to justify our belief as true or normative. In questions of valuation, we appeal to reason to justify our choice. We consider evidence, we take into account consistency and consequences, and there is a body of previously tested ethical principles upon which we draw. I know that if I have a headache, and I take two aspirin tablets, I may alleviate my pain. This is a prescriptive recommendation that has been verified empirically. Similarly, I learn that, if I were to lie to another person, I wouldn't be trusted, and that if another person were to lie to me, our relationship would be jeopardized. Thus, I learn that telling the truth is the most prudential policy to adopt, and as a mature adult I come to feel *strongly* about this common moral decency on both cognitive and attitudinal grounds.

What I have been describing is the constitutive role that deliberation can have in the process of decision-making. Thought becomes essential to the very fabric of the ethical life, and we thus have some role in developing our own ethical sensibilities. We are able to resolve moral questions without necessarily deriving what we ought to do from fixed or ultimate principles. The "ought" cannot be easily deduced from the "is," yet in any process of intelligent deliberation it can be a function of a process of valuational inquiry. What I decide to do is relative to the facts of the case, the circumstances before me, the various alternatives I face, a consideration of the means at my disposal, and the likely consequences of my acts. Intrinsic to the valuational base in terms of which I make my choices are value-laden data: my previous prizings and appraisals, the common moral decencies, the ethical principles of my society, considerations of human needs, comparative excellences, and my own unique wants and desires. We need not deduce our duties from absolute universal rules. Moral reasoning is not the application of simple recipes, nor is the process one of drawing inductive generalizations from the past. Ethical reasoning involves a process of what I have called *act-duction*.[7] By this I mean that we infer the actions that are most appropriate—we act-duce—given the valuation base at hand. On the basis of this, some choices may thus be said to be more reasonable in the situation than others.

ETHICAL FALLIBILISM

Ethical knowledge has a degree of probabilism and fallibilism attached to it. We need to recognize that there are alternative lifestyles and a wide variety of human values and norms. This presupposes some comprehension of the fragility of the human condition and some skepticism about our ultimate perfectibility. Thus, ethical wisdom recognizes that life is full of uncertainties. In one sense, it is permeated by indeterminacies. We can very rarely, if ever, be absolutely certain of anything. There are few finalities that we can grasp onto. There are always new challenges, new problems and conflicts, new discoveries and opportunities that confront us. The pervasive character of human existence is the fact that we are forever confronted by ambiguities. No one knows for sure what will happen tomorrow, or next year, or during the next century. We can make predictions and forecasts, and these may or may not come true. We note regularities and trends, and we find some order in nature and society (in the sciences and ordinary life), on the basis of which we can make wise choices Alas, life is full of surprises: An unexpected accident upsets our best-laid plans; a freak storm fells a tree and it lands on our house; the bizarre suddenly intrudes into our life-world. There are sudden breaks or chance contingencies. Anomalies beset us, like a typhoon suddenly blowing in on us, or a hailstorm in the summertime. Thus one can never rely entirely on one's past experiences or achievements. There is always something new to contend with. We encounter paradoxes, dilemmas, and puzzles. And we may be faced with insuperable odds or excruciating choices. Our options may be awesome and terrible. We may suffer great financial losses and be close to bankruptcy. Or we may have an over-whelming victory in politics or war, although we cannot sustain heroic efforts indefinitely without becoming exhausted. Other persons or soci-eties may emerge to challenge our hegemony, and this may lead to con-flicts. Polarities are ever-present. The virtuous may become corrupt; the corrupt may be reformed; the good turns out to be bad; our grand suc-cesses may be followed by ignominious defeats. For every move we make there is a counter-move by someone else. Life is replete with sorrow and tears, but also with laughter and joy.

Given these indelible generic factors about the human condition, we cannot escape from making choices, however painful or exciting they may be. And what we ought to do depends on the situation. Often the dilemmas we face have no solution. We sometimes have to make a choice between two unmitigated evils, or between two goods, both of which we cherish but cannot have. The skeptic or the cynic or the pessimist is wont to point out that any effort to achieve utopia, ultimate perfection, or nirvana is an illusion and bound to fail. Yet some optimism is war-ranted. We may be inspired by the steady progress and achievements of the human species in history. This may be attributed to the humanist virtues of courage and endurance, the will-to-become in spite of obsta-cles, the use of critical intelligence (mingled with compassion) to solve our problems, and the determination to lead the good life as best we can. This ethical position may be described as *melioristic*. It does not hope to attain the unattainable, whether in this life or in the next, but it does believe that we can improve the human condition and that we can achieve the better, on a comparative scale, if not attain the absolute good. But to succeed in life requires the constant use of ethical rationality. We do the best we can, given the limitations and the opportunities discovered within the situations of life. In making choices, we can draw upon our knowledge of the common moral decencies, our moral heritage, and the fund of human wisdom. But ethical inquirers must be prepared to modify their beliefs in the light of altered circumstances.

There is thus a *revisionary* character endemic to morality, for new principles are constantly being discovered and introduced. It took a long time in human history to finally eliminate slavery and to begin to liberate women from male domination. It is only relatively recently that the ethical principle that "all persons are entitled to equality of consideration" has been recognized. In the field of medical ethics, the principles of "informed consent," "voluntary choice," and the "autonomy of adult patients" now provide guidelines for medical practice. A whole new constellation of "human rights" is now being recognized worldwide. Thus there is a continual revision in our ethical values and principles as we learn from experience and make new discoveries in the sciences. Yet we are constantly confronted by moral absolutists—conservatives or reactionaries, on the one hand, or radical innovators on the other—who wish to substitute moral fanaticism for ethical inquiry.

Some degree of skepticism is thus a necessary antidote to all forms of moral dogmatism. We are continually surrounded by self-righteous moralists who claim that they have the Absolute Truth or Moral Virtue or Piety or know the secret path to Progress, and they wish to impose their convictions on all others They are puffed up with an inflated sense of their own rectitude and they rail against unbenighted immoral sinners who lack their moral faith. These moral zealots are willing to repress or sacrifice anyone who stands in their way. They have unleashed conquering armies in the name of God or the Dialectic or Racial Superiority or Posterity or Imperial Design or the Free Market. Skepticism needs to be applied not only to religious and paranormal fantasies, but to other forms of moral and political illusions. These dogmas become especially dangerous when they are appealed to in order to legislate morality and are used by powerful social institutions, such as the state or church or corporation, to enforce a particular brand of moral virtue. Hell hath no fury like the self-righteous moral fanatic scorned.

The best antidote for this is some skepticism and a willingness to engage in ethical inquiry, not only about their *moral* zeal, but about *our own*, especially if we are tempted to translate the results of our own ethical inquiries into commandments. The epistemological theory presented here, the methodological principles of skeptical inquiry, has important moral implications. For in recognizing our own fallibility we thereby can learn to *tolerate* other human beings and to appreciate their diversity and the plurality of lifestyles. If we are prepared to engage in cooperative ethical inquiry, then perhaps we are better prepared to allow other individuals and groups some measure of liberty to pursue their own preferred lifestyles. If we are able to live and let live, then this can best be achieved in a free and open democratic society. Where we differ, we should try to negotiate our divergent views and perhaps reach common ground; and if this is impractical, we should at least attempt to compromise for the sake of our common interests. The method of ethical inquiry requires some intelligent and informed examination of our own values, as well as the values of others. Here we can attempt to modify attitudes by an appeal to cognitive beliefs and to reconstruct them by an examination of the relevant evidence. Such a give-and-take of constructive criticism is essential for a harmonious society. In learning to appreciate different conceptions of the good life, we are able to expand our own dimensions of moral awareness; and this is more apt to lead to a peaceful world.

By this I do not mean to imply that anything and everything can or should be tolerated and/or that one thing is as good as the next. We should be prepared to criticize moral nonsense parading as virtue. We should not tolerate the intolerable. We have a right to strongly object, if need be, to those values or practices that we think are based on miscalculation, misconception, or are patently false or harmful. Nonetheless, we might live in a better world if *inquiry* were to replace faith; *deliberation*, passionate commitment; and *education and persuasion*, force and war. We should be aware of the powers of intelligent behavior, but also the limitations of the human animal and of the need to mitigate the cold and indifferent intellect with the compassionate and empathic heart. Thus I conclude that within the ethical life we are capable of developing a body of melioristic principles and values and a method of coping with problems intelligently. There is a form of *eupraxia*, or good practice, that we can learn to appreciate and live by, and this can be infused with *sophia*, or wisdom. When our ethical judgments are based on ethical inquiry, they are more apt to express the highest reaches of excellence and nobility, and of civilized human conduct.

Chapter 6

THE VALUATIONAL BASE I

The Common Moral Decencies

THE BEGINNINGS OF ETHICAL INQUIRY

Ethical inquiry can begin at different stages of life. Some people, hidebound by their religious codes, resist this. They are opposed to ethical inquiry because they fear change. It is threatening to them, and they seek to block it; yet no one can resist inquiry entirely. To live and function is to be challenged in one's moral beliefs and in how to apply them to concrete situations. The task of critical philosophical ethics is to engage in such inquiry directly and consciously. Virtually the entire history of philosophical ethics has been devoted to the effort to establish ethics on rational grounds. It is the quest for knowledge of good and evil. Where shall we begin this inquiry, we may ask?

Some important distinctions need to be made between normative ethics and metaethics. Normative ethics is concerned with issuing prescriptive recommendations of how we ought to live and with assisting us in framing value judgments. The normative ethicist will tell us what is good, bad, right, or wrong, and what is the just society. Philosophers from Plato and Aristotle to Spinoza and Mill have made an effort to provide practical wisdom to guide conduct.

Metaethics is one step removed from the actual decisions that people make. It is an effort to understand *how* people make ethical choices, and how they go about justifying them. There are two central problems to metaethics. The first concerns the definition of moral terms and concepts: Can we define *good, bad, value, right, wrong*? The second is concerned with the methods or criteria for establishing ethical truths; what do these moral concepts refer to, if anything? The problem of definition has been a complex one for philosophers. As we have seen, Platonists consider such concepts objectively real, and have postulated an ideal realm that may represent them. Such theories are tied to general theories of the nature of language. G. E. Moore considered the term *good* to refer to a non-natural property known by direct inspection but not capable of identification with any empirical or natural property, and hence, indefinable. Any effort to define it, he said, committed the "naturalistic fallacy."

Other philosophers, such as A. J. Ayer and Charles L. Stevenson, believed that such terms have no objective reference at all. They are emotive and imperative, simply expressions of our attitudes that are used to influence the behavior of others. This form of ethical skepticism has been hotly debated in the twentieth century. Critics maintain that its interpretation is too narrow, since value terms have many functions other than the expressive and imperative. There are many nuances governing their uses, and they make sense not simply as descriptives but are used to perform many functions.

Some philosophers have nevertheless attempted to provide naturalistic definitions of terms by reference to behavior; the task here is to seek to understand the phenomena. Values emerge where there is life, and in human affairs, where there are conscious processes of selection. Values thus refer to forms of preferential behavior; to say that something has value for an individual or society means that it is esteemed and has positive worth. This applies conversely for disvalue. Values are therefore the object of any interest or need. Given the wide diversities in behavior, however, certain questions have been raised: whether all values are equal in worth—this would mean a kind of subjectivism—or whether it is possible to offer some kind of critical standards by which to judge them. Although values are relative to the valuer, there are degrees of objectivity concerning their moral worth.

I submit that to say something has value need not mire us in subjectivity. In simply describing the behavior of humans, we find a wide range of preferential activity: People value everything from chocolate ice cream to ice hockey, from sexual pleasure to the *Mona Lisa*, from cricket to moral sympathy. The question is whether normative standards can be used to evaluate the diversity of likes and wants on a comparative scale of values. Here the ethical ingredient intervenes not only for the individual in terms of his personal life, but for the society, where values either come into conflict or harmony.

A second major problem of metaethics is to ascertain whether there are criteria for judging competing systems of value. Are certain normative standards more appropriate than others? If so, how do we go about validating or vindicating our value judgments? A significant number of criteria have been introduced by philosophers to help us in the decision-making process.

In one sense, this inquiry is epistemological, for we are concerned with ethical knowledge and the question of truth. Is there any such thing as an ethical truth—analogous to an empirical or scientific truth—and if so, how do we go about establishing the veracity of an ethical claim? Ethical truths appear to be far more difficult to establish than ordinary factual truths. We can prove to someone that a table is made of wood or that it is hard, but not as easily that it is beautiful or valuable. I think that there are objective criteria to which we can refer and that it is not simply a question of caprice or taste. The facts of the case are relevant to our ethical judgments, but not sufficient in themselves, since normative attitudes are present. Apples and pears may be graded on the basis of objective qualities, and this does not depend solely on the taste of the beholder, although that is an essential ingredient. There are objective properties of the fruit, on the basis of which we make a value judgment. Similarly, we may judge the moral worth of an action in part by relating it to the facts of the situation. Complete skepticism or nihilism are indefensible, for we make normative claims throughout life. Someone who refuses to examine the objective factors intended by a normative claim we may say is normatively blind or deficient.

Philosophers have introduced criteria for making value judgments: Aristotle defined happiness as the ultimate good, Bentham and Mill used the greatest good for the greatest number criterion, and Kant employed the categorical imperative. I do not think that the effort to find a single standard or criterion as the touchstone of ethical choice has succeeded. All these efforts are simplistic, for they attempt to reduce ethical choice to an ultimate principle or value, whereas ethical choice is pluralistic. It is far more complicated than most ethical philosophers have allowed, for it involves a multiplicity of considerations that we need to draw upon within a situation. The great philosophers have made contributions to ethical inquiry, but the principles they have introduced usually provide only one criterion to be considered along with others. I am here suggesting a kind of ethical eclecticism, in which we draw from the best insights of a variety of theories.

For purposes of our analysis I wish to focus on the fact that there usually are a great number of moral principles to which we may be committed. Indeed, in an ethical situation, it is often the clash of our values and principles that is at issue, and we need to weigh and balance all of them in making our choices. Societies have evolved any number of moral principles to which people become committed: it is our task, often, to adjudicate between them.

But what do I mean by the term *principle*? I would define an ethical principle as a rule we appeal to in order to guide conduct. An ethical principle is *general* in that it designates an entire range of actions which comes under its rubric. I am unwilling to say that it is absolute or universal, for any one principle may clash with others, and there may sometimes be exceptions. The term *general* is sufficient, for principles can be generalized in the sense that they are introduced to govern various forms of conduct that have similar characteristics. W. D. Ross used the term *prima facie* to apply to the general duties to which we are obligated, at least presumptively, unless other considerations outweigh their application. I would extend his terminology to say that there are sets of *prima facie general principles* to which we are obligated in the sense that we ought to follow them.

These principles are not actual or concrete obligations. Whether or not we have an actual obligation can only be determined after a reflective evaluation of competing principles and values within a context of inquiry. These principles are normative in the sense that they establish norms to guide our conduct. They are recommendations for action, and have an "oughtness" attached to them. Moreover, they are both emotive and cognitive in force and function. To say that someone is committed to a set of moral principles means that these have some internalized influence upon his motivation; they have the force of a psychological disposition. To say that a man or woman has principles that he or she stands by suggests some deeply rooted convictions.

These principles are also cognitive—or at least can function as such—for they can be tested in part by their consequences and modified or altered as the result of a process of inquiry. Thus, reason can be constitutive in the attitudinal state and be deeply interwoven with and influenced by psychological attitudes. Deliberative thought enters into the process by which we validate and vindicate our ethical principles and make them part of our being.

I submit that there are two main sources for the ethical life. First, there is a set of ethical principles, which are general rules governing our behavior and to which we are *prima facie* committed. And second, there is a wide range of values to which we are also devoted. How our principles and values relate to one another is a problem I shall address; I would only suggest for now that we need to weigh both our principles and values in any situation in which we have embarked upon a course of ethical inquiry.

PRINCIPLES, MORAL AND ETHICAL

I will focus now on moral and ethical principles and the role that such principles play in the life of the individual, especially as he or she relates to others in society. Although the terms are often used interchangeably, there is some difference between them: *Ethical* principles may be said to differ from *moral* principles insofar as the former have been explicitly modified by critical cognition and intellectual inquiry. Both moral and ethical principles, however, are rooted in human behavior.

Are there any general ethical principles that apply to human beings, no matter what the society? Do we have an obligation to follow them? Can we, in other words, discover any *common moral decencies* that have emerged in human conduct?

As we have seen, our moral and ethical principles are general *prima facie* guides for conduct. Etymologically, the term *principle* comes from the Latin *principium*, which refers to the beginning or foundation, that is, the source or origin, or primary truth. To refer to a person's *principia* in the moral sense is to designate the most basic norms by which he lives, those he cherishes and considers most fundamental in his life. A *principled* person has moral principles, which he is willing to stand on, and support when need be, and perhaps, if he has the courage, even to fight for. He is faithful to his moral convictions as to how life should be lived. He is reliable and trustworthy—unless he is excessively self-righteous. One may not agree with the principles he lives by, but at least he can be counted on to behave in 93 terms of them. An *unprincipled* person is without scruples; he has no qualms about violating the standards of equity and probity.

Individuals whose principles fit into one kind of morality—that is, a religiously based moral code—take their principles to be absolute and universal God-given rules that they are duty-bound to follow. For critical ethical inquirers, a principle will not be taken as an unalterable regulation; it does not lay down a directive for everyone to follow uniformly. One has a conditional, rather than a categorical, duty; it is more like a hypothesis than a dictate, amenable to critical interpretation and appraisal before it is applied in a concrete context. This does not mean, however, that a general principle can be easily violated; once it is discovered or developed it cannot be taken lightly or abandoned. If it is deeply rooted in conduct, it cannot be blindly ignored or rejected without some justification. A general principle ought to be followed unless good reasons are given to demonstrate why it need not be.

We recognize a number of moral decencies that should apply to our conduct, especially in relation to other people. I am referring to forms of conduct that are generally appropriate and fitting. Our moral principles indicate what these are. In principle, for example, we ought to be kind, but sometimes an individual may take advantage of one's good will or be undeserving of our largesse. In principle, we ought to be appreciative of what others may do for us, though the recognition of their help or recompense for it may be insufficient or too late in coming. That there are general rules of human conduct is one thing that a developed moral being recognizes; how these relate to one another, especially when they conflict, and which should be fulfilled, is another. We may, for example, make a sincere promise which in a time of adversity or altered circumstances may be difficult to fulfill or, were we to do so, would make it impossible for us to realize other equally binding principles or values.

Among the reasons we give to demonstrate why we ought or ought not to do something is the relevance of the principle to the case. Utilitarians emphasize the fact that in deciding what we ought to do we judge an action by whether or not it maximizes good and contributes to pleasure or happiness. This is an important consideration we need to take into account. There is a danger, however, that some utilitarians, especially in regimes tending toward the autocratic, may be willing to compromise certain elementary and well-established moral principles in order to achieve what they consider to be a greater good, or certain social goals they perceive to be desirable.

But moral principles have an autonomy of their own, in the sense that they are not simply instrumental, to be appealed to or dispensed with at will. They have an intrinsic worth, and are not to be considered simply as means to fulfill certain ends; they are part of the ends themselves. Our moral principles may indeed function as values treasured for their own sake. We cannot, for example, choose to be honest or dishonest simply to serve our own purposes or even a greater purpose; honesty is valued in itself as part of a person's character and is a high principle on the scale of human values. Principles and values may thus overlap. Still, principles and values are not necessarily the same thing, for values are not general, nor do they lay down *prima facie* rules of conduct.

The central question about moral and ethical principles concerns their ontological foundation. If they are neither derived from God nor anchored in some transcendent ground, are they purely ephemeral? If they are simply relative to human interest, can they be violated with impunity? What happens if they clash or conflict; how do we decide which have higher priority and legitimacy? Will morality collapse if there are no ultimate first principles resident in the womb of reality?

I think not. The moral and ethical principles that we live by and to which we are committed are "real"; that is, we can make factual descriptive statements about their centrality in human behavior. In that sense, they are part of *nature*, as are all qualities. Second, such principles are *relative* to human beings, to their interests, needs, values, and concerns. To say that they are relative does not mean that they are purely subjective, or that they can be dismissed at will, or abandoned by caprice. It simply means that they are functions of human behavior, and that they emerge in human interactions. It makes no sense to talk of them in an isolated abstract way, separate from their consequences in human conduct. Indeed, the commitment to moral principles becomes so significant in human civilization that they begin to take on a special kind of objective reality and are an integral part of the bio- and socio-cultural spheres. They have natural and objective foundations.

OBJECTIVE RELATIVISM

The term *objective relativism* perhaps best designates ontological status: moral and ethical principles have some kind of *transactive* function, applying to men and women as they interact in a natural and sociocultural environment. This applies equally to so-called transcendental systems of morality; even though believers may choose to attribute them to some abstract divine order, these too are products of human culture.

When I use the term *relative*, I do so in three senses. First, moral and ethical principles have social and cultural referents and some deep institutional framework. Second, they take on meaning and force only because they are based on inherent propensities developed or inculcated in specific persons. Accordingly, they are also relative to a given individual. Third, such principles are *relational*; that is, they take on meaning and have content only because they *relate* to human beings.

The term *relativism* has been used as a term of opprobrium by its critics, and the adjective *mere* has been applied to relativism because of the fear that to consider the foundations of our moral code relativistic might lead to its being gravely weakened or endangered. Relativism should not be confused with subjectivism, however, for relativism refers to the empirical fact that principles are rooted in human experience and are not separate from it, whereas subjectivists can find no basis for criticizing or appraising principles. But I should point out that I think there are objective criteria for doing so—hence the term *objectivism*. Thus objective relativism is distinct from subjective relativism, and although the latter may lead to utter skepticism or nihilism, the former does not.

The term *cultural relativity* has been introduced by anthropologists to describe the wide range of principles and norms in human culture. Out of this has come the view that we ought not to impose our standards on other cultures—certainly not when studying them—and that one set of standards is as morally viable as another. That meta-normative theory does not follow, as we shall see, and although principles are in some sense relative to cultures, this does *not* mean that we are led to cultural relativism in the sense that cultures are immune to critical ethical scrutiny, or that they are all at the same point in their level of ethical development. Again, there is a kind of *objective* cultural relativity distinct from subjective cultural relativity.

What are some of the objective features of relativism?

First, moral imperatives have some *socio-biological* basis; they are rooted in the nature of the human animal and the processes of evolution by which the species adapts and survives. Human beings are social animals, and our young require an extended period of nurturing for survival. Given this, a number of moral rules that govern behavior have developed. For example, ingrained in the species is maternal care, the instinctive urge of the parent to feed and protect its young. Another is the relationship between the sexes, which includes some affectionate regard for the object of one's amorous advances (delight in warmth and touch, fondling, embracing), as well as a number of concomitant psychological affections. These instinctive tendencies are not unique to the human species. E. O. Wilson found similar rudimentary patterns in other social species: Ants will die to defend the queen ant, and their relation to the corporate entity is such that they cannot exist apart from the colony. Of course, this is instinctive and not self-consciously ethical, but similar patterns can be found in higher-level species, such as the bonds of affection of primates, wolves, lions, and other species, for their young and for each other.[1]

The roots of moral conduct and the recognition of the elementary moral decencies requisite for face-to-face interaction thus already lie deep within the biological framework of the human species. Although there is diversity in the kind of moral rules accepted by different social groups, *some* such rules emerge—for example, in the relationship of parents to their young, or of sex mates to each other. Given the fact that individuals have common biological needs and face similar problems of survival, common norms have developed in spite of wide cultural diversity. Humans need to gather or hunt or plant food to survive, to shelter and clothe themselves against the elements, to protect themselves from predators or other marauding tribes, to relate to each other sexually, to reproduce, to deal with the aged who are no longer capable of self-care, and to face adversity and death with equanimity and fortitude. Given the common tasks of living, some common moral rules have developed. Given the nature of the human being as a social animal, it is thus essential that social groups establish certain rules governing the way in which the members would live and work together and delineate the parameters of acceptable social behavior, so that some clear sense of roles and expectations are understood.

Moral codes thus have an adaptive function; one can postulate that those groups which had some effective regulation for conduct were better able to survive, reproduce, and compete with other species or human groups, and thus transmit this favorable trait and these learned behavioral responses to others. One can imagine a possible scenario in the dim past of our forebears, when the glimmerings of what I shall call the common moral decencies emerged: be kind and considerate to the members of your tribe; be honest and truthful; do not maim, injure, or harm them needlessly; be sincere and keep your promises, etc. The test of the truth of these principles was their consequences. Those tribes that developed such rules had less discord and could better survive than those that did not. It is far more beneficial for everyone to cooperate; it works pragmatically in the long run. This is not a universal characteristic which has always dominated, for our propensity for moral behavior has to compete with other tendencies and temptations in the human breast. Still a minimum of moral relationships needs to operate if the social group is to survive.

We can see analogous forms of moral behavior in other species that bear striking resemblances to human conduct. For example, a mother duck will furiously seek to protect her ducklings from harm. Moreover, species establish pecking orders. Groups of chimpanzees, for example, are ruled by a dominant male who protects his females against other threatening males. Eventually he may be ejected by another male, ousted from his group, and left to die. Socio-biological and genetically rooted behavior has its analogue in the first development of moral patterns in primate groups and extended families. Thus there is a kind of biological relativity for morality conditioned by the constraints of adaptation and survival.

Second, of course, is the emergence of complex *socio-cultural* rules that go far beyond the basic biological imperatives. In the human species, it is sometimes difficult to distinguish the full range of social functions from simple socio-biological functions, but at some point, complex socio-cultural systems evolve. With the development of language, especially the use of symbols and metaphors, human mentation expanded, and learned experience could be preserved and transmitted to future generations. This especially applied to the development of sets of moral rules. In time, morality became nuanced with complexity. Higher levels of moral rules developed, superimposed still further, as it were, on our basic biological equipment and needs, or the immediate survival function of the rules. It is at the level of culture that morality acquires a new dimension, for it is elaborated upon, extended with finesse and distinction. It becomes ingrained in human conduct. Although within the tribe certain moral rules needed to be enforced if the entire tribe were to survive, these did not always apply to other tribes as they interacted and often battled.

It was then that a new stage of morality developed: We should treat the stranger in our land as our brother; we should not mistreat the alien in our midst. One can see this noble affirmation of a new moral principle in the Old Testament, discovered and enunciated by the Hebraic prophets. The first glimmerings of the universality of morality began to appear.

This points to the fact that moral principles are relative to the level of civilization that has developed. The emergence of a higher stage in moral awareness was no doubt forced on our forebears by the fact that as tribes of people intermingled, there were various forms of intercourse, including commerce and trading. When warfare and conflict threatened, there was the perceived need for establishing some conditions of peace and harmony, or no secure life would be possible.

Narrow tribal moralities thus had to be transcended. That this moral truth has still not been fully apprehended today is one of the great tragedies of the human condition; for nations, religions, and ethnic groups still are at war with one another and are willing to use dastardly means to gain an advantage. Yet ethical cognition points to the need for a universality in conduct, and it speaks to all men and women no matter what their social or cultural backgrounds.

Third, moral principles that have emerged have deep *historical* sources: they are the products of civilization, and eventually sweep over nations and become the common heritage of large sections of the globe. A good illustration of this is the revulsion against slavery. The moral principle emerged: Do not enslave another human being, even though he is of a different race, or comes from a poverty-stricken class, or is a member of an ethnic group too weak to resist capture and enslavement. The fact that there is little or no condemnation of slavery in the Bible or Koran, and that it was accepted and was widely practiced well into the nineteenth century by Christian and Arab nations vividly demonstrates the point: Many moral principles have developed only late in human history. This is also true for the recognition that females have equal worth and are thus entitled to equality of treatment, although this is by no means universally accepted or even practiced where it is given lip service.

Moral principles emerge at certain stages of historical development. They are relative to the culture and civilization in which they first appear and are given a hearing. They cannot be violated with impunity by a tribe, nation, or race, without condemnation by a major portion of the community of humankind. Today they have a profound claim on human conscience. To deny them a transcendent or divine basis does not mean that they are any less deeply rooted in human history.

The recognition of a moral or ethical principle may require a long and arduous struggle. Indeed, some principles are deemed so crucial in certain epochs of human history and the opposition to them is so intense that they can only prevail after long and bloody battles. This means that the moral decencies we come to recognize as necessary, at least on a minimal level, are enunciated and extended to all humans, and that a doctrine of human rights is developed for humankind in general. The moral codes of various cultures are not equivalent, and we can with some justification maintain that some have reached a higher level of ethical awareness than others.

One of the most profoundly disturbing facts about the human species is the partiality that individuals have for their own kind. There is perhaps a natural and even necessary favoritism that individuals display to members of their own breeding community. Parents have a unique obligation to protect and nourish their own children, and this is a stronger obligation than to the children of others; filial obligations are felt in return. This close relationship is no doubt advantageous and necessary for the survival and growth of the species. The same favoritism is generally shown also to the extended family: sisters, brothers, grandparents, grandchildren, cousins, nephews, nieces, aunts, and uncles. Again, this no doubt has some kind of bio-sociological function, particularly where members of consanguineous groups have a bond based on common interests and needs, and are confined to a common locality.

What is unsettling is the extension of this bond of loyalty to the wider community—the tribe, nation, or race of which one is a part—at the expense of other groups. This marks some moral advance, for at least it takes us beyond our immediate, face-to-face encounters and parochial attachments and brings us to a wider community. Nonetheless, a cause of much misery in human affairs is the fact that intense hatred can develop toward those not within one's own group, and this can erupt into violence.

Konrad Lorenz has found that members of a rat colony are able to tell by their common nesting smell which other rats in the colony are blood relatives, and to afford them more pacific behavior, while they will display intense aggression, kill, and tear apart unrelated rats who might stray into the nest from another colony.[2] One would hope that there is no strict analogy between human and rat behavior in this regard, but empirical evidence suggests a similar human affection for the inbreeding tribal group and hostility to perceived aliens. That this is not simply rooted in consanguinity, however, is clear from the fact that large nation-states sharing a common cultural heritage may in fact contain a multiplicity of breeding groups, and that they can maintain group loyalty within and exude venom outside with equal strength. Witness the bloody carnage in Europe between France and Germany in three wars and in the bloody war between the two Islamic nations, Iran and Iraq.

There are fortunately less dangerous forms for group rivalry to take, such as the competition between sports teams. Football teams from two different cities or countries may be locked in battle for victory or glory, and their fans, in viewing them, are aroused to intense levels of often irrational fervor, but warfare does not ensue.

The clash of group loyalties and the emergence of moral claims over and beyond parochial identities has been a slow process. And there is still a long way to go before a truly moral community of all humankind can or will be established. Is human behavior aggressive and destructive by nature, and is partiality and loyalty to one's own kind so deep that it can never be overcome? The history of civilization clearly evidences the indelible influence of ethnicity in human affairs, but it also demonstrates that it can and has been overcome, at least to some extent. The strict rules prohibiting intermarriage between different religious, ethnic, or racial stocks have broken down in some societies, which enables the development of new nationalities and loyalties. In this regard, economic, political, and social interaction—and especially mobility and travel—make it possible to meet people of different nationalities. In addition, critical ethical intelligence plays a vital role, for there has been the emergence of the recognition of universal (or general *prima facie*) human rights.

This is related to a key ethical principle: *Each person is entitled to equality of consideration as a person, and as such has equal dignity and value.* This claim is independent of his or her group membership, racial, religious, ethnic, class, national, or sexual orientation. Thus there are a set of human rights we can delineate that realize the fulfillment of basic principles. The term *right* means that persons are entitled to recognition and respect within the community of humankind, and their liberties and opportunities should not be denied or transgressed. In chapter 7 I will specify what the most basic human rights are; these include not only ethical rights but economic, political, and social rights as well.

THE JUSTIFICATION OF ETHICAL PRINCIPLES

The question that can now be raised is this: If we grant that moral principles, including the common moral decencies and a doctrine of human rights, have evolved and are related to our biological human condition and to our cultural history, how do we determine which should be accepted and what is the standard by which they can be warranted? This is a difficult epistemological question, which philosophers have debated. Let me suggest what is *not* the case:

1. *Ethical principles cannot be deduced from the concept of God.* First, the existence of God is questionable. Second, not all men and women of different cultures share the same religious beliefs. Third, granting the fatherhood of God is no guarantee that uniform moral codes will emerge. Theists have "deduced" any number of moral codes at variance with those held by other believers. For instance, witness the sharp differences of opinion held by Jews, Christians, and Muslims regarding marriage and divorce.

2. *Ethical principles are not self-evident or intuitively certain.* The difficulty we find with the argument of intuition is that not everyone finds ethical principles self-evident. Often what is taken as intuitively obvious is simply a mask for established cultural attitudes, customs, habits, and beliefs, or for uncritical common sense. The appeal to self evidence is not without merit, however, for ethical principles come to play such a vital role in human culture and are considered to be so important that those who flout them or fail to see their obligatory character are rightfully blamed as immoral.

3. *Ethical principles are not simply subjective emotional attitudes or states unamenable to any critical justification.* There are important objective criteria that we use to evaluate ethical principles.

How then would one go about appraising or justifying a principle? Even to ask for a justification is to initiate a course of ethical inquiry and is to presuppose some degree of objectivity. In this process of deliberation, cognition assumes an important role, supplementing mere faith or authority; it means that reason, in some sense, becomes constitutive in any judgment that emerges from the inquiry. Insofar as rules and principles are tested by rational considerations and by the relevant evidence, they are transformed from unexamined moral assumptions and principles into critical ethical principles. The moral principles that govern our behavior are rooted in habit and custom, feeling and fashion. Ethical principles emerge in the same rich soil of human experience, but are now consciously watered and pruned by critical intelligence.

In this process, one does not begin at the beginning, but *in rem*, in the midst of life and in the context of established and antecedent sets of the rules and norms. Intelligence translates arbitrary rules into informed judgments that are fashioned in the light of reason. This point is vital. The radical revolutionary, particularly in corrupt societies, wishes to destroy all preexisting social structures that he considers morally degrading; he wishes to wipe the slate clean and begin anew. One can appreciate the abhorrence of corrupt, oppressive, and hypocritical *ancien régimes*; and at times, drastic actions may need to be taken to restore social justice. Still, this does not mean that all norms, principles, and values can be overthrown; only some should be, and others should be retained as expressions of the collective ethical wisdom of the race.

Hence, my first point is that humankind, including the specific societies within it, already possesses a number of principles that are recognized and accepted as binding. This refers to precedence, to common law, and to the acceptable modes of conduct approved of by a social group and perhaps even enacted into law. The moral experiences, values, and principles already accepted by humankind in a historical context provide a starting point for morality.

If reason begins here, it does not mean, however, that it must remain here, because what is given is based on the problems of the past and on the solutions of earlier generations. The moral behavior of the past functioned in accordance with the philosophical and scientific outlook that then prevailed; and insofar as the scientific or practical knowledge may have been mistaken or limited, and has since been revised or added to, so the moral conceptions of the past may require modification. Similarly, many moral principles were introduced or slowly evolved to help people cope with their problems, but they may no longer be effective today, and indeed may be dysfunctional. Moreover, new problems may emerge, which the old-time religion or morality is unable to deal with. The old verities may not apply to present realities.

There is a glacierlike lag that persists in the moral domain: habits become so deeply entrenched that they are difficult to change. *Some* principles of moral order, no matter how archaic, are no doubt better than none, and are, in any case, essential for social cohesion. Yet many habits, no matter how venerable, ossify into mere prejudices and may need to be revised or abandoned if the society is not to stultify in repression.

How shall we change and for what reasons? First, I submit, by an appeal to *factual evidence*. To illustrate: Many people believe in capital punishment as the general moral principle that applies to the treatment of murderers. They may support their beliefs by referring to the old biblical adage "An eye for an eye and a tooth for a tooth," which they utter as an article of deep-seated faith. The belief that murderers should be executed by the state, however, may also be related in part to the conviction that only capital punishment will deter murder, and that if a society were to abandon this method of punishment, the community would be at risk.

The factual question can only be resolved, if it can be resolved at all, by scientifically conducted sociological and psychological studies. Do societies that enforce the death penalty have lower rates of murder than those that do not? This is an empirical question. One can speculate about the answer, but only detailed scientific inquiry can resolve the question. But another key point is this: Would a person who believed in the death penalty because he thought it deterred crime be willing to abandon his belief if it were definitely established that it did not? And, conversely, can those who are opposed to capital punishment as a barbaric and ineffective method of treating murderers be persuaded to change their minds, if it could be shown that capital punishment did significantly deter crime?

I shall not present the evidence pro and con. I am merely pointing to the significance of factual data in modifying moral attitudes. I do *not* wish to argue that one can deduce ethical principles from the facts—that would be a form of the naturalistic fallacy—but only that our knowledge of the facts is relevant to our judgments. One cannot simply derive what "ought" to be the case by knowing what "is" the case. Nonetheless, knowledge of the full facts in a situation does help us to make wiser decisions.

Another illustration of the point concerns the question of whether homosexuals should be entitled to the same rights as heterosexuals, and whether, for example, sodomy should continue to be prohibited by the law, as it now is in many states and in some other nations. A crucial factual question is relevant: Is homosexuality genetically determined? Are those who express a preference for members of the same sex so disposed by biological causes that in effect a person's sexual orientation has been established at birth? There is some evidence that homosexuality exists in other species, which might suggest a genetic basis. E. O. Wilson has even postulated a possible socio-biological adaptive function for the appearance of certain homosexual members of the species. Whatever the truth or falsity of this claim, if people were born with their sexual orientation or developed it so early that they have little or no control over it, is it right for the community to condemn and/or prohibit such conduct?

The Roman Catholic church considers homosexual conduct sinful and urges continence and celibacy for homosexual individuals. Similarly, the effort to stamp out homosexuality by legislation is based on the premise that such individuals have voluntarily selected their lifestyle and can choose not to be gay. No doubt some element of choice does enter into the picture: Everyone must choose how to express their sexuality, regardless of their sexual orientation; one must decide whether to be promiscuous or to pursue a monogamous relationship. Also, under certain conditions, such as in the army, in prison, or in a monastery, homosexual conduct may be exacerbated among individuals who otherwise might not express a same-sex preference. But still, some scientific knowledge of the causes of homosexuality are relevant. For if we were to find that such individuals are unable to change their sexual proclivities, it would be oppressive of their rights as human beings to expressly deny what is for them part of their "natural" selves.

This does not mean that society may not regulate homosexual conduct that is overtly promiscuous, especially where the health of the community may be at stake, nor that it should not seek to protect the young from nonconsensual behavior. The issue of health especially raises factual questions. For example, the high incidence of certain diseases, such as AIDS, among homosexuals introduces questions of social control: Should bathhouses be closed, male prostitution regulated or prosecuted, or mandatory testing and treatment be required as a way to control the disease? If many or most homosexuals are unable to change their sexual orientation, should they have the same rights as heterosexuals to satisfy their needs? Such complex issues must be approached through fact-finding and analysis, and decisions should not rest simply on whether heterosexuals find homosexual behavior repugnant.

A second important test of an ethical principle is *comparative*: it lays down a general prescription for treating people or for behaving in relation to them. But principles may have to be modified if better principles are to be discovered. Some people no doubt think that there are, ideally at least, a set of ethical principles—such as those relating to justice or fairness—which at some point we can discover, and that these would reflect the norms of all human beings. This was Plato's quest in the *Republic*, as he sought an ideal, utopian definition of "the Good." I think that we need to be very cautious in this regard, for there is great danger that a fixed authoritarian model may be imposed. As I have said, morality and the principles of ethics should be open to modification as societies encounter new problems different from those of the past. Hence the need for revisionary and experimental approaches to many ethical questions. However, it is clear at the same time that many of the moral and ethical principles that have evolved, insofar as they deal with common human problems and needs, will remain the common heritage and moral wisdom of the human race and cannot be tampered with easily or abandoned in a cavalier manner.

Third, the most significant test of an ethical principle has not been stated yet, and that is the need to examine the *consequences* of proposed rules of conduct. We can judge principles not simply by what they state or enunciate, nor by our pious fidelity to them, but by how they work out in practice. The biblical adage is relevant: It is by their fruits that we best may know and judge them.

This appeal to consequences is a pragmatic test. A principle may seem fine on paper, but once put into practice, its end result may be disastrous.

An illustration of this is the idea of participatory democracy, to which many people in the modern world are committed. The ethical principle postulates that all individuals in an organization should have an equal voice in determining the policies of that organization and the manner in which they are governed. Does that mean that everyone should have an equal vote? This seems eminently fair at the political level, particularly in guarding against oppressive governments; for the right of dissent and the legal right of opposition are strong bulwarks against tyrannical regimes.

But whether the participatory principle can be extended without qualification and in the same way to all institutions of society is highly questionable. For example, the movement for unlimited participatory democracy in universities and colleges can bring about confusion and lower standards of excellence. Students should participate in discussions of policies and curricula. They should not be treated as mere passive consumers without the ability to intelligently evaluate the content of the education being offered. Bright students, in particular, will be demanding of course offerings and quality of instruction.

Still, the application of participatory democracy, without recognizing the demonstrated competence of faculties in evaluating the educational content of programs, can lead to foolhardy behavior, as was the case in the 1960s in many universities.

By referring to the test of consequences, I do not mean simply the utilitarian greatest-happiness principle. If taken literally, this can lead to unfortunate results. Can a majority, for example, deny rights to recalcitrant minorities, if this would lead to the greatest good for the greatest number? Surely not, for there are certain principles and rights that should not be eliminated, no matter how beneficial the results would be to the majority. Some might say that the reason we are unwilling to deprive minorities of their rights is because of the long-range negative consequences, and that the ultimate test is still the greatest-happiness principle. This argument has some merit, but one might respond that one ought not to deprive others of their rights on intrinsic and not simply utilitarian grounds.

In any case, I would argue that the test of consequences is plural and not singular, for we cherish *many* values and principles that we wish to preserve; and hence to seek to derive a single principle may endanger the entire body of our values and principles. As a matter of fact, a wide spectrum of values and principles in a particular context of inquiry may be at stake; we may desire to preserve or enhance them, and it is important to examine carefully what a particular principle will do to them.

Here the consequentialist test is also empirical, because presumably the results can actually be observed in the world. We may, it is true, speculate about what might happen if a certain principle were adopted, but only concrete testing of the principle is decisive. Sometimes we may not be able to embark on such a course of experimental action, for it may entail too much risk; and so, our only test would be a hypothetical one. For example, a powerful political leader might ask, in weighing options, what would happen if a nuclear exchange began between the major powers? Would the human species be annihilated? Such a test would hardly be feasible.

There is a fourth criterion for appraising the worth of a principle, and that is the appeal to *consistency*. Kant's famous test of the validity of an ethical principle was its universality; before we commit an act, he said, we must ascertain whether the maxim under which we propose to act could become the universal rule for all mankind. He considered this a purely formal logical test. If the rule would contradict the entire framework of morality, we would not be entitled to make an exception for ourselves. We cannot lie, cheat, or commit homicide, for example, for if these were to become universal laws, moral conduct would be impossible.

Critics have pointed out two main difficulties with Kant's criterion. First, it is difficult to maintain that any maxims are absolutes, for exceptions may be justified on ethical grounds. This is especially the case where there is a conflict of duties. Hence, rules should only be interpreted, as I have already argued, as general *prima facie* duties and not absolute imperatives. Whether we actually have an obligation to do something would depend upon the context. Kant's categorical imperative is thus too formal and empty to serve as the sole guide for conduct. Second, the test of a rule is not formal consistency with the moral order, as Kant thought, but depends upon the examination of the consequences of action. It is because consequences are viewed as destructive to morality in an empirical sense that a rational agent decides to forbear. Kant's categorical imperative does serve us in ethical decision-making as one factor to consider, among others, but not as a decisive or single criterion.

Nonetheless, there is a logical test that is important, and that is the test of the *internal* consistency of our principles. No single ethical principle should be judged in abstract isolation without considering its logical effect upon other principles to which we are committed. Thus, we need to ask whether a new or old principle contradicts other principles we hold. If so, we may find ourselves to be hypocritical or holding a double standard. If, for example, we posit that all human beings are entitled to equal consideration but exclude women from this principle, we are limiting our definition of human beings to males, and it is obvious that we are disregarding half the human species. Thus we either have to abandon our general principle or reinterpret it to extend it to women. The appeal to consistency is a fundamental method for evaluating, revising, and extending principles. It is used by judges and courts of law, particularly in democratic societies, and has historically been involved in the battle for the recognition of new liberties and rights. Consistency thus is an essential criterion in addition to the appeal to facts and consequences in appraising principles.

One caution needs to be introduced at this point: it is the need to guard against the tyranny of principles. A moral principle, once it is enunciated and reaffirmed, may be considered so vital to human justice that it is thought no exception can be made to its application. In some cases, however, the rule of consistency can become oppressive, for when applied in actual life a principle may be destructive to the constellation of other values and principles that we cherish, a kind of self-righteous fervor may take over and moral fanaticism may rule.

One can think of firmly held moral principles that became slogans for radical revolution or reactionary repression. "All power to the people" may sound fine in theory as a universal rule, but when put into practice by an unruly mob or a revolutionary tribunal, it may lead to despotism.

"All abortions are wrong" is declared universally binding by the right-to-life groups seeking to preserve what they view to be the sanctity of life. They wish to defend the "life of an innocent fetus," but are willing, in a cavalier fashion, to undermine women's rights to reproductive freedom. In some situations, bringing a pregnancy to term might harm the woman (as in the case of rape or incest), or produce a seriously deformed fetus; right-to-lifers do not propose to pay the medical bills in such situations or raise the infants themselves. Still, these pro-life groups insist on absolute fidelity to their principle. Their opponents point out, using the consistency criterion, that many of those who are against the killing of fetuses defend other forms of killing such as capital punishment or the killing of innocent civilians in times of war.

Another illustration of the appeal to consistency is the attempt to apply the libertarian principle with nondiscriminatory universality and without viewing its consequences. That "individuals ought to control their own lives" seems a persuasive rule to govern our conduct, one that we ought to respect. Yet if it is taken as an absolute and without exception, it may in some cases harm both the individual and the community. I remember questioning a well-known libertarian who insisted that all addictive drugs, including heroin and cocaine, should be legalized; to be consistent with the primacy of individual liberty, he argued, the state should not seek to regulate private conduct in any way.

"What if the legalization of such addictive drugs would most directly harm disadvantaged minority youth living in poverty in the ghettos?" I asked.

His reply was, "I guess they'll have to learn their lesson. Perhaps an entire generation of young people will have to be lost." He thought this policy was consistent with his libertarian philosophy, but it seems to me that in not allowing any exception, he was a victim of his principle, unwilling to appraise it in the light of other principles and values he undoubtedly cherished and failing to judge it by its actual consequences.

In summary, even if we abandon transcendental morality, and even if the new ethics are relative to human interests and needs, we are not thereby led to subjectivism in ethics. There is a kind of objective relativism that we can and do appeal to, and there are objective standards for judging the ethical principles that govern our lives.

A CATALOGUE OF THE COMMON MORAL DECENCIES

Can critical ethical intelligence discover any *prima facie* general principles that transcend the limits of cultural relativity and apply to all human beings, no matter what their social condition? Are there any ethical principles that we can affirm to be objectively true, independent of whether there is a God who has declared them to be binding? I submit that there are and that they are so fundamental to human intercourse that they may be characterized as the "common moral decencies." Indeed, virtually all human cultures have now come to recognize their significance, for they lay down moral imperatives necessary for group cohesion and survival. Individuals who abide by them are commended and praised, and those who flout or transgress them are condemned and blamed as immoral, wicked, or evil.

To state that certain forms of conduct are decent, admirable, or proper, and that other forms are indecent and improper, even despicable, is not simply subjective caprice or an expression of cultural bias, but is, I think, a function of a level of moral development that has crosscultural dimensions. There is still wide diversity in human conduct; there are numerous disputes about what is considered decent or indecent behavior, and there is much variation in moral judgment. Nonetheless, there is a basic core of principles that we have come to recognize as binding in human conduct. We may apply the term *common* to these "decencies" as a qualification, for we speak only of the most fundamental principles that are widely held, leaving many other layers of moral principles open to further critical examination. I use the term *moral* rather than *ethical* because I think the recognition that there are fairly basic moral principles that ought to govern conduct between civilized individuals has become deeply ingrained in long-standing social traditions. These principles are supported by habit and custom, are enacted into law, and are even considered sacred by various religions.

Far from being derived from some transcendental source, the moral decencies are taken as divinely revealed precisely *because* they are considered so basic to the human community. The fact that they have been converted into the language of divinity is a further sign of how highly esteemed they are. They can, however, have an authentic cognitive and independent ground; these principles are justifiable by rational considerations and are based upon practical ethical wisdom. Indeed, they express the deepest wisdom of the human race and can be discovered by anyone who digests the fruit of the tree of knowledge of good and evil. Interestingly, theists and humanists share in their commitment to the moral decencies, for people of all persuasions inherit a common wisdom, even though they may dispute the ultimate foundations of morality.

The following catalogue of moral principles should not be taken on a scale of ascending or descending priority. The order in which they are listed is simply one of convenience, for in any particular situation, one or more may assume higher priority than another. They should be interpreted as general guides for conduct rather than absolute or universal commandments, but this does not mean that their obligatory force is weakened; for a rational moral being can recognize their significance no less than can a God-intoxicated believer. It is important that we present them explicitly, since ethical philosophy should not be a metatheoretical and abstract exercise but should have a normative relevance to conduct. It is especially important for humanism to provide a catalogue of the moral decencies, in order to counter the unfounded charge that it has no moral principles.

Moral principles concern our relationship to other human beings living in communities; they would have little meaning for a hermit living in isolation in a cave or on a desert island. Some can also be applied to other sentient species, so that it makes some sense to talk about animal rights. Although moral principles are forms of social behavior, they need to be structured within the character of the individual if they are to have any efficacy or force. There is some overlapping of these principles, and some are subsumed under others. Nevertheless, it is important that they be separately defined and classified. The following list should not be taken as exhaustive or complete. There are no doubt other principles that might be added. But at least the following provide a basic framework for ethical conduct and choice.

I. Integrity

1. *Truthfulness*: the quality of being truthful; veracity; accuracy in representing reality. This quality is basic to all human social relationships, for people cannot live and work together if there is a deliberate effort to withhold, falsify, or erase the truth. Negative: to lie; to be deceitful.

Interestingly, this principle does not appear in a forthright statement in the Ten Commandments, although one variant does appear: "Thou shalt not bear false witness against thy neighbor." Nor is it central to the Sermon on the Mount.

Nonetheless, telling the truth is a common moral decency expected in all civilized communities and probably in the majority of so-called primitive societies. When people deceive each other, it is difficult to count on them. Lying makes true communication impossible. When we do not know when to believe a person, we cannot rely on any aspect of his or her behavior.

People may disagree about what the truth is. They may differ as to what the facts of a particular case are, or how to interpret them, or what their causes are, but they are obligated to state the truth insofar as they know it—or believe they know it—without any deliberate intention to deceive others. The person who does not follow this principle is a liar.

The question of telling a harmless white lie is not an issue here; nor are the moral dilemmas that may arise when lying to someone may be considered—that is, not in one's self-interest but for the other person's good, especially when *not* lying conflicts with other general ethical principles equally binding. There are exceptions to any general rule, but such transgressions need to be justified before the rule can be overridden. Still, this does not deny the widespread human recognition that, all things considered equal, we have a *prima facie* obligation to be truthful.

In social contexts, one may swear an affidavit, take an oath, certify that one is telling the truth, or even take a lie-detector test, if it is believed that such will guarantee truthfulness. Truthfulness is basic to science, philosophy, and any discipline concerned with discovering the truth. It is fundamental to an open and free society but lacking in totalitarian and authoritarian societies, in which the elite attempts to cover up inadequacies, suppress dissent, and censor any attempt to speak or publish the truth. Such lying is a violation of a basic moral principle, not only from the standpoint of the individual but also from the standpoint of the community.

2. *Promise-keeping*: honoring a pledge; living up to one's agreement. In everyday life, if one makes a promise in good faith to another person, then it would be immoral to break that promise. Negative: failing to honor one's commitments; to be derelict and unfaithful; to not be true to one's word; to exhibit bad faith.

A promise is a declaration made to another person, who then expects that it will be fulfilled in the future by either performance ("I promise I will repay you") or forbearance ("I promise not to tell anyone"). It is a commitment other people may rely upon. It may include a solemn oath, vow, or assurance. The one who makes the promise has a responsibility to the person to whom he makes the promise. Implicit in this is the recognition that in some cases circumstances may become so altered that one does not have the means to fulfill a promise made in good faith.

This may involve the fulfilling of *contracts*, where two or more parties enter into an agreement or pact, in which both parties agree to perform or avoid certain acts, and in which one party, should he fail to fulfill his contractual obligations, stands in breach of contract. We not only have a moral but a legal duty to abide by agreements entered into freely and without duress. These include covenants entered into freely between contractual parties such as oaths of office and vows of marriage. If one party to a contract violates it substantially, then the other party may not be bound to honor the terms of the contract. Some people make some promises they cannot possibly keep. They may do so to please others, in which case their motives are beneficent; or perhaps they do so to deceive others, in order to get them to buy a product or contract for a service, in which case their motives are malevolent.

3. *Sincerity*: the quality of being candid, frank, free of hypocrisy, and sincere in one's relations with others, especially on a one-to-one, personal basis. Negative: to be insincere, hypocritical, false, deceitful.

Sincerity is essential to building trust. It is a sign of moral integrity. A sincere person is truthful in his dealings with others; he is not disingenuous or artful in concealing ulterior motives. Between lovers and friends, sincerity is essential if confidence is not to be broken. If a person cannot trust what another says, then it is difficult to cooperate on common tasks. An insincere person takes another in and misuses him for his own purposes. In extreme cases he may be cunning. On the other hand, there may be some limits to the degree of sincerity possible in human relations. One may be artless and too self-effacing in his dealings with others. He may confide too quickly in another or confess his affection or love too readily, so as to disarm or embarrass the other person, who may not share his feelings. Sincerity is a necessary bond in human relations, and we have an obligation to follow it, though we need not bare our inner soul to anyone and everyone at the first opportunity.

4. *Honesty*: the quality of integrity or fairness in dealing with others. "Honesty is the best policy" is an aphorism widely accepted in common parlance, but often flouted in behavior. If no one could be trusted, all social interactions would break down. Negative: to be dishonest, deceitful, fraudulent, false, crooked.

I am using the term *honesty* here to pertain primarily to not using deceitful means to take material advantage. In human relations, it is important that we be able to trust another person's word. If someone says one thing and then turns around and does something else, such a person is without integrity. If he conceals a hidden motive, and is seeking to beguile or deceive another, then he cannot be trusted. Dishonesty is distinct from insincerity, though these vices overlap, because it is resorted to in order to gain some advantage. A dishonest person is willing to commit fraud. He may cheat or sell out for a price. His behavior is not honorable and he soon loses his credibility and our respect. The temptation to dishonesty is for the profit or prestige that one can reap. Dishonest people are hypocritical and duplicitous; they are insincere and willing to lie and break promises. Conversely, an honest person will tell the truth and fulfill his contractual obligations insofar as he is able to do so. Probity in dealing with others is essential if we are not to lose our reputations. Once one has a reputation for false dealing, his career may be ruined.

In the economic sphere, selling adulterated products, lying to consumers, or cheating them are pernicious forms of dishonesty. On the political and economic level, the opposite of honesty is graft and corruption.

II. Trustworthiness

1. *Fidelity*: the quality of being loyal; showing allegiance, fealty. This principle applies to one's attachments to friends, relatives, and the community. Negative: infidelity, treachery, perfidy, or betrayal.

In human relationships we build up bonds of common interests, we share values, and we are committed to similar goals to which we all strive together. A person is expected to continue his loyalty to another in a one-on-one relationship, or to a group if he has pledged allegiance and has received mutual benefits. He is not to betray the trust—particularly for personal gain or advantage—unless he has an overriding justification. Our obligation to be faithful is based on our previous commitments, which we have the responsibility to uphold.

Fidelity is an essential principle in a viable marriage, where the partners have demonstrated trust and love for each other. It also applies to brothers and sisters, parents and children, and other members of the family. Fidelity is the bond that also holds friends together through adversity or prosperity. This means that there is some constancy of commitment and steadiness of attachment, rather than capricious or infantile behavior. Fidelity not only applies to persons but to an individual's commitment to a cause, to his principles, or to the group or nation. We are not talking about blind allegiance or fanatic loyalty, but fidelity that is responsible and devotional. It is a mature commitment, opposed to fecklessness, vacillation, and disloyalty. No matter what a person's relationship to others or to a group, he or she is expected not to betray them. The principle of fidelity needs to be extended to ever-wider communities of humankind, though it has its origin in small interpersonal relationships.

Where the trusted individual or group has committed a grave moral transgression (e.g., treachery, murder, etc.), then one may deem it permissible to waive fidelity in the name of a higher principle or cause, but a clear justification must be given for this.

2. *Dependability*: the quality of being reliable and responsible. The importance of reliability in human affairs is well-recognized. Negative: to be untrustworthy, undependable, irresponsible.

We depend on other persons to do the things they promise to do, for which they are employed or with which they are charged. People assume different roles in society, and in the division of labor we come to expect that they will discharge their obligations and duties honorably. Parents have responsibilities to properly nurture and care for their children. Teachers are charged with the education of the young. People in public life have the duties of their offices to discharge. We expect that workers, office personnel, doctors, lawyers, administrators, etc. be trustworthy and do their jobs well. If they are undependable, lazy, indifferent—if we cannot count on them—especially when they have agreed to assume a job, then they are negligent and can rightly be criticized. In human relations we bestow confidence on certain individuals; if they betray our trust in them, then it is difficult to live or work cooperatively with them. Irresponsible behavior is blameworthy. Accordingly, once one is specifically entrusted with certain duties, he is obligated to fulfill them or to responsibly notify the appropriate person if he cannot.

III. Benevolence

1. *Good will*: to have noble intentions, a virtuous disposition; to demonstrate trust. In our dealings with others, it is important that we have a positive attitude toward those who are deserving of it, and that we express good intentions toward them. Negative: to be malicious; to show ill-will, hostility; to be distrustful, suspicious.

This principle means that we should have good feelings about others, wishing them well and not seeking to do them harm. It suggests that we should always think the best of others unless they are scoundrels, and even then, they may have some redeeming virtues that we can discover. We should always try, if possible, to find something good to say about another person, and seek to appreciate his virtues rather than to criticize his faults. Moreover, we should be glad when he prospers and be pleased when he is happy. We should not exult in the misery of others. In general, it means that we show some care, concern, or thoughtful regard for the needs of others.

The antonym of this is *malice*, to wish people to make fools of themselves, to fail in their efforts, or indeed to suffer harm. The Tenth Commandment says that we should not *covet* another person's belongings. Among the most difficult of human vices to control is *envy* of what someone has, or *jealousy* of his achievements, talents, or possessions. This passion may be all-consuming and destructive to viable relationships of trust, or to effective learning, working, and functioning. If allowed to grow unimpeded, it can destroy persons and corrode nations. The principle of good will is the willingness to allow others to live and let live. A person with good will does not wish to deny other persons good fortune or success because he himself may lack them. Instead he hopes for the best for everyone. A person of genuine good will often finds that his motives are misinterpreted by people who lack good will; though he is sincere in his aims, others may accuse him of the same perfidy to which they are prone.

The opposite of good will is *hatred*, which can lead to an all consuming and seething rage between enemies, jilted lovers, former friends, or competitive rivals. Though one might compete against rivals in a sports contest or commerce or in time of war, one should strive to maintain *some* degree of fairness and courtesy toward one's opponents. If one loses, it should be with some grace; one should not wish to get even or bear undue resentment. This means that *vindictive* conduct is patently wrong. One should not seek to retaliate, or to make others pay for their wins or for one's own misfortunes.

One form of good will that is more general than its expression on the personal level is *benevolence*, the love for humanity and the desire to increase the sum total of human happiness. This is expressed in a philanthropic, charitable, and humanitarian devotion to worthy projects.

2. *Nonmalfeasance as applied to persons*: refraining from harming or injuring others. This principle is related to good will; it denies the right to inflict harm on other persons, without necessarily requiring that we confer benefits upon them. Negative: harmful or malefic actions or evil deeds against others.

Nonmalfeasance involves the following important list of prohibitions that are necessary in any civilized community. Anyone who flouts them transgresses the most basic principles of moral conduct. This applies not only to the members of our own inner circle, tribe, or nation, but to all men and women, whatever their ethnicity. It is the principle of brotherhood, which unfortunately is violated constantly in times of war, when the rules of decent behavior are usually abandoned.

Do not kill other human beings. Do not inflict physical violence or bodily injury on them.

Do not deprive them of food, shelter, clothing, or other necessities of life.

Do not be cruel, spiteful, vengeful, or vindictive.

Do not inflict harsh or inhuman punishment on anyone, even those who have severely transgressed these principles.

Do not torture or inflict unnecessary psychological suffering upon them.

Do not kidnap persons, take them as hostages, or hold them against their will.

Do not terrorize innocent persons by threats to life or limb.

Do not rape (see "Sexual consent" below).

Do not libel, slander, defame, or seek to destroy the careers of others.

Do not harm others by gossip or innuendo; do not spread false rumors or calumny.

Do not abuse children, the helpless, the weak, or the disadvantaged who are unable to fight back or defend themselves.

Do not harm by revenge or carry on a vendetta for past wrongs.

3. *Nonmalfeasance as applied to private and public property*: showing respect for the property of others or of the community. Persons have a right to possess property they acquire honestly, without fear of theft or plunder. Negative: to rob, steal, plunder.

The act of theft of lawful possessions is considered a crime punishable by law in all societies that sanction the holding of private property. The most extreme form of robbery is the use of force or intimidation to compel a person to give up property through acts that may involve threats to life or limb. Plunder or pillage in time of war involves spoilation and extortion, often on a vast scale. In extreme cases, this involves sacking and ravaging an area. It may also occur at the hands of bandits who loot, pirates who seek booty, kidnappers who seek ransom, or even arsonists who maliciously destroy property.

Robbery may occur surreptitiously when the victim is absent, but it is obviously still wrong. Another form of robbery is the deliberate effort to defraud persons of what is rightfully theirs.

When we say that persons ought to respect the property of others, we are referring to property that is rightfully obtained and not unlawfully gained by misbegotten means.

The principle similarly can be extended to public property. The prohibition here is against the purposeful looting, defacing, misusing, or neglecting the common property of a group or association, or the public property of the state.

4. *Sexual consent*: to have mutually consensual, voluntary sex. This is a form of the nonmalfeasance principle as applied to private sexual conduct between adults. Negative: to rape, require sexual submission, to abuse or harass sexually.

The act of rape is a violation of an individual's rights as a free person and is abhorred by the civilized community. This means that sexual relations depend upon consent given by both parties. It means that there will be no use of physical coercion to seize or force a person to have sexual intercourse. Included under this is the use of intimidation or duress to force a person to submit to any degree of penetration of any orifice of the body. Whether this applies to marriage partners is open to dispute. Generally, it has not been applied to marriage partners, and those who force their partners to have sex have not been considered rapists; today many women think that the definition of rape should be extended to protect them from brutal husbands—and certainly from estranged ones.

Included in this principle is the recognition that sexual consent explicitly excludes children below the age of consent. The use of force or deception in order to have sexual relations with children is specifically proscribed and considered even by hardened criminals to be the worst crime. It is severely punished by the civilized community.

A broader form of the principle of sexual consent is now under intense debate, and that is whether society should permit private, non-marital, and especially homosexual, relations. Historically, many societies have regulated what they consider to be deviant forms of sexual conduct, prostitution, anal or oral intercourse (whether hetero- or homosexual), and sadomasochism, even though it is difficult to police most forms of sexual conduct, since most sex acts occur in private.

The extended principle would permit any type of sexual relationship between consenting adults and prohibit the state from intruding into the bedroom and prosecuting the varieties of sexual preference. Another problem that emerges is whether the state should regulate sexual relations between adult members of the same family (brothers, sisters, aunts, uncles) and all forms of sadomasochism, even where there is consensual agreement between the parties. These expressions of sexual orientation, however, are generally not recognized under the common moral decencies, and the extension of the principle of sexual consent to them is a recent development.

5. *Beneficence*: kindness, sympathy, altruism, compassion. To perform a good deed, to be helpful or thoughtful, to be humanitarian, and to bestow gifts are acts of beneficence. This is the positive desire to help others, to improve their lives, to confer benefits, to reduce misery, to spread happiness. Negative: to be malevolent, harmful, selfish, uncharitable.

A beneficent attitude toward others is deserving of the highest praise. Some individuals may be so limited in means that they are unable to contribute very much to charity. But a beneficent person is willing to go out of his way to do a good deed. This involves empathy with the needs of others. It means that we ought to be considerate of the feelings of other human beings and seek to assist them if we can. This may not cost very much: to give up one's seat on a crowded train or bus, to help a blind person across the road, to lend a helping hand to someone injured or in need of solace are all beneficent acts. It means also that one should do what one can to reduce a person's misery or suffering, and even, if possible, to contribute to his care, education, nourishment, pleasure, or happiness. Many people discover that it feels better to give than to receive and that the pleasures of altruistic behavior outweigh the pleasures of self-seeking gratification.

Moralists have pointed out that the principle of beneficence, or doing good to others, is less binding than the principle of nonmalfeasance, or not harming them. Within the family unit, however, relatives have an obligation to assist family members in distress, and if possible, to afford the means for them to prosper. The more spontaneous this is, the more satisfying it is; the more satisfying it is, the easier it becomes. Altruism among friends and relatives is expected, and one condemns egocentric behavior in this context. We call upon those we love to assist us in time of need, to make sacrifices of time and money. Jesus' admonition that we should "love one another" is the noblest expression of this principle. A morally decent person recognizes, for instance, that if we are all seated around a table, no one in our midst should want for food; he will willingly break bread with others.

Beneficence has two dimensions: (1) an injunction to assist mercifully in order to alleviate pain, suffering, or deprivation for those we are able to help, and (2) a positive prescription to increase the sum of the goods a person can attain in life. The real question, again, is how far the principle of beneficence shall be extended: to all men and women including the starving in Africa and the diseased in the slums of Asia— or only toward those within our range?

The state can enact legislation to protect individuals from harming one another; for example, force or fraud is considered a crime and can be punished. Thus although the state can regulate negative behavior, it can hardly legislate altruism in those individuals who lack it. In some societies, it provides tax-incentives for voluntary contributions to charity, thus encouraging beneficent action. The principle of nonmalfeasance is considered too important to be left to private action and is thus enforced by the state. The principle of beneficence, on the contrary, cannot easily be enforced.

IV. Fairness

1. *Gratitude*: the quality of being grateful, of having friendly and warm feelings toward a benefactor. In human relationships, it is important that we show some appreciation for favors done for us. Negative: ingratitude; to be ungrateful, unappreciative.

Many individuals are pleased to bestow a gift or a favor, or to lend a helping hand to someone who needs or wants it. They may not wish recompense nor expect anything in return, but would welcome some sign of appreciation. The recipient should manifest some gratitude, by thanking the person or acknowledging his help. Perhaps at some future time, he may return a favor in kind or render a service. Those who are oblivious to good deeds bestowed and act as though they believe they have favors coming to them are ingrates, insensible to what others have done for them. If a good society is to prosper with beneficent actions, the quality of beneficence is watered by signs of appreciative response. In some cases, the help proferred may be long overdue, niggardly, or inadequate, and may not deserve recognition. Where it is worthy, however, it merits gratitude. The recognition should be dignified, without obsequiousness or groveling; for the benefactor to demand this would itself be indecent.

2. *Accountability*: the quality of being answerable for conduct. There

is a deep sense that a person who commits a foul deed that harms another, particularly an act such as murder, robbery, or rape, should not be allowed to remain unpunished. Negative: not being answerable for conduct.

Implicit in this principle is the idea that individuals should be held responsible for injuring others and should be called to account for it. For a grave moral crime to go unanswered may be considered unjust. Moreover, there is the conviction that if a criminal is allowed to go unpunished, the societal order will degenerate. The victim or his relatives or the community at large may feel so aggrieved that unless some accountability to the public is rendered, moral outrage may only be compounded.

In the strong form, this includes the demand for revenge, whereby one inflicts equal suffering, pain, or loss so that the punishment fits the crime. The penalty imposed either may be invoked as an act of retribution for its own sake, or, in more developed moral communities, may be used to deter future moral transgressions and crimes. In this way society attempts to protect itself, and if possible, to reform the criminal. In civilized communities, cruel and unusual, barbarous, or degrading punishment is deemed inappropriate.

One form the principle of accountability takes is the demand for damages. Where culpability has been established, and particularly where there has been an attempt to harm another through malice, it is felt that some form of reparation ought to be made. When someone has injured another person or harmed his property, the victim can sometimes sue for damages.

The whole effort of civilized conduct is to establish procedures for determining guilt and then seeing to it that there is a just application of the laws. In extenuating circumstances or for first-time offenders, society recognizes that there are some grounds for mercy. Related to this is the need to forgive and forget at some point and to avoid vindictiveness or revenge, especially when a person has made a mistake and admits it, shows some remorse, or has learned from his errors. In such cases the better part of valor is to be forgiving, not carry a grudge, and even at some point to welcome the reformed criminal back into the community.

3. *Justice*: fairness, equity, rectitude. That justice ought to prevail is widely held in civilized communities, even though there may be widespread disagreement about what it is. Negative: injustice, unfairness, partiality.

In its simplest sense, justice refers to meting out just deserts, that is, punishment for misdeeds and reward for merit. The principle of accountability enters here, as do notions of equity and rectitude.

Also involved in the principle of justice is the idea of equitable compensation for work performed or services rendered. This involves a normative standard for distributing the goods and services of society. People should be paid an honest wage for an honest day's work; income and/or wealth should be equitably divided among those who have earned and/or deserve what they have received. The principle of fairness is present here. In democratic societies, other manifestations of justice have emerged: the rule of law, equality, and liberty. All individuals are considered equal before the law and should not seek to obtain special privileges and immunities which others in the community lack.

The modern democratic principle thus suggests equality of consideration: each person is equal to all others in dignity and value. Similar is the principle of liberty and the opportunity to pursue happiness without undue interference. New ideas of economic equality have been introduced in modern society. Implicit in the principle of justice is the belief that there ought to be penalties for discrimination based upon racial, religious, ethnic, or sexual differences. Should those who are unable to work receive some support from society? Should the basic needs of the disadvantaged be satisfied? Should society help those who through no fault of their own are unable to care for themselves? The dispute between capitalism and socialism takes us far beyond the elementary moral decencies to a more complicated doctrine of human rights and equality of opportunity and of treatment. Justice also requires an appeal to the use of peaceful methods of adjudicating differences equitably and harmoniously. It means that we should reason together in order to solve our problems and not resort to force or violence.

4. *Tolerance*: the quality of sympathetic understanding and broad-mindedness. The toleration of individuals or nations who differ from us in values, manners, customs, or beliefs becomes an essential method of achieving peace and harmony in a civilized world. Negative: prejudice, bigotry, hatred, discrimination, narrow-mindedness, mean-spiritedness.

One of the faults of human beings is the tendency to reject and deny equal access or rights to individuals or groups who do not share our beliefs and practices. This can happen within the community, where we may disapprove of the lifestyles or values of other individuals; or it can apply to other groups, cultures, races, or nations, whose customs and beliefs we find alien to ours. We may disapprove of their tastes or norms, and think that their beliefs are false, bizarre, or wicked. The tendency is to seek to censor or prohibit differing values and beliefs. We may even fear them or believe that they are a great danger to our community. We may feel that if they are allowed to go unchecked, our own cherished values would be undermined. Thus the desire is to suppress them.

The tolerant person may differ with others in his community, yet forbear any effort to suppress them. He believes that he has a moral obligation to allow diverse styles of life to express themselves. To tolerate does not necessarily mean to approve; it merely means that we will not seek to prohibit differences by legislation, nor use force to root them out. Tolerance need not imply permissiveness. An open and pluralistic society will permit some measure of freedom so long as those to whom it is extended will not seek to prevent others from enjoying the same rights. It does not necessarily mean that "anything goes" and that no standards of criticism are possible.

Tolerance applies to a broad range of subject matters: moral and religious beliefs, practices and ethnic customs. It is opposed to any discrimination on racial, religious, economic, social, or sexual grounds. It also applies to philosophical, scientific, or political forms of belief.

To tolerate means that we accord other individuals or groups some respect—not that we agree with them, only that we recognize the rules of the game, and allow them some degree of liberty of belief, taste, and pursuits. In biblical terms, to tolerate the alien or the stranger in one's midst is to recognize that one may sometime be an alien in another land, hoping for the same measure of sympathy. Tolerance is a basic humanistic virtue. In modern times, humanists have defended the right of dissent of nonbelievers and heretics against the demands for conformity. It is a generalized moral principle and an expression of moral decency.

5. *Cooperation*: working together for peace, harmony, tranquility, or the social good. Maintaining a state of peace and amity between individuals within a community, between factions or states, is essential for the human social order. Negative: the inability or unwillingness to work with others to prevent or diminish war, hostility, strife, conflict, discord, and enmity.

That we should attempt to keep the peace and not resort to violent means in order to achieve our ends is a cardinal rule that all individuals and nations recognize in principle but unfortunately all too often violate in practice. We should use every effort to work out our differences peacefully. Negotiation is preferable as a mode of preventing strife or conflict, but to resort to power or force in human affairs is common. The moral principle is that we should seek to avoid this and not impose our will upon other individuals or nations. Aggression against others with whom we cannot agree is destructive to all human values, if allowed to get out of hand, it leads to the killing or maiming of individuals or the despoiling of their property. Defensive measures of self-protection are justifiable against an aggressive enemy.

Warfare, though common, is hardly the best or most effective method for resolving differences. Aggression or the fear of it leads to retaliation or encourages preemptive strikes. It engenders intense hatred against one's enemies and a seething desire for revenge. People have resorted to war for any number of reasons: for territorial expansion, financial profit or plunder, to promote a cause, to convert heathens or barbarians, ostensibly to aid mankind, and to bring down tyrants or madmen. The toll of violence often can be terrible in human suffering and misery.

We ought to beat our swords into plowshares, says the Old Testament. "Turn the other cheek," says the New Testament. But both injunctions have been violated with impunity by Judeo-Christian nations. The Koran has been used as a justification for the Jihad, or the Holy War in the Middle East.

The principle of cooperation beseeches us to find an appropriate resolution for our differences, to strive as mightily as we can to negotiate, and to reach compromises that all parties to a dispute can accept. We need adjudication rather than confrontation. Unfortunately, men and women often sing praises to peace as they march off to war.

Under certain conditions a war can be a just one. This is particularly the case when it is a war of self-defense. It is difficult to justify a war of aggression, undertaken in order to achieve one's political ends or to seize power or amass riches. Under certain conditions, one may not be able to reach an understanding with an invading army or a menacing individual. One should try to negotiate or compromise, and war or violence should only be a last resort. It is only in a situation of clear and present danger and in order to protect oneself that appropriate force can be justified. The general rule of moral decency is to cooperate as best we can, to tolerate the differing views of others, and to negotiate. Whether in fact it is always possible to do this remains to be seen, but it should be both the rule and goal of conduct.

Although the preceding list of common moral decencies has merit and is widely accepted, at least in principle, by most civilized communities, how they work in practice will depend upon individual circumstances or different social situations. That they are not fully realized in human conduct should be evident to everyone. No one is perfect. These general principles only establish norms of decent conduct; they do not promise that everyone will observe them. Indeed, given the conflicts that may sometimes arise in life, individuals may violate their norms and principles. But this should not weaken our obligation to recognize their binding nature, and whenever possible to seek to live in the light of them.

Many more ethical principles have lately emerged in some societies, and some that we have discussed are still open to dispute in others. Both are products of a revisionary humanistic morality.

These include the doctrine of human rights, the right to privacy, an ecological concern for the environment, an imperative to seek to preserve other species on this planet, obligations to future generations, the need to transcend the limits of ethnicity, and a need to extend our ethical concerns to the wider world community.

THE VALUATIONAL BASE II

The Ethics of Excellence

WHAT IS VALUE?

Thus far we have been discussing the common moral decencies that civilized communities have recognized and that critical ethical intelligence should take into account in order to reach wise decisions. Although we have dealt with the individual's moral behavior, we have left aside the question of the personal realization of the good life and the role that values play in ethical choices.

Some moralists have ignored questions concerning value, for they have thought that the center of morality must be our obligations to one another and the relationship of the individual to society. Kant fits into this category, for he believed that morality must be concerned with fulfilling the moral law, and not with considerations of personal happiness or of the good. But he was mistaken, for we do not live simply so that moral commandments be obeyed in and of themselves; rather we obey them because of their instrumental role in contributing to the good society, in actualizing individual human happiness. There is something disingenuous about deontological theories, whether religiously motivated or not, that take virtue and duty as the center of the moral life and minimize the need to realize the widest constellation of values that we cherish.

Many philosophers historically have focused on the good. They have sought to define its nature and delineate what it is and how it can be enhanced. A paradox has emerged, particularly sharp between human-istic and theistic approaches to morality: Is the central question of ethics maximizing goods, or doing what is right; realizing values, or obeying moral principles? Both the good and the right are, no doubt, essential to any complete theory of ethics, but central to our concern is the need to discover some measure of creative enjoyment and enrichment in life.

Value has a more specifiable meaning than the classical idea of the good, and it can be given a behavioral or operational definition. Good is a far more abstract concept, often related only to the moral good, whereas value encompasses a wider range of human activities (economic, social, æsthetic, etc.). Value, as I interpret it, does not exist independent of the processes of preferential behavior expressed by an organism. Wherever there is selective teleonomic activity,[1] valuing is going on. The worm has value for the bird, the carrot for the horse, the T-bone for the dog. Organisms engage in a number of focused activities, such as fer-reting out objects and consuming them. Here, value has a biological basis; it is mixed with instinct and conditioned response. Certain goods have functional survival value for the organism, and it learns to strive after and appropriate them for its own purposes. Pleasures that accrue in the process of consumption also serve as a motive for future action, and there is an effort to engage in activities and seek out objects from which enjoyment is derived.

Valuing activities are also essential for the maintenance of human organisms. Built into the genetic endowment of the species are biolog-ical processes essential for its survival. During the processes of evolution, certain forms of behavior contribute to survival and have adaptive value. Eating, copulating, fleeing from danger, and fighting all trigger appro-priate responses in behavior and have important biological functions. Every normal member of the species develops deep-seated somatic and homeostatic needs, and these have to be satisfied if the human organism is to survive and function. Pleasure is attached to the satisfaction of our basic needs, such as feeding and copulation. Human beings, as complex social animals, can only survive in groups; they have built-in bio-cooperative mechanisms to enable them to do so. Our biological stimuli are modified, however, in socio-cultural contexts, and new values emerge in civilization. Food and liquid are essential to sustain life, and humans embellish them in a variety of ways. The variety emerges from the geographical regions and socio-cultural traditions under which we live: from spaghetti or rice to escargot or filet mignon.

Similarly there are a whole range of bio-psychological needs and interests: sexual activities, art, music, poetry, sports, politics, and philosophy. We thus have a double nature: Our values are structured by our given genetic endowment, but they are also malleable and modifiable as conditioned and learned responses. Indeed, there are virtually unlimited varieties of tastes and appreciations cultivated within the cultural contexts in which humans are born and flower. In complex social systems, economic activities are geared to producing and distributing an incredible number of goods and services consumers will find enticing. Humans become so dependent upon such goods that they actually come to need them to live. Their worth is given a price and we engage in barter and trade in order to obtain them. We come to crave and exult in the fineries, delicacies, and luxuries afforded by civilized life.

Value may be defined as the object, or goal, of any interest, desire, or need on the part of the human organism. Value is biogenic and psychosociogenic in origin, content, and function. In any valuing process, there are goals (ends, purposes) that we seek to attain, and satisfaction and/or pleasure in their consummatory achievement. Valuing involves both objectives and activities. It is a transactional concept, for we interact with objectives in an environment, and the objects and experiences are fused and intermingled. Thus valuing is relational. It includes a perceived or imagined objective (expectation), a conative striving process, and some immediacies of enjoyment and satisfaction in achievement.

Some values are largely instrumental; that is, we pursue goals because of their results. We mine for coal or work the soil not for mining or digging's sake, but for what such acts lead to: warmth and food. The concept of intrinsic value refers to that which we seek in itself. There is rarely a sharp delineation between instrumental and intrinsic values, but rather a continuity. We may come to like our work and find it intrinsically worthwhile. Moreover, intrinsic experiences have consequences and are themselves instrumental, positively or negatively, to what follows. We may enjoy good food, music, wine, sex, or play for their own sakes, but some of these activities have physiological and psychological consequences, especially if taken in excess. There is a means-end continuum in behavior. Although we seek out means to achieve our goals or objectives, our ends are themselves functionally related to, influenced by, or modified by our means. What we wish to achieve is contingent upon what is possible or probable.

In human behavior, valuing processes are not simply instinctive or unconscious; these are surely present (as in the newborn's sucking response), but most involve conscious awareness. Our motives and intentions thus are expressed in emotive attitudes and are fused with cognitive states of consciousness. Processes of deliberation and reflection intervene to structure our values. Valuings that are purely conative or motor-affective are thus transformed into purposeful *valuation* processes, whereby we come to define, interpret, and evaluate our values. We seek to appraise them in the light of knowledge of the situation in which we act. We learn that to successfully fulfill our desires, we need to calculate the likelihood of achieving them. We thus weigh the consequences and costs of our actions. We make predictions of what will ensue were we to embark upon a course of action. And we formulate various strategies to attain our ends. The objects we choose to pursue often depend upon our estimates of the likelihood of achieving them. In Edwin Arlington Robinson's poem "Miniver Cheevy," a man longs to be a knight of old or a Medici prince. And because he can't be, he abandons rationality, lapses into self-pity, and becomes a hopeless drunkard.

Rationality is essential to the processes of human valuation and volition. How does it proceed? By considering the facts of the situation, the objectives desired, the goals we wish to achieve and how they fit in with other motives, the circumstances under which we act, and an estimate of the effort, time, or cost needed to achieve our ends. A wise choice involves balancing the worth of one object against others, a prediction of the consequences of achieving it, and an imaginative exploration of its net effect on the other values that we and others hold. We often ask ourselves whether we need an object or merely want it, and, if the goal is difficult to obtain, whether it is really worth the effort. Here the evaluative process brings in short-range and long-range considerations.

A reasonable person will not wish to place in jeopardy or risk a long-range interest (for example, a marriage or career) for an immediate and transitory value (for example, an affair). He learns the economizing principle, namely, to forgo expenditures and enjoyments today for capital investment in tomorrow. On the other hand, he asks, should he sacrifice all immediate enjoyments for a future that might never come? The essential question, given the wide range of human interests and values, is to balance competing values and interests and to judge which ones are worthy of attainment. A rational person soon learns that if he wishes to preserve his health, restraints on eating, drinking, working, and even playing are essential, and that if he wishes to achieve mental equilibrium, some temperance in his passions is necessary. Or, as the ancient Greeks said, nothing to excess, in all things moderation.

There are many disputes about values and about the objectives that are worthy of pursuit. One can catalogue the great number of valuable things that we enjoy experiencing—virtually all of the goods for which people express preferences. Which of these ought to be considered most beautiful, satisfying, or fulfilling, and which are ugly, unsatisfying, and worthless? At this point, considerations of ethical values emerge, and we may attempt to develop a hierarchy or scale of values, a set of priorities, a hedonic calculus. Is there a *summum bonum* that we should seek above all else?

I may like watching football games, going to the opera, taking vacations in the Caribbean, collecting stamps, reading Wittgenstein, singing in a chorus, working for a cause, making love to my wife, exercising daily, supporting a worthy charity, doing my job well. But I cannot do them all at the same time and may have to sacrifice some for those with more enduring ends.

Why do I seek these goals? Is there some ultimate goal that I desire more profoundly than any other? At this point begins the philosopher's quest, and the most common response to the query is, yes, there is a highest good: it is happiness. But what is happiness and how is it achievable? Is it creative self-actualization, hedonic pleasure, service to our fellow human beings, or the attainment of a state of eternal bliss in the hereafter?

What is the humanist response to these questions? Given the wide diversity of interests, values, and tastes, and the different motives expressed in human culture, it may be thought arbitrary to seek to define one set of values as superior. Which is "better": shooting dice or reading poetry, basking in the sun daily or hard work, a life of dedication to the service of others or solitary meditation, heroic adventure or withdrawal from the world? Students in my philosophy classes always resist the question. In wishing to be fair-minded, they end up as subjectivists: "Who are *we* to say that one style of life is *better* than the next?" I ask, "Is there a difference between the life of great nobility and enterprise in which a statesman conducts the affairs of a nation, and that of a lush who spends his days on a barstool consuming vast quantities of alcohol?" Granted, we risk the danger of exalting one set of values over a wide range of experiences and enjoyments and perhaps even of censoring tastes by legislative or cultural dictate.

Yet we may ask: Is there a difference between a Florence Nightingale, who dedicated herself to caring for wounded and dying British soldiers in the Crimea, and a prostitute who also ministers to soldiers in other ways and for other reasons? Is there no way of comparing the life of an Albert Schweitzer, for example, with that of an S.S. trooper? To claim that there are no criteria for evaluating interests, tastes, and preferences would reduce us to nihilism, where all values are equal because there are no values, and no distinctions can be made, and where there are no differences in quality and nobility. Is that a reasonable posture to take?

This debate has raged for centuries. It is central to the history of ethics. Plato and Aristotle denied that all pleasures were good, and found that only some were; John Stuart Mill made a distinction between higher and lower pleasures. From the standpoint of humanistic ethics, both sides of the argument have merit. We need to tolerate alternative lifestyles and the richly diverse range of human enjoyment, and not seek to prohibit or legislate them out of existence. Nor must we identify that which is simply accepted as a higher form of life by an Establishment that may be blind to its own hypocrisies and rail against meaningful nonconformity. Still, there are some norms that we can use as guides, and some standards of evaluation. Would a Bluebeard who dissolves bodies in lime or a drug addict qualify equally in dignity with a Jesus Christ or an Abe Lincoln? It would be ludicrous to argue that anything is as good as anything else, and the fact that some sentient being is interested in an object or activity and enjoys it does not thereby mean that it has value equivalent to some other object or activity.

Some values are more precious than others; some interests are demeaning and unworthy of human attention. Some forms of life are vulgar and banal, and others have sterling qualities that evoke our admiration. We recognize that certain kinds of activities are trivial, and that others are more significant and ennobling. Indeed, we critically appraise values all the time, and in a wide range of fields. Within each field we use comparative judgments: we say that there are good and bad artists, poets, skiers, chefs, political leaders, musicians, mechanics, philosophers, and scientists. And we appeal to æsthetic and moral standards of criticism. The standards we appeal to may not be fixed or absolute, and they may be relative to the context or field of inquiry, but nonetheless we assume that they exist. They are the standards of civilized taste, discriminating appreciation, cultivated connoisseurship, and professional competence.

STANDARDS OF EXCELLENCE

Indeed, criteria for grading values and performances are introduced in virtually all fields of human endeavor; these involve qualitative standards of excellence. What is excellence? How do we know it when we see it? How can we attain it? These questions are particularly important for the ethics of humanism. Its critics, especially the theists, charge that it has no

standards or values, and that insofar as it advocates tolerance, it is permissive toward the vagaries of human tastes, including those of volup-
tuaries and egotists. But this is not the case.

There is, as Mill pointed out, a difference between the levels of taste
of a developed adult in comparison with that of a child or a savage. Mill
says, "It is better to be a human being dissatisfied than a pig satisfied;
better to be Socrates dissatisfied than a fool satisfied."[2] If the pig or fool
differs with this judgment, it is because he knows only one side of the
question. The fully realized human being has tasted both kinds of pleasure—the developed (intellectual, aesthetic, and moral), and the underdeveloped (purely physical)—and according to Mill, invariably prefers
the former. Thus, basic to the concept of value is the idea of realization,
for this enables us to distinguish levels of maturation and growth. The
standard here is what a person who has fully actualized his talents would
judge to be worthwhile. This leaves room for the higher reaches of intellectual, aesthetic, and moral pleasures.

Although Mill's argument is not unreasonable, I think it can be
overstated; one should take a balanced view. It is not always the case that
intellectual, aesthetic, and moral pleasures are superior to the natural
biological pleasures derived from food, drink, exercise, physical contact,
or sex, and that if given the choice, most people would prefer the former
to the latter. One might say that it depends on the time, place, and circumstances. Sometimes one would prefer to make love rather than visit
an art museum, jog rather than read a book, enjoy a good dinner and
drink fine wine rather than listen to a lecture by a colleague, or spend
money at a football game rather than contribute to the Salvation Army.

Many so-called moralists are deceptive, especially when they label
the so-called biological pleasures as "lower" forms of human experience.
There is an underlying *hedonic phobia* gnawing at the bowels of such

moralists, who, though they may have developed the capacity for enjoying literature, the arts, mathematics, or spiritual pursuits, are incapable of enjoying good food and drink or experiencing an orgasm. These individuals are so repressed that they cannot appreciate the excitements of physical and biological pleasures without a sense of guilt or sin, and they live out their lives in impoverished sublimation, spiritual substitution, or other forms of ascetic desperation.

I would argue that in order to achieve the full life, a person has to satisfy his or her basic biological homeostatic and survival needs, and this includes the need for sexual love and orgasm. When these needs are dammed up, the potential for tragedy simmers. In the past, diseased views of sex—such as St. Augustine's—have been celebrated and emulated. The Roman Catholic or Buddhist emphasis on celibacy and asceticism is essentially pathological. To fight against natural desires or consider them evil, to be at war with one's own body, or to turn in wrath and hatred against it will often produce serious illness. What untold misery and desperation this view has caused the poor souls whose bodies were considered so corrupt that they were forced to suppress their natural desires! Perhaps I have overstated the case. Some people have resorted to sublimation seemingly without ill effects. Some say that orgasm might not be necessary for everyone. Some people claim to lead fulfilled lives as celibates, whether by deliberate choice or the inability to find a suitable partner. Perhaps "pathological" is too strong for all of them. Yet is a celibate not like a person who would rather be blind or deaf because of the quiet afforded him; and may not we say that his capacity for enjoying physical pleasure is underdeveloped?

Nonetheless, if there are disturbed individuals who are incapable of appreciating their biogenic tendencies, there are also those who have never developed other potentialities—intellectual, aesthetic, moral, and social values, the so-called civilizing virtues. No doubt the terms *higher* and *lower* are here misleading, for we wish to develop fully as personalities, and it is difficult to assign priority or posteriority on a scale of values. It is not either/or, but *both* that we ought to cultivate in any kind of rounded life. I have elsewhere called this the *exuberant* life, or robust hedonism, for it does not involve simply passive enjoyment but creative actualization. The ideal here is the person who is able to realize and appreciate a wide range of biogenic and sociogenic values. One must be cautious, however, about defending a hierarchy of values, as A. H. Maslow did,[3] unless one makes it abundantly clear that biological pleasures are as essential to one's well-being as those of higher levels of creativity.

The normative concept of *excellence* is applicable here; it refers to the various dimensions of experience. We say, for example, that a person enjoys excellent health, meaning that his physiological system is functioning well. He gets proper nutrition, takes sufficient exercise, and is free of any major ailments or diseases. By contrast, another person may be in poor health. These categories have some objective basis in testable fact. Although conditions of health are relative to each person, some empirical criteria are relevant to the evaluation. We can also appraise a person's social relationships, to see if they are dysfunctional or harmonious. There are, for example, some families rent with emotional conflict. A husband and wife may be incompatible and live in constant friction, and their children may suffer as a consequence. Although such normative judgments are relational in the sense that they refer to specific individuals with diverse idiosyncratic tendencies, we nonetheless can characterize some relationships as healthy and others as unwholesome.

The philosophers have traditionally referred to the vital role that reason plays in ensuring happiness. But a key element they have sometimes overlooked is the need for developing emotive compassion. In mature relationships, some affectionate bond is present, and there is some empathy for the needs and interests of other persons. All of this suggests a double normative standard. First, there is the need to satisfy our basic needs and desires, both biogenic and sociogenic. The inability to do so leads to unhealth. Second, there is the need to achieve some degree of harmony or compatibility in the social environment, particularly in the intimate, face-to-face relations of the family.

It is apparent that the idea of excellence can also be applied to the so-called higher creative functions, to our intellectual skills, for example. Some individuals are slow learners, poor readers, or are unable to do mathematics or science, whereas others seem gifted, well-motivated, and capable of high performance. We grade students on a scale of academic achievement. We praise aesthetic creativity. We recognize the musical genius of a Mozart or a Beethoven, and the artistic talents of a Leonardo or a van Gogh. Standards of critical judgment enable us to appreciate a work of art and to evaluate it in terms of its aesthetics. Thus we use standards of excellence throughout life.

ETHICAL EXCELLENCE

The central question is whether there are standards of *ethical* excellence. Is it possible to contrast and compare the wide variety of tastes and appreciations, and to adjudicate between them? Can we judge between various styles of life and apply to them the terms *better* or *worse*? If so, on what bases?

The first point to make is that all evaluating procedures are *comparative*. Few absolute standards can be discovered. All standards, thus, are relative to a class of persons and their performances. We can, for example, rank track-and-field athletes, but only in relation to the performance of other athletes. We might do this by first examining the Olympic records. Only those who have broken new records or been awarded gold medals, such as Roger Bannister, Fanny Blankers-Koen, Paavo Nurmi, or Rafe Johnson, would qualify for excellence in the field. *Excellence* is thus a thoroughly relative term, applicable to human beings engaged in some activity and used to compare their capacities and achievements. Here we are talking about athletic excellence, not ethical excellence, but analogous processes apply.

Another test of excellence is *consistency* in performance. It is not a single success—important as that may be to record—but achievement over a period of time that most impresses us. A child prodigy, however great a talent, may burn out early and be heard from no more. Not everyone is a Yehudi Menuhin, who displays virtuosity throughout his life. Thus we say that Wordsworth and Whitman are great poets, that Mies van der Rohe and Frank Lloyd Wright are great architects, that Einstein and Newton are great scientists. Such individuals are considered geniuses in specific fields of endeavor because their work broke new ground. Their performances or discoveries came to be recognized as pre-eminent, towering, or unique, and eventually each was publicly acclaimed. Does excellence require public approval? They are considered excellent not because they achieved recognition, but because of the intrinsic qualities of their work, which manifests creativity, innovation, discovery. They are noteworthy because they have exceeded our expectations, and have made an outstanding contribution.

I should add that there are countless creative persons who have not been recognized during their lives but whose excellence and creativity are eventually acknowledged. Van Gogh, for example, was not recognized as a genius during his lifetime, and Nietzsche was reviled as an evil man.

No doubt we can also quantify some forms of excellence, as when a person receives a perfect score on an examination. Often the evaluative concept is qualitative and difficult to characterize numerically; yet the excellence gleams through, much as a polished crystal, and we are dazzled by its sparkling beauty. Standards of ethical excellence are relative to a person's own level of talent and accomplishment. A person may not be a genius, nor make new breakthroughs, yet working with the materials he has, a kind of excellence may emerge. In focusing on excellence, I should make it clear that we should not concentrate on only a small elite. We should not judge the quality of a person's life by his or her fame or eminence, nor by the criterion of whether he or she is a genius or has made significant discoveries or contributions to the world.

Excellence is a relativistic standard applicable to the individual on his own terms, given his personality, the biological and environmental factors in his life, and the social circumstances in which he finds himself. The life of nobility that I am talking about has a dignity and grandeur, not as befits only monarchs and presidents but also persons of the lowest station. Excellence emerges whenever there is a harmonious blending and symmetry. Even through pain, suffering, adversity or tragedy—and perhaps in spite of it—the life has been worthwhile. Such a person does not live in a degraded state of failure and self-deceit. His life exudes exquisite qualities. His life is *precious*, to himself and to those about him. One doesn't have to paint a Mona Lisa to excel in life, but only one's own home. Nor does one need to build a monument; it can be one's own career nurtured with loving care. A person can express a kind of artistry and virtuosity in living, even if it is in modest circumstances.

Perfection cannot be attained by any person; all humans have flaws. It is in spite of a person's limitations and character defects that a kind of qualitative worth may still express itself. A human life, if well-lived, is a wonder to behold, a sublime and illustrious entity, like a splendid chestnut tree or a stately lion. We need to appreciate what it means to be a human being, and not mistakenly believe that one has to be a genius or a saint—for we are all only human.

We come back to the question: From the standpoint of *ethical* value, in what sense is it meaningful to apply the standard of excellence? Can we apply the terms *exquisite qualities* and *high merit*? Yes, we can. Here we appraise: (1) the *kinds* of values that a person cherishes and that activate him or her, (2) the *style* of life that he or she has adopted, and (3) how he or she *relates* to other persons within the sphere of interaction. In dealing with ethical excellence, I am not referring simply to a person's chief occupation or career—as important and satisfying as that may be in achieving the good life—but to the total constellation of values and principles manifested throughout the entire life. A person can be a great physicist and lead a miserable life, a great mathematician and not know how to get his car started, a sensitive poet and a terrible husband. I do not wish to focus on the part-man or part-woman but on the total life of the developed personality. What are the ingredients in a life which enable us to say that the person is exemplary, and/or that he or she is capable of some nobility? What are the admirable qualities, the signs of perfection and excellence that manifest themselves?

From the standpoint of the humanist, the fruition of life is to live well and to achieve some modicum of happiness. For the individual, happiness involves some sense of achievement and of having reached the fullness of one's being. A person's life is like a work of art. We are involved in the creative process of giving form and structure, unity and harmony to our plans and projects. We have blended colors, tones, shapes, and forms, and affixed them to the canvas. Our life is in part our own creation. What results is due to the choices and actions we have taken over many years and decades. Is the end product our own doing? Are we able to bring the parts together, to complete our dreams and projects, and to give a kind of unity and coherence to our world? Not everyone can create a masterpiece, build a noteworthy career, or lead an exemplary life. Many persons have failed. Their lives are wasted, they are overcome by fear and timidity, they are drowned by years of sorrow. They can never find a niche for themselves in the scheme of things. And so, they are condemned not only by the fates (to speak metaphorically) but also by their own inability to achieve great things. By this I do not mean social expectations, but their own. How many failed careers, dissolute marriages, and lives of quiet desperation are there?

Could a person's life have been otherwise? Yes, perhaps to some extent, but if so, how and in what sense? The full ethical life, measured in personal terms, involves a sense of achievement and accomplishment, a conscious recognition that we have, however modestly, contributed to the world, expressed our talents, and done something useful and productive in terms of our own ideals. To be able to do so can lead to a joyful and creative life, the bountiful, outgoing, adventurous life. Happiness, in some sense, can be achieved by most men women, but it depends upon what we do. It depends on our being able to fulfill our basic needs, but also in our being able to express our creative talents in whatever fields we choose.

There are, of course, great tragedies, unforeseen accidents, and calamities. Someone is struck down by the ubiquitous tide of events, and through no fault of his own is unable to complete his life satisfactorily. Thus luck plays a key role in life: being in the right place at the right time, or being absent from the wrong place at the wrong time. But still, what happens to us depends on what we do, how we respond to challenges, whether we deal with them wisely, how we plan our lives, the choices we make, the people we relate to, our interests and activities, our occupations and careers, how we adapt and persist in spite of adversity, and how we respond to new opportunities.

Some of the classical religious models, I submit, are in a profound sense antihuman, and the source of deep-seated misery and unhappiness. I am referring to those systems of morality that preach withdrawal from this world, such as some forms of Buddhism, which advocate the extinction of desire in order to achieve a state of quiescent nirvana, or some aspects of Christianity, which emphasize salvation in the next life. The Promethean ideal is to challenge the gods and the fates, to adopt the outgoing posture, to dazzle our own world with achievement. Living outside the Garden of Eden, having eaten the forbidden fruit, we need the courage to persist despite adversity. That is what human culture is about; it is the product of our hopes and inspirations, of our imagination and resourcefulness, and of our determination to fulfill our highest visions. The sum and substance of the creative life is expressed in the heroic virtues: the unwillingness to accept defeat, and the determination to create a new world in which we realize our aspirations.

The key to the life of excellence is not found by simply satisfying our needs, or even in fulfilling our nature, but in exceeding it by leaping forward and performing courageous deeds. Ethical nobility best exemplifies itself by taking the first step into the unknown when all others fear to do so, by lighting a candle instead of suffering the darkness, and by seeking to reach new horizons for ourselves. A creative person is capable of *existential* choice, is willing to master his or her fate as far as possible, to dream of new frontiers, and to expend the effort to bring all of this into being. The creative person is not fixated on the past, nor is he overwhelmed by the present moment, but instead focuses his energies on attaining his future. He does not bask in Being nor is he mired in Nothingness, but he is eager to enter into the exultant process of Becoming, for that is the dynamic key to life.

In writing these lines, I am not unaware of the possibility for some skepticism, for I have described a style of life that has been emphasized in certain cultures but not in all. It is expressed in contemporary American and European life, where creative scientists, artists, entrepreneurial builders, and high achievers are praised. But not all cultures have focused on this; some have sought other ideals, such as religious quietude or spiritual release. Is what I am presenting universal in the sense that it expresses a common human capacity, no matter what the culture? Not all individuals in all careers are capable of high achievement. Yet I say it applies to everyone. Would it apply to the office typist, farm laborer, or factory worker who has a job to do that leaves little room for creativity? Some individuals seem to exult in the adventurous life of challenge, while others would prefer comfort and security. Is the ideal I have presented only available to a creative elite?

These objections are worrisome, for, if true, they would mean that the exuberant life is an expression of my own personal predilections (or even physical makeup), and though I may have found such a life exciting and ennobling, others may find it stressful and tiring. Is there any objective justification for it, or is it simply a matter of taste? Some of these criticisms appear to have merit. Perhaps I am only talking to those individuals who have a Promethean temper and who can find grandeur in a life of risk-taking and exertion. Yet, in support of my argument, I submit that if one scans the entire human drama, one finds that creativity plays the key role as the mainspring of civilization, and that each person can contribute to creative development, no matter how modestly. It is the creative surge that marks the indomitable human spirit, the fact that men and women are not content to rest, but can strive to master events and turn them to advantage. The human animal is a builder and doer, and is by its very nature creative. I readily concede the need for order, harmony, for savoring the immediacies of experience, and for times of release and relaxation from the strenuous life. Nonetheless, creative activity and the achievement motive are deep impulses within the human species, the sources of greatness and inspiration, which enable us to transcend the limits of our nature and to build culture. Many theists war against such impulses; they wish to save us from the ambiguities and challenges of living by postulating an eternal life of blessedness. But insofar as they try to deny the creative adventure they are antihuman and the enemies of human realization.

EXCELSIOR

Can I be more precise? What constitutes ethical excellence? It is not simply a life of pleasure or enjoyment but one of creative achievement. Is it possible to delineate the qualities and characteristics that such a life of excellence entails? Perhaps the term *excelsior* best describes this state of creative fulfillment. No one can attain perfection, and yet there are degrees of magnificence that each and every person may discover and express. I shall adopt *excelsior* to mean a concrete, empirical state, one that can be achieved here and now. One doesn't have to wait for nirvana or salvation in the next world.

First, we may distinguish those states of excellence that apply to the individual as he seeks personal realization and exuberant achievement. Second, there are excellences that apply to the individual as he relates to other human beings within the community. For no one can fully achieve a state of excelsior without sharing values.

I. Excellence Primarily in Regard to Oneself

1. *Autonomy.* Among the highest human excellencies is a person's ability to take control of his or her own life. This means the willingness to accept responsibility for his own future and the recognition that it is the person himself who will ultimately decide how he wants to live and what he wants to become. This is not to deny that by living in communities we make cooperative decisions, but since we have only one life to live, we should not waste it by refusing to make our own choices or by forfeiting that opportunity and allowing others to choose for us. The autonomous person thus has some sense of his own independence. He is self-directed and self-governing. His autonomy is related to the affirmation of his freedom.

Can he control his own destiny? Can he change or redirect events? Is he so structured by impersonal forces that he can do nothing other than submit to them? The great failure in life is an individual's acquiescence to his fate, his willingness to escape from freedom, and his refusal to make choices about his own vital interests. Theists demean human power when they maintain that we are nothing in ourselves but are dependent upon God at every turn. They insist that we can do nothing outside of God's dictates. We cannot overcome the tragic character of the human condition; the only solution for man is divine salvation.

The humanist differs with this pessimistic appraisal and psychological retreat by providing a positive alternative. We *can* cope with the problems of living. But we need to deal realistically with the world as we find it, and not seek to flee to a mythological deity for help. Only by extending our best efforts can we hope to overcome adversity, conflict, tragedy. We need to be willing to do what is necessary to understand the processes of nature and to seek to redirect them for our own purposes. If we are to succeed, we need to have some confidence that we can make a difference, that our activities will be effective, and that at least we will try.

Thus autonomy is personal freedom extended to control the events that impinge on our lives. I am not talking about our ability to influence other people or society at large, but to control our own private life and the acceptance of this as an ongoing project. One must think: I am at the center of choice and decision, and I must decide what I wish to do with my life. I will make my views known, and when possible I will attempt to act upon them. This involves courage, not simply the courage to be, but the courage to become. It involves audacity and verve.

The opposite of this attitude is conformity, withdrawal, and in its extreme, fear and trembling. Here one is defeated before one begins. A person feels that there is nothing that he can do except submit to his fate and the Furies. Yet a person with an autonomous, self-affirming, assertive outlook refuses to give in without a fight. The autonomous person has pluck, energy, and some strength of will, which enables him to forbear and to prevail.

Autonomy is not antisocial; indeed, the open, democratic society encourages the growth of autonomous persons. The best society is one in which people are willing to accept some responsibility for themselves and to behave intelligently in making their choices. Autonomy does not mean that I may not work in concert with my wife or husband, sister or brother, mother or father, friend, colleague, or fellow-citizen. Insofar as I am autonomous, I can respect other persons as equally entitled to autonomy over their lives.

2. *Intelligence*. Classical philosophers have emphasized the essential role that reason plays in the good life. In doing so, they have perhaps underestimated the significance of the conative and passionate dimensions of human experience. Aristotle delineated five intellectual virtues

that he thought contributed to rational excellence: philosophical wisdom, scientific demonstration, intuition, art, and practical wisdom. Our intellectual abilities are far more complex and extensive than that. I have elsewhere catalogued twenty-one such intellectual qualities, including everything from abstract intelligence and logical ability on the one hand, to technical skill, artistic virtuosity, and mechanical dexterity on the other.[4]

Aristotle perceptively recognized the significance of practical wisdom in making ethical choices. One can possess high intellectual skills and manifest significant intellectual attainment in one area, and lack it in others. It is difficult to find one person possessing all the intellectual talents. From the standpoint of the ethical life, however, the most important quality is that of practical critical intelligence. Common sense, or native understanding, enables us to cope with the dilemmas encountered in life and to make sensible choices. I call this *good judgment*, the ability to evaluate alternatives and make intelligent decisions.

Whether this ability is a gift of the gods (that is, genetic) or a product of experience, capable of being cultivated by education and training, has been debated by the philosophers. Why are some people able to hit the bull's-eye, as it were, and to know the best thing to do in a situation, whereas others are *taugenichts* (good-for-nothings), poor fools constantly embroiled in disasters and unable to make wise choices? Practical wisdom is probably a result of both talent and training; fortunately we can learn to improve our capacity to engage in critical thinking and apply it to ordinary life. What I have in mind here is prudential intelligence; that is, the ability to make plans, fulfill projects, and reach decisions after a deliberative process. This includes an estimation on our part of the costs and consequences of alternative actions. Cognition becomes constitutive of the process of choosing. The ethics of excellence depends upon our ability to make *informed* judgments based upon knowledge of good and evil.

We had better be honest about this excellence. No one is perfect, and even the most rational person may at times succumb to passion. It is surely appropriate to fall in love, cheer the home team, or enjoy oneself at a banquet. Intelligence provides an ideal model, a comparative method for evaluating values and principles, and balancing competing claims within a situation. Critical ethical intelligence is not purely formal or abstract. Its content is concrete: One should not counter reason against desire. It is not a question of cognition mastering or dominating desires, as the ancient Stoics would have it, for all motivation involves our wants and is deeply bio-psychological in content. Our motives, fused with desires and reasons, stimulate us to action, not to thought alone. All that awareness can do is bring about an equilibrium between the various phases of our psychological impulses. Intelligence itself is a biological state. It is not an interloper; it is an intimate part of our entire physiological makeup, though only one ingredient in the preferential process of valuing. Nonetheless, we may say that we ought to prize intelligence as an excellence, for insofar as it can play a causative role in helping to modify intentions and interests, it can contribute to a better life. It is essential, for it is the fullest and the most complete expression of what we are as human beings.

Intellectual activities are a deep source of enjoyment and enrichment. This is surely the case with pure research, the quest for scientific explanations of how nature operates, historical investigations, philosophical understanding, and so on. Many individuals have dedicated their lives to intellectual pursuits and have discovered the intense satisfaction they can afford. Aristotle recognized that one needs some measure of leisure in order to pursue the life of the mind. Every man and woman is capable of some degree of intellectual activity, whether it is going to school, reading books, listening to lectures, or trying to discover something for themselves. There is a fascination in attempting to solve problems and puzzles; some of the most challenging games test our mettle as we become engrossed in their solutions. Man is a curious animal and he wishes to know. Some people are so eager to be well-informed that they wish to learn everything they can about a certain subject. They may travel or read widely; they may wish to meet new people or go to exhibitions or lectures. This expression of our intellectual interests points to the fact that we place a high value on knowledge, both for its value in our lives and as a source of enjoyment.

3. *Self-discipline*. This is an important virtue to develop. It is related to intelligence and good judgment, but it goes beyond them. It applies to the life of desire and passion. Unless one can control his emotions and direct his efforts to constructive purposes, his energies are apt to be squandered and dissipated in unproductive and self-defeating activities. One is in danger of being obsessed with a given pursuit, like the food addict, who eats to exhaustion, or the nymphomaniac, whose desire for sex is uncontrollable. The habit of self-discipline needs to be cultivated by education and training. Once achieved, moderation is used in satisfying one's desires. Self-discipline also enables one to channel his efforts creatively in order to achieve his purposes in life. Discipline draws upon intelligence and practical wisdom. It fuses thought and desire. More than a cognitive state, it applies to the character of the whole person. It involves strength of will and the determination to persevere.

The undisciplined person is prey to every haphazard whim and fancy; his lusts and cravings dominate him. He may be overwhelmed by his desires for sex, food, drink, drugs, or trivial entertainment, to which he may give in with abandon. Self-restraint is an essential guide for mature individuals, who are able to resist the lure of momentary temptations for long-range goals. It may entail some measure of stoic resignation, but also involved is the ability to face adversity and the determination to overcome challenges. This does not mean that one does not enjoy life or ever give in to desires. Rather, he seeks to balance the various desires and decide which ones will be fulfilled. To lead an effective life, one needs to guide and control external events, but also to learn how to master and control one's inner drives so that they do not dominate.

4. *Self-respect*. The ethics of excellence involves the development of a decent respect for oneself. We are constantly being told that we ought to respect other human beings, our elders, the law, and those dependent upon us. This may be well and good, but in the process some individuals forget that they are entitled to the same kind of care and consideration they confer on others.

The focus on self-respect can become exaggerated if an individual develops an over-inflated sense of his own worth. These are the egotists and egoists. I am not talking about them, for their self-concern has been inflated beyond reasonable measure, and society has a right to complain about this and guard against them. These individuals often behave in an infantile fashion, which may lead to megalomania and self-glorification.

Contrasted with this state is absence of self-esteem and an impoverished sense of identity. Having been beaten down by others, perhaps over-criticized by censorious parents or teachers, a person may rebel and flout even the most reasonable demands of society, or, on the contrary, he may withdraw, lacking any sense of independence. Such a person simply conforms to what is expected of him. I find that a deep and abiding concern of college students is whether their talents compare favorably with those of their peers. Poor or average grades or parental disapproval can arouse great anxiety. They have an underlying fear that they may not succeed in life.

Some individuals, lacking self-confidence, give up early. Unfortunately, such individuals often find it difficult to live fully, because they lack minimal respect for themselves, their talents and abilities, and what they can achieve or attain. Those who lack self-assurance may constantly need to prove themselves, and so they wear themselves out in fruitless efforts to seek approval in the eyes of others, and abandon what they would like to do in life. The opposite of self-respect is self-hatred. For some individuals it can so corrode their sense of worth that they constantly criticize themselves for failures or defeats—or even for their inability to succeed gloriously. They may be perfectionists, never content with the tasks they have chosen or their level of accomplishment. They have no inner peace. They may even give up in quiet desperation, seeking to find some quiet haven that will afford them warmth and security. Despite the lip service paid in our culture to openness, tolerance of differences, and emphasis on individuality, there is an appalling pressure to conform, which is not conducive to self-respect.

No one can succeed in everything he undertakes in life. One tries his best, hoping to learn from defeats. But the person who lacks self-respect can never accept failure: he turns against himself. Although he can make allowances for those about him who fail, he will not do so for himself. He may love others, but he doesn't love himself. Christianity certainly helps to foster this self-guilt by advocating values that are completely unobtainable on earth, such as perfect virtue, and then castigating its adherents for not obtaining them.

The humanist responds to the perfectionist: You are the only person you have to live with all your life, from the beginning to the end. Hence, you might as well come to terms with yourself, enjoy yourself, and think well of yourself. Although hopefully you can recognize your virtues and limitations, you may need to make some allowances. This doesn't mean you are not accountable for your errors of omission and commission, or that you shouldn't constantly strive to improve.

Some self-respect is necessary for building one's identity and to expanding one's powers of autonomy and independence. Pride in oneself is not a sin. Self-effacing humility is not an appropriate response for a free, autonomous person capable of some action in the world and desirous of deserved respect.

5. *Creativity*. The creative person exemplifies the most eloquent expression of human freedom: the capacity for originality. Creativity is intimately related to autonomy and self-respect, for the independent person has some sense of his own power. He does not submit to the obstacles he encounters in nature. He is able to invent or to bring into being something new. He not only can apprehend new possibilities but bring them to fruition.

Creativity has many different facets. One often thinks of the creative scientist on the frontiers of knowledge who makes some monumental discovery or proposes some new and daring theory. It is also the driving force of the great artist or sculptor, who is able to take the raw materials of nature and impose new forms that fulfill his creative vision. The poet, novelist, and composer, using the materials of language or harmony, weave captivating works of art that inspire us. Similarly, the inventor or engineer creates a new instrument, machine, or device. Statesmen who draft constitutions, builders of new industries, explorers of uncharted seas, continents, or galaxies all express similar creative impulses. The designation *creativity*, I reiterate, should not be confined to exceptional geniuses, for it applies to ordinary people who display talent for innovative behavior.

In one sense, all organic life has creative dimensions. The first union and fertilization of egg and sperm and the processes of creative growth that flow from it illustrate the creative processes intrinsic to organic matter. Wherever there is learning and adaptation by life-forms to environmental problems, there is some degree of creativity. Creativity is one of the defining characteristics of the human species. No one is entirely without it, for it is the necessary means by which we overcome adversity and adapt or respond to stimuli in the environment. There are, however, degrees of creativity; perhaps it best manifests itself in teleonomic activities consciously directed.

Creativity involves both insight and imagination. It appears wherever thought strives to solve problems by introducing alternative means, and manifests itself wherever we seek to combine old materials in new ways. It is the key stimulus to culture-building. Insofar as each person is unique, some creativity is expressed in his idiosyncratic behavior, and in how he learns to cope with and adapt to the world on the everyday, pedestrian level.

There are degrees of excellence attached to creativity. Some persons are more adept than others at discovering new possibilities. They are overflowing with new ideas; they have fertile imaginations. Unfortunately, someone can be a creative genius in one field of endeavor, or show enormous talent and achievement at one time, yet lack the creative outlook outside his field or for the remainder of his life. Thus we should focus not on narrow creativity in a specific area but on the creative life in general, which is approached adventurously and openly.

The uncreative person tends to be a conformist, prone to follow rituals or be obsessive in observing rules. A creature of habit, he is unwilling or unable to try something new. He resists change or novelty. The creative person, on the contrary, is a fountain of ingenious ideas. He is fruitful, constantly bubbling over with new thoughts, schemes, and plans. A problem with one form of creativity is that people have brainstorms but end up as visionary dreamers who never implement their ideas. An effective creative person is one who can follow through. He is not simply an ideas man but a doer, able to realize his dreams. To be effective, his ideas must be grounded in reality. The great creators of history have not simply had random flashes of insight, but have been able to express them, give them form, and ground them in reality. They do not simply conceive or apprehend in their inner souls alone, but can give birth to their offspring. Creativity thus involves a generative process of organization and realization. Many creative persons are not on the frontiers of knowledge, nor do they contribute to civilization's advance. They may not be gifted with special talents, yet in their chosen areas they are creative: finding and following new recipes, redecorating a room, planting a garden, repairing the roof, breeding horses, or teaching a course. I am not talking about pseudo- or pop-creativity, which follows the whims of fashion, but genuine creative expression. The creative person has some confidence in his powers and willingly meets the challenges of life with self-assurance and zest.

Creativity ought to be encouraged in the young, and nourished and cultivated throughout life. Unfortunately it has its enemies. Creative persons often arouse envy and jealousy, and since they are at times unpredictable, they may be difficult to live with. If allowed to vent all their enthusiasms, they can be exhausting to those around them.

From society's standpoint, the most important use of creativity is its application to work. Some forms of work are drudgery. The creative person is able to make his work exciting. His work is not separate and distinct from himself, but flows forth as an expression of his own interests. Drudgery most likely ensues when means are disconnected from ends, and one is given orders to fulfill that hold no interest. A slave or peon has no mind of his own, or at least is not permitted to introduce his own purposes and fulfill them. His labor is thus humdrum, rote, or mechanical. Creative activities thrive best in a free environment, where people's efforts are directed toward their own goals. Given the division of labor, it is often difficult to permit creative persons free rein to luxuriate in their inspirations. One needs to work to make a living, and this work may be boring, yet it needs to be done. That is why developing opportunities for creativity in the marketplace is important. But if this is not entirely feasible, then the expression of creativity in leisure time becomes all the more important for the ordinary person. A creative person, in any case, is resourceful, in that he can deal with life's problems, using both imagination and effort to achieve what he wishes.

6. *Motivation.* Some individuals are highly motivated. They are always ready to undertake projects without wasting time or engaging in delaying tactics. They are resourceful in both ideas and deeds. Other individuals are lazy and ineffective. They never seem to have sufficient energy or interest in doing something, but get by with a minimum of effort. They have low levels of motivation and hence low levels of activity. They do not wish to stand out. They would much rather rest quietly in a garden than weed and plant it or venture outside of it. They seem to withdraw from the hustle and bustle of living.

The motivated person, on the other hand, is self-directed. He has courage, stamina, and the will to do something. He is not loath to dirty his hands and do the things necessary to get the job done. There is an old saying: "if you want something done, ask a busy person." A lazy person never succeeds because he lacks the determination and drive to do so.

There is an excellence that characterizes the well-motivated person. He is able to gather together the things he will need in order to attain the goals he appropriates as his own. He has autonomy, self-discipline, self-respect, and a capacity for creative, inventive, and adaptive response. But he also has the ability to fulfill his goals, whatever they are. Individuals often shy away from tasks they do not like or that are given to them by others. They are only happy when they are doing what they want to do. Unfortunately, some people are limited by narrow horizons and restricted interests. They demonstrate, not only at work but even at play, that they have impoverished imaginations. Low levels of motivation characterize them. They never seem to find themselves. Their drives are wanting. They never develop a career—for them a job is a job, not a profession.

A well-motivated person *professes* a specialty or expertise, and is committed to it. He is achievement-oriented. But more, he finds some pride and satisfaction in his accomplishments. The underachiever is bankrupt as a person. He is easily bored, which means that he is boring. His reactions are infantile, for his only interest seems to be "having a good time." Unless he can point to some contribution he has made to his own life, some deed or accomplishment that is creative and rewarding, then he is underdeveloped and will clearly have a lessened sense of self-respect. Well-motivated persons are dependable, for you can count on them to get something done. The unmotivated person is given to sloth and indecision. In extreme cases, he literally ends up a bum.

7. *Affirmation*. Living the full life depends, to a great extent, on a positive outlook. This means having some degree of optimism, believing that life can be good and bountiful, that it can be ameliorated and improved. Opposed to this is negativism, pessimism, and a tragic sense that life is difficult, that things cannot be changed and will only get worse. There always seem to be impossible Bastilles to storm. This attitude is defeatist and depressive.

The affirmative person takes life as a challenge. He looks upon it as an opportunity. He wishes to do many things and to experience widely. Exuberant happiness cannot be achieved without some sense of one's own power and the ability to solve one's problems. An affirmative person's attitude is apt to be a cheerful one, for he looks to the future with high expectations. His attitude also expresses humor, laughter, and an appreciation for fun. If we have self-respect and some creativity and are well-motivated, then our outreach is ongoing and there is a willingness to explore, experiment, innovate. The optimist tends to look at the positive side: he focuses on the good in people, not their faults. Living is exciting; horizons are unlimited; there are not enough hours in the day to do all the things he wants to do.

The pessimist is forever focused upon the tragic aspects of life. He worries about, without seeing solutions to, the problems of the world hunger, suffering, pain, and sorrow. He is timid and fearful of what people will say about him. Thus he is permeated by negativity, paralyzed by fear, and more apt to retreat than to advance.

The affirmative, outgoing, optimistic, buoyant person finds life to be joyful. There are so many wonderful things to accomplish, so many future achievements that beckon us. Life is full of great promises and opportunities: whatever ills we now encounter can be improved upon and ameliorated. The optimist is never bogged down by feelings of impotence, but has a sense that human effort can be effective, and that we can make this a better world in which to live. A new turn of events is taken as a propitious opportunity, a bright prospect for success. He willingly meets new challenges with anticipation and enthusiasm. He is full of the will to live, to overcome, and to attain new heights of creative enjoyment.

8. *Health*. High on the scale of excellence, perhaps even first, is the realization of personal good health. Perhaps it is a truism to emphasize health (though philosophers have often overlooked it), but any realistic view of happiness must take health as its starting point. If one is to live

and live well, one must be in reasonably good health. If a person is grossly handicapped, sick, or in constant pain, he may not be able to function well, nor be able to accomplish all that he wishes to, yet many individuals have been able to live significant lives in spite of debilitating pain or physical handicaps. In situations of poor health, a person should attempt to do the best he is capable of doing. It is interesting to note that many professed humanists lived long and comparatively healthy lives. What's more, they remained active until their deaths. John Dewey pursued a vigorous career until the age of ninety-three and Bertrand Russell, who died at ninety-seven, was arrested for demonstrating against the atom bomb when he was in his nineties!

There are important principles we should follow if we wish to live healthy lives. It is particularly essential that health education be an important part of our upbringing, and that children should learn from the earliest age about their bodies. The widest dissemination of scientific knowledge should be readily available. This means that there be adequate information about (1) proper nutrition; (2) the importance of daily exercise in maintaining physical and mental fitness; (3) ways of avoiding unnecessary stress and attaining periods of relaxation and rest; and (4) exercising moderation in the life of pleasure. All of this is within the range of preventive medicine. For the humanist, the neglect or abuse of the body is immoral, particularly by those who seek the idle pleasures of hedonism, or who waste their talents in indolence and sloth. This means that drug addiction or gluttony in food or drink—growing obese or eating or drinking to reduce one's anxieties—are also to be condemned.

The test of whether an action is good or bad lies in its consequences. The emphasis in medical science has been on diagnosing and treating illnesses once they occur, and though this is vital, we also need to understand how to avoid risks to health and prevent illness. We now know that the excessive intake of alcohol, cholesterol, or cigarette smoke is dangerous, and only a foolish person ignores the warnings. In any case, every individual is responsible for his own health. The body is the most important possession that we have, and it is our responsibility to see not only that it is not abused and that preventive measures are observed but also that proper care is taken once an illness develops.

The achievement of good health is not simply physical or biological; it involves an important psychological dimension. Psychiatric disorders are the bane of human existence, the source of anxiety and depression, misery and unhappiness. The treatment of the whole person is essential: no doubt many mental illnesses have their origins in biochemical malfunctioning. Psychiatry needs to seek the causes of manic depression, schizophrenia, and other debilitating illnesses. Which of the various methods of drugs or psychotherapy are most effective in treating mental or emotional disturbances remains to be determined. Severe cases of psychosis may have a biochemical basis, so the sick individual may not be helped much by counseling, although his family may benefit from it. Such illnesses are tragic in their destructiveness, rendering the victim unable to cope by simple acts of will power.

The fulfillment of a person's psychosexual needs seems to be an important factor in health. Does the satisfaction of libido fantasies and the avoidance of repression enhance a person's ability to enjoy life? The answer appears to be yes, though of course within reason. It is difficult to discover a single model of sexual realization, for tastes and enjoyments are wide-ranging. Different individuals are "turned on" by different fantasies. What appears odd or vulgar to one person might be exciting to the next. Richard von Krafft-Ebing, who in the late nineteenth century catalogued "deviant" sexual practices, devoted an entire chapter to foot fetishes. Without delving into intricate questions here, I merely wish to state that the capacity to satisfy the sexual libido, culminating in orgasmic release, seems to be an important contributing factor to health.

9. *Joie de vivre.* The French terms *joie de vivre* and *bon vivant* refer to joyful living. All work and no play is not the be-all and end-all of life. The affirmative outlook, important as it is, focuses primarily on the future. Yet the present moment is intrinsically worthwhile, and we need to appreciate fully the immediacies. The *capacity* for enjoying life is an important excellence; it manifests itself in the hedonic and the erotic. The ability to enjoy pleasure without excessive guilt or the sense that it is evil is a positive virtue. I am thinking primarily of those pleasures in personal life, innocent and robust, that do not injure or harm others.

Many moralists have exiled hedonism, eroticism, and the *bon vivant* from their moral universes. Theists have railed against the body and condemned sexual pleasures. In so doing, they betray their own *hedonic or erotic phobia*, which expresses a disease of the soul. Various terms describe the failure to appreciate hedonism: asceticism, self-denial, repression. The inability to savor the delicacies of life is a corroding psychological malady, and can be a source of neurosis and misery.

There is a wide range of pleasures that we should enjoy as part of healthy living. First are those that involve the satisfaction of our basic urges and needs: food, drink, sex. Built on these are the developed pleasures of moral, altruistic, intellectual, aesthetic, and even spiritual joys. A person with *joie de vivre* can find pleasure in a wide range of activities. He can enjoy a feast, drink heartily, make love, read books, travel, listen to music, work for a cause, enjoy sports, poetry, the arts—indeed, experience everything that is worthwhile.[5]

However, excessive concentration upon hedonistic delights, abstracted from the activities of life and to the detriment of other excellencies, is not conducive to the well-lived life. The glutton, fleshpot, drug addict, or libertine mistakenly focuses on the immediacies of enjoyment as the sole end of life. Fixation on the hedonic-erotic is infantile and destructive to the total personality, especially insofar as it dominates other creative activities. The hedonist is the prisoner of his own pleasure-seeking desires; there is an inner tyranny at work.

One must steer a course between two extremes: on the one hand, theistic morality, which rails against the body and makes war on natural enjoyments, and on the other hand, amoral hedonism, which abandons all self-discipline and allows us to become prey to our cravings. One cannot fulfill all of one's fantasies. Self-restraint and moderation are signs of personal maturity. Still, the satisfaction of one's sexual needs must be rated high on the scale of values, and this means some orgasmic pleasure and sexual release. Masturbation is a common method of sexual enjoyment. Kissing, petting, sexual foreplay, and sexual intercourse involve the fullest expression of the libido, for these relate to other persons.

No doubt the strength of sexual passion is connected to the need of the species to reproduce itself. But in human affairs, reproduction is no longer the primary reason for sex; the desires to achieve pleasurable orgasm and to enhance love and intimacy are the chief motives. These matters become enormously complicated, given the wide range of pleasurable activities people seek; thus what is "normal" or "natural" is not easily determined. Romantic love is no doubt among the highest of human pleasures. Infantile forms of love wish to possess or even use the other person as a source of sexual gratification. The intensity of psychosexual longing can drive men and women to madness and desperation—especially in the case of unrequited love (such as in *Carmen*)—but also to the most rewarding forms of fulfillment. In one sense, an individual is never fully realized unless and until he or she is capable of achieving some kind of romantic attachment to another.

Is man polygamous and is promiscuity to be accepted? Mankind has long since discovered that jealous rivalries for sexual partners could lead to constant warfare. The institution of marriage, a monogamous relationship, with divorce as a safety valve, is a sensible solution. Although sexual pleasure can be derived from the physical act itself, one soon discovers that some kind of emotional attachment provides the most enduring form of satisfaction, especially when it is based on sincerity and trust. Sexual enjoyment appears to be more complete when it is experienced in a loving relationship with another.

Love is twofold: first, it helps to actualize our deepest yearnings, needs, and desires, especially to be loved by another human being; and second, if we are able to love another person, we wish him or her to prosper on his or her own terms. There is a general concern for the good of the other person, not for the reflected glory that he or she brings. Mutual love is both sexual and altruistic.

10. *Aesthetic appreciation.* Included in our capacity to enjoy life fully is an appreciation for the finer things of life as perceived by the senses and enhanced by the intellect. The term *aesthetic* best describes these pleasures, which include the fine arts, poetry, drama, literature, and music. One's ability to appreciate great beauty enriches life. Unfortunately, some individuals never seem able to develop an understanding of the arts. They may be tone-deaf or color-blind or disinterested, totally unable to enjoy classical music, art, literature, or the theater. The appreciation of aesthetic values is a product of education, and parents should expose their children to these values at relatively early ages.

Appreciation presupposes a kind of growth and development of the personality: one admires the natural beauty of a brilliant sunset or a beautiful woman, and this does not require training. But the highest reaches of the arts require some exertion. To learn how to read requires early effort, and what a great source of satisfaction and joy it is to the person who masters it.

One's aesthetic sensibilities need not be limited to the arts, for tastes can be cultivated in other areas—in fine delicacies that the gourmet appreciates, in exotic varieties of flowers, or in embellishments in fashion. The aesthetic touch can be added with finesse and expertise to almost any field of human interest. The connoisseur of fine wine is able to discern subtleties that bring pleasure to his sense of taste. A simple farmer may not be able to tell the difference between a chablis and a bordeaux, but may have a subtle and distinctive appreciation for breeding blue-ribbon horses or show dogs.

II. Excellence as Related to Others

We have been discussing excellence primarily in regard to the individual. But we are social beings, and among the highest human values are those that relate to others: the excellences of ethical development. Although we are discussing the ethical excellences last, this in no way indicates any order of priority; moral or ethical development must stand high on the scale of values, and anyone who lacks it is missing something essential.

Some individuals are apparently blind to the moral decencies, much the same as some individuals are deficient in health or intelligence. Hence they may be said to be morally handicapped. Whether this is due to social and environmental conditions or some biological insufficiency, and whether moral decencies can be cultivated or taught are questions we have touched on. It may be that no human is fully deficient in this capacity, else he would be as a wild animal. Sociability is part of our being and defines our very nature. Perhaps morality is only a question of degree. We all need to belong to some community. Behavior outside it would be self-centered, autistic, or hermitlike. Our language and the symbols and metaphors by which we function are all transactional, the products of culture and community. The civilizing component of morality is as much a part of our definition as is our biological equipment. For example, we need to be loved and cared for by other human beings (parents, relatives, lovers) if we are to develop and flourish. Concomitantly, we need to love others, to be concerned about their needs, to share their values and dreams, to learn to live and work with them cooperatively. We not only need parents and sexual mates, friends and colleagues with whom we can identify, but in a broader sense, as fully developed moral beings, we need to be a friend to each and every person, within our community and outside of it. There is a kind of moral excellence that comes to fruition as we develop our ethical capacities.

Since the moral decencies are central to our social natures, they need to be internalized as values within the person if they are to be effective. Values and principles overlap, for in living by general rules, we incorporate them as part of our preferential structure, and learn to cherish them for their own sakes. They become moral excellencies for us to live by.

Values thus are not simply private soliloquies or idiosyncratic preferences. Nor are they selfish expressions of desire. They involve our sharing of common objectives and goals. Although one must respect the domain of privacy, among the finest values are those shared with or involving others; they are the moral decencies, which become part of our character and being.

The following list of the ethical excellencies is not complete, but enumerates those which lie at the core of our ethical behavior.

1. *Integrity*. This term encompasses a whole set of the moral decencies. A person who expresses this excellence in his life is morally sound and uncorrupted. We can count on his being consistent.
   - Such a person is *truthful* and is not given to lying or deceit.
   - He keeps his *promises* as best he can, does not break agreements, fulfills his contracts, and pays his debts.
   - He is *sincere* in his relations with others, not duplicitous or two-faced.
   - He is *honest* in his dealings and will not deliberately cheat, steal, or seek to take unfair advantage.

2. *Trustworthiness*.
   - A person with this quality shows *fidelity* to his friends, relatives, and colleagues who are deserving of it; he will not betray their principles or values out of self-interest and without rational justification.
   - He is *dependable*, reliable, and responsible, and someone on whom we can count.

3. *Benevolence*.
   - Such a person has a genial disposition and *goodwill*. He does not have ulterior motives, evil designs, or vested interests. He generally wishes only the best for other persons and is happy when they are happy, and pleased when they prosper.
   - He bears *no malice* toward others, carries no ill will. He does not harbor hatred, jealousy, envy, animosity, resentment. He has no bitterness, anger, or rancor. He does not carry grudges. He has no desire to purposely inflict any harm on another person or upon another's lawful property, possessions, or family.

- He will not seek to force his attention on another person or seek to dominate her or him sexually; he bases sexual relationships on *consent*.

- He is *beneficent*, sympathetic, considerate, thoughtful, and compassionate. He makes a positive effort to reduce needless suffering or pain in others and to distribute, as far as possible within his means, some benefits. He strives to be altruistic. He is kind, charitable, and wishes to be helpful. He is friendly and shows affection. He is especially sensitive to the needs of the weak, the helpless, the forlorn, the disadvantaged, and the handicapped. He is not over-impressed by those who have wealth, power, fame, or position.

4. *Fairness.*

- A person with this quality will express *gratitude* to individuals who have helped him or deserve thanks. He will express appreciation for a job well-done, a deed well-performed, or a benefit rendered. He is not vindictive or given to petty jealousy or envy.

- By the same token, he believes in some measure *of accountability*. He believes that those who commit immoral deeds or inflict injury to others should be held responsible. Thus he has a sense of right and wrong, and seeks as far as possible to be equitable in his dealings with others. He follows rules that will establish a *quid pro quo*, harmony and order. He bears no resentment, does not seek revenge, and is willing to forgive and forget.

- He tries to fulfill, as far as he can discern them, principles of *justice* in his dealings with others. He wishes to treat each person with equal dignity and value. He attempts to be even-handed, to apply the principles of fairness to others, and to give rewards for merit.

- The fair-minded person will be *tolerant* of other lifestyles and will respect the right of others to be different. Though he may disagree with or find odd or offensive others' values, tastes, beliefs, or practices, so long as they do not harm others or impose on them, he will forbear. He will accord to other individuals the same rights he asks for himself, and though he may criticize and/or persuade, he will not seek to stamp out, denigrate, or suppress other styles of life, points of view, or value systems.

- The fair individual will not resort to the use of violence, force, or power in his dealings with other human beings. He will be *peaceful* and *cooperative*. As far as is possible, he will seek to negotiate differences and to work out compromises in which all can live together. He lives by the spirit of fair play and reasonableness.

Chapter 8

LOVE AND FRIENDSHIP

Many critics of humanism believe that it is primarily concerned with the individual's personal satisfaction and creative fulfillment. This they charge is too self-centered and egoistic. But this is far from the case; for the autonomous human being cannot find life completely satisfying unless he or she can relate to other human beings. Sociality is so basic to our nature as humans that unless we can share our joys and sorrows, we are condemned to lead narrow and futile existences. The purely autistic person has limited horizons. His or her life lacks full body and flavor; it misses the most important ingredient of the full life, without which we can never feel complete: *les autres*.

We are defined as persons by the objects of our interest. If our interests are narrow, then so are we. Insofar as we can extend the range of our concerns, we are able to expand the dimensions of our being.

There are several ways in which we can broaden our horizons. On the simplest level, I have already pointed out the need for intimacy with at least one other person. The fullest expression of this need is in loving someone else. Love can be possessive, especially when we consider another human being an object and seek to monopolize him or her for our own consummatory enjoyment. Here the primary motive may be selfish: we wish to be loved, stroked, and caressed, to receive pleasurable stimulation. But there is another sense of love: the ability to *give* love without necessarily receiving it in return. Here, we derive satisfaction simply because we do something for someone else, not because that person responds fully in kind. Possessive love is infantile. It says, I want you to love me, I miss you, or I need you. The ego dominates this relationship. The possessive person becomes insanely jealous because he believes that the relationship will be threatened if another person enters the scene. Historically, husbands possessed their wives, who were considered little more than chattel. For the wife merely to look at another man would provoke jealous rage. Similarly, women had a smothering attitude toward their husbands and lovers and could not tolerate any sign of interest in another woman. But matrimony should not mean the extinction of our personalities or interests in others as friends, colleagues, or even lovers—difficult though it is for most people to overcome the consuming flames of jealousy.

Many relationships are simply contractual; that is, we agree to do someone a favor knowing that it is good policy and that they will reciprocate. This is an important ingredient in a relationship; it involves prudential self-concern. Yet there is another kind of relationship that is based on the ability to give of oneself without any thought of direct gain. This kind of feeling especially manifests itself in the relationship of a lover to the person loved. A person who truly loves someone would, under certain conditions, virtually give one's life for the other person. He or she is willing to do things, day in and day out, for the loved one. No one compels him or her to do so; it is not forced but is an act of genuine affection. One gladly goes out of his way for the sake of the partner and does so because one wants to, because doing so gives intense satisfaction. I am not talking about dutiful acts that are done grudgingly because one believes one ought to do them, but about freely performed deeds of merit.

I surely do not wish to argue that one should always act selflessly. Relationships are not one-way streets to be used by another for his own advantage. A person who does not recognize another's needs as a human being is destructive both to oneself and to the other person. Indeed, it is the ability to share with another some loving devotion that can bolster personal strength and autonomy. An individual who has not developed this other-regarding love remains dwarfed as a human.

The sharing of a full life with another human being—as in marriage—can be a special source of profound affection. Granted that some marriages fail; yet where marriages are viable they are cherished relationships (for however long they last—one year, five, ten, or a lifetime). One person relates to another on many levels—not only through sexual passion, but also through altruistic love, the joining together of careers, the raising of children, living together and sharing a home, pursuing activities cooperatively, and so on. To be alone in life and to do things by and for oneself is, of course, common; some individuals do not wish to enter into relationships they consider confining. But to partake of life with another can be a source of deep fulfillment. If one has someone to love—and that love is returned—one can remove the mask worn in the world, and one can experience the joys and sorrows of life with another and without the need for pretense. The ability to share intimately with at least one other human being (whether inside or outside of marriage) is a priceless adornment of the good life.

II

Another form of other-regarding love is, of course, the attitude of parents toward their children—their devotion and their willingness to make sacrifices for their children, even though the children many not appreciate them. One doesn't say, *I* am more important than my children; nor does one calculate what one's children will give in return—whether they will love me and appreciate what I am doing, or even support me in his old age. Rather, one gives of one's self without thought of gain; I worry about my children's health, education, and welfare. My family is a *whole*: I am identified in everything I do with them. My bounty belongs to them. We share cooperatively our food and shelter. My deepest hopes and dreams involve them. Their prospects for success in life are mine and their trials and tribulations also are mine. If my child is sick or languishes, I am troubled; if he or she does well, I beam with pride.

There exists, of course, parental love that is selfish. All too frequently children are viewed simply as an extension of the parent's self. Many parents project all of their unrealized dreams and aspirations onto their children. All of the things they were unable to achieve themselves are wished for their children; conversely, if parents succeed in their careers, they often want their children to follow in their footsteps. Such demanding attitudes are infantile and self-indulgent; adults who have them are trying to dominate their children. They require submissiveness and acquiescence. Where children do not live up to the parent's values, or where their love is unrequited in kind, they may be rejected, disowned, or disinherited.

A genuinely loving parent will attempt to do the best for the child, if one wishes the child to be a person in his or her own terms. Let the child become whatever he or she wishes. One may provide guidance and sustenance where it is needed, but if one loves one's child, one should want the child to develop its own unique personality. One can love one's child even though one disagrees fundamentally with the choice of a mate, career, or lifestyle. One should make allowances for one's children, recognize their limitations as well as their virtues, not demand the impossible, but love them for what they are. One ought to try to do the best for one's child, nourishing his or her physical and mental growth. At some point, however, one should let him or her go out into the world alone, to discover and create their own destiny.

To love someone in a healthy sense (whether a husband or wife, a son or daughter) is to want that person to flourish in his or her own terms and to develop his or her own autonomy. I am not arguing for self-sacrificing devotion beyond the limits of human endurance; nor am I saying that parents should give without limits to their children and never expect anything in return. Such a relationship would be debilitating to both the child and the parent. One wants one's child to be a *mensch*; yet some children may turn out bad, become self-centered, be incapable of loving. In such cases to continue to spill one's life's blood for a good-for-nothing is the height of folly. We should do the best we can for our children; but if after all is said and done they are mean and inconsiderate, there should be limits to what we should continue to do for them. An unremitting giving without end may be more harmful than helpful: "my child, right or wrong" cannot apply forever. If parents have obligations to their children, the children in return bear certain responsibilities to their parents. If they fail consistently in their concern for their parents, the time may come for the parents to call a halt to their unquestioned giving.

As parents we should try to develop creativity in our children, to cultivate their individuality, assertiveness, independence, freedom. But we also need to cultivate in them the ability to relate to others. If we do not succeed in teaching our children to give love as well as to receive it, then we have indeed failed. However, if children turn out bad, it is not always the parents' fault. There may be other influences at work: bad friends, poor schooling, different psychological tendencies and needs. Doting parents who are too good to their children often unknowingly ruin them. To give our children everything they desire may be more destructive of developing responsible personhood than allowing them to earn what they want. To work and save, to plan and conserve are important qualities of character that need cultivation. To go overboard in showering children with favors, toys, and trinkets that they did not themselves earn is to spoil the child—at least it contributes to a distorted view of the world. One reason that the children of affluent parents often turn sour is that they have been reared on an immediate-gratification demand basis. The child never becomes the adult. The parents are always there to help them if they falter, to make excuses if they fail, to gratify their hedonic needs as they demand.

Such children, overwhelmed by their own need for self-gratification, are self-centered; they take everyone around them, including their parents, for granted. They believe that they can always count on their parents to help them, no matter what they do. But what they lack is the ability to give love, not for a reward or out of habit, but out of genuine and loving concern. The question of how children should relate to their parents is a perennial problem that all human societies have faced. There are societies that have emphasized complete filial piety. This is best illustrated by traditional Chinese society. The parents were venerated by their children and grandchildren. Their word was final; they controlled money, power, and privilege. They demanded obedience; if their children did not follow their advice, they would be cast out. In this authoritarian family the entire life of the child was often dictated by the parents, including the choice of a mate and a career. This family structure hardly exists in modern society.

At the other extreme there is the youth-oriented culture in which the old are abhorred and their wishes and desires ignored. The extended family was able to provide members of the family with many more bonds of security and affection; the nuclear family often has ostracized grandparents and divested them of virtually all rights and dignity.

It is clear that for healthy relationships children need to develop a loving concern for their parents, a concern that will remain even after the children have gone out on their own. The desire of parents not to interfere with the lives of their children, to avoid any suggestion of authoritarian domination, has had the reverse effect of emotionally starving the parent. And their elderly parents or grandparents, having little contact with their children and a lack of love and endearment, are gradually strangled by their need for affection. Children should—even when they are older—demonstrate their love and affection for their parents. In order to do this, they need to develop an appreciation for the fact that their parents are themselves human: like everyone else, they have their own defects and limitations, their own needs and desires. Parents should not be placed on a pedestal as either models of perfection or as unquestioned authorities. Thus it is essential for children at some point in life to come to appreciate their parents as unique persons and to love them in spite of their foibles and idiosyncrasies. To be able to assist one's parents, especially to be concerned for them as they grow older, is important not only for the parent but for the child, whether he be a teenager or a middle-aged adult.

Similar considerations apply to other members of the family, to sisters, brothers, aunts, uncles, and cousins. How sad that the ties of family affection have been narrowed and loosened in modern society. The nuclear family, divorce, and geographical mobility have uprooted individuals from the broader family. Belonging to the tribe or clan had provided rich soil for the development of the human species. Those who are cut off from strong kinship relationships lose a great deal: the wider bounds of joy and affection. Can the values of the extended family be recovered?—that is a dilemma of our time.

The family, whether nuclear or extended, has many functions to perform: biological at first, then as a basis for the economic division of labor. It is the psychological function of the family that needs emphasis as a source of security and affection. A basic educating force, the family provides the nourishment for stable growth and for the development of the ability to relate to others.

The best family, in a sense, is the egalitarian one. By this I do not mean that each member functions with equal power and authority. Parents have a greater role to play, and they should not abdicate their responsibility. Yet children have rights as well. Each member of the family should count for one person and have equal dignity and value. A truly just family is democratic; it is one in which there is an equality of consideration for each member. Individuals have different needs and interests, power and resources; and each family must allow for these differences. The family should provide the basis for the self-actualization of its members; it should appreciate common needs, but recognize diverse ones as well. The family can become a growth matrix for all its participants. But to do so, the family must itself become actualized as a unit. Its members need to work in harmony and do things cooperatively.

As this implies, the best family is the joyful one: a group that works together, shares defeats, celebrates important family events, exults in common pleasures. It is exuberant. How unfortunate are troubled families, full of hatred and strife, divorce and alcoholism. How damaging they are to tender minds and delicate souls. How beautiful is a joyous family, full of loving relationships, happy, zestful, overflowing with bountiful interests and affection.

A good family is active, involved, creative, interesting; it provides an environment for both individuality and sharing. It does not suppress Anne, who plays the piano; Valerie who is into Zen; Jonathan, who loves sports; mother, who is constantly redecorating and has her career; or father, who is an active professional. It allows each latitude and quietude, while at the same time providing support and strength. It is open and flexible; the growth potential of everyone is at stake. It is a wondrous foundation for warmth, sincerity, closeness, loyalty, humor, laughter, seriousness. It is life-affirming, and a vital nourishing ground for the fuller flowering of a meaningful life. A person may be able to achieve a good life, even if he or she had a deprived childhood or bad marriage; but not to have enjoyed a family life is to have missed so much that life has to offer.

III

Blood kinship is a powerful binding force; it gives rise to emotions that hold humans together. Kinship has its roots in biology: sexual reproduction stimulates passion and love, maternal nurturing provides the milk to sustain the young, and parental care provides the psychological warmth and physical security necessary for the survival of the offspring. Moreover, the family provides a biological and economic basis for joint survival. Out of common needs grow the bonds of love and affection.

However, if consanguinity were the only basis of human affection, the human species would be in a bad way. The problem for society is to extend the range of affection and caring. Plato thought that familial love was so important that it needed to be generalized throughout the entire polis. He deplored selfish attitudes that reserved loving concern to those within the family. Hence parents in *The Republic* did not know their children and thus would relate to all children as their own.

It is the ability to care about those outside of one's immediate family and to build ties of friendship and congeniality that are important for human fulfillment. Familial love has its roots in biology and instinct, but relating to strangers can often present a problem. Sexual attraction is usually between those who are not blood relatives. But how far can the bonds of friendship and of moral concern between individuals outside of the family be extended?

Aristotle recognized the importance of friendship as a source of immediate appreciation and of lasting significance in life. One must have *some* friends; to be unable to relate on the level of friendship with other human beings is to lead an impoverished and deficient life. We may develop many different kinds of relationships with others, and on many levels. A friend is one whose company you enjoy, one whom you help gladly without any thought of return, and one with whom you can develop trust, sincerity, honesty. A true comrade accepts you for what you are.

Since personal friendship is on the level of face-to-face encounters, we are limited in the number of true friends that we can have, though we can continue to make new friends throughout life. Childhood chums are important to one's sense of well-being. Indeed one's peer group may be more influential than one's parents and teachers in developing values. Childhood friendships give meaning and depth in life: there are things that a child will confess to a friend but not to a parent. Exploring streams and woods, playing games, going through school, reaching puberty, discovering puppy love, suffering adolescent crushes are all part of friendship; children learn about life and the world together.

In modern mobile societies it is sometimes difficult to maintain permanent relationships. We do have, however, the opportunity for meeting many new people, particularly if we move about: colleagues at work, their wives or husbands, one's neighbors, members of the same clubs and associations. There are various kinds of relationships. If we are fortunate, we can find others whom we can relate to, who will become our confidants, our close and faithful friends, trustworthy and constant, and whom we can rely upon in time of need and distress. They may be schoolmates, playmates, teammates, roommates, shipmates, colleagues, neighbors, or companions.

There are important moral dimensions to friendship that, if violated, can disrupt the bond. Basically, friendship is built on a spirit of mutual benevolence for each other. It is a relationship of amicability, conviviality, congeniality, cordiality, and harmony. Friendship, to be true, must be based upon a general concern for the other. This means that a number of moral virtues are present: caring, honesty, sincerity, trust.

One must not misuse a friend to one's own advantage, though one will do a friend a favor gladly. Nor may one betray a friend, or else the friendship is over. Jealousy, pride, and vindictiveness are absent among friends. Instead there is a genuine concern for the other, an acceptance of his or her faults, and a joy in his or her prosperity and achievements. A friend is one who knows your faults, yet loves you in spite of them.

Some of our social relationships are disproportionate in terms of age, power, money, influence, and prestige; but friends, as friends, are equal. They do not erect barriers but seek to break them down as they reach out to touch the other soul.

There are some persons who are so timorous and diffident that they make friends with difficulty. Their hearts ache for sympathetic companions, but they cannot relate easily to others. There is also the extreme case of the friendless person who suffers a destitute life in sorrow and tears. How sad not to be able to make friends. How essential it is if one is to enjoy life.

We can be friends with members of the same or the opposite sex. Historically, men banded together in hunting groups or as warriors, and comradeship was essential for survival. Thus friendship, no doubt, had adaptive value; today it seems necessary for our psychic health. Indeed there remains a kind of masculine bond that remains strong. Men like to get away from women at times: to work or play together on the team, to associate in business or in the army. They seek private clubs or bars to escape. Women also find intimate relationships with other women, without male intrusion, sometimes desirable.

One may have many acquaintances, but they are not one's friends. For friendship is a special moral relationship held together by empathetic concern. Like love, however, friendship is not a relationship in which one simply receives favors; one must also be willing to give them. Indeed it is the ability to give to another person without question or complaint, and to share life's blessings and sufferings, that is perhaps the highest sign of human nobility.

Chapter 9 ⁓

CARING

It is clear that independent and resourceful persons are capable of exercising autonomy in their own lives. No longer willing to submit passively to the blind forces in nature, they go forth boldly to create new worlds, using rationality to fulfill their aspirations and achieve their goals. They will exercise contingent rationality wherever possible, and in most situations of life both contextual and reformist rationality, and they will apply the latter to social contexts in which rational thought can play a role.

It is clear, however, that we do not exist as solitary persons floundering in private egoistic soliloquies and that the full realization of what it means to be human is in terms of *les autres*, other human persons. I can best actualize my potentialities because I can share the stores of truth, beauty, goodness, and love with others. We are inherently social animals, dependent for our very survival upon the nurturing care of other human beings. We relate to other persons throughout life in a variety of ways. Indeed, the highest flowering of the human potential in art, philosophy, and science is found in the fabric of social and cultural traditions, which makes these possible. The arts of communication by which we express our ideas and values are realized because of the development of language and culture. The mind evolves because our brain makes cognition possible and because we assume the role of others in social transactions, reacting to their experiences and thoughts; they in turn respond to ours. We imbibe the linguistic signs and symbols of our culture, and they serve as wings to carry us to wider horizons beyond the isolated self; we are not confined to our immediate spatial-temporal location. Language focuses our cognitive and perceptual powers by providing the tools of discrimination and generalization, and it enables our imagination and fantasy to soar to new heights. It is by means of social transactions that both self-consciousness and critical thinking are enhanced,[1] and it is through this process of communication that the self is more precisely defined.

It is also out of social interactions that morality emerges. In the natural world we compete with other humans for goods and services. Sociocultural normative standards emerge to regulate conduct. We learn from experience that if we are not to be destroyed in the ensuing struggle for survival, we need to establish some conditions of peace and harmony.

Human beings come to recognize that we share common interests with others and that there are elementary precepts that we have to respect, if we are to survive. It is wrong to kill or maim other persons without due cause, and we ought to care for them if they are in distress—at the very least in the small face-to-face communities of interaction. We should be truthful, sincere, honest, loyal, and dependable, and keep promises. I have catalogued the basic "common moral decencies" (in chapter 6), which have come to be recognized by most societies. These moral decencies are so essential for civilized conduct that those who transgress the cherished norms need to be called into account. Systems of law have developed to protect the principles that are considered to be vital to the public good. These basic duties are deemed so important to human welfare that they have been mistakenly interpreted as sacred and divinely inspired. Human beings are prone to invest nature with their fondest hopes and values and they seek to find some kind of divine sanction for their moral codes.

From a humanistic standpoint this is an expression of the transcendental temptation. Religion no doubt had an important function historically; it provided an imperative that compelled obedience to moral rules. You will be punished by the civil authorities if you break the moral code embodied in law, and you will incur divine wrath; or conversely, if you are truly moral, divine love will be your reward. Thus, both law and religion develop systems of rewards and sanctions to ensure compliance.

CARING DEFINED

Humanists are often challenged: If we dispense with the classical religious foundations for moral behavior, what will replace them? Are there naturalistic grounds for ethical conduct? My response to these questions is two-fold: First, *empathetic feeling* is the originative source of moral awareness, and second, *ethical rationality* emerges to further develop a mature sense of responsibility. In this chapter I wish to focus on the nature and source of the central moral imperative: *caring for others.*

A person may abide by the moral rules of his or her social group and outwardly conform to what is expected, but this may be motivated by fear of punishment from parents, teachers, the state, or God. Surely we cannot consider this motive for conduct to be fully moral. It is, of course, important that people not violate the moral rules, and it is especially important that courageous Prometheans respect the rights and needs of others within the community. Prometheus, according to the ancient myth, so loved humans that he wished to share with them the gifts of fire, science, and the arts. The key to moral conduct and a vital humanistic virtue is the presence of a genuine state of *caring*; by this is meant both the inward and outward expression of some moral regard for other persons. A caring person is not indifferent to what happens to others, to their interests and needs. In a limited sense, one may take care of another person, that is, minister to his or her wants—as a nurse cares for a sick patient in a hospital or a mother suckles her infant. In a broader sense, to express a caring attitude is to be interested in the well-being of some other person or persons—as, for example, a teacher helps her student to master grammar. In some cases a person may care for someone, be interested in their well-being, or be disposed favorably or sympathetic without necessarily doing anything about it overtly. I may be interested in someone's career or marriage and hope for the best, even though he or she may not be directly involved. There is a moral principle that is implicit in our discussion: *a rational person recognizes that one should care about the needs and interests of others*.

There are various aspects of *caring* that may be distinguished. The first is *compassion*. Here a person has a sympathetic awareness of another human being's distress, and a desire to help reduce or alleviate suffering. Compassion may involve some degree of pity concerning the discomfort that someone is experiencing. If a person is in pain and calls for help, I may out of compassion attempt to do what I can. For example, a missing child lost in a department store may arouse my compassion, and I will do whatever I can to help the child find its parent. The compassionate regard for other people can become the be-all and end-all of life for many persons. "If I can stop one heart from breaking, I shall not live in vain; if I can ease one life the aching, or cool one pain . . . I shall not live in vain," wrote Emily Dickinson.[2]

Compassion is rooted in empathy, a powerful stimulus to sympathetic moral awareness. The Greek root for the term is *empatheia*, which means literally *passion*. This term is derived from *empathés*, meaning *emotional*, which is a combination of *em* plus *pathos*. Insofar as I am able to read the inner experiences, desires, or thoughts of another human being, I can empathize with that person. If I can help, I do. Empathetic emotions enable us to recognize the plight of other persons and take on some of the burdens they face; kindness is aroused. In some cases, I may be able to accomplish very little or nothing at all because those who need assistance may not be within the compass of my activities. For example, I can feel compassion for the starving children of Ethiopia or the poor people of Bangladesh, and this sympathetic identification may be felt within my heart and mind. Thus, a person can have compassion yet not do anything to help. Compassion is an attitude or belief that someone is in need and a concomitant wish that the deprivation be reduced. In one sense this is *negative*; that is, I wish to mitigate the suffering of others. This applies not only to humans, but also to animals. I may have some compassion for the deer who are starving in the winter; thus, I may attempt to feed them or even attempt to thin out the herd. I may be concerned about needless pain being inflicted on animals in scientific experiments, and I may urge that experiments with animals be designed so as not to subject them to unnecessary pain. Compassion, therefore, evinces a *humane* attitude to various sentient forms of life.

There is a second sense of moral caring that is *positive*: the desire not simply to reduce the suffering but to contribute to the happiness, joy, or well-being of others. This is a form of *benevolence* whereby I wish to bestow goods on others. They may not necessarily be suffering, but they would benefit from my acts of commission. I might, for example, support the building of a beautiful public park for the common good, or the construction of a new library, or even take part in the distribution of gifts to children during the holidays. I am playing the role of the benefactor, and I may express benevolence by acts of generosity. The moral concern is to increase or enhance the treasury of goods available for a person or a community of persons, and this may involve feelings or thoughts of affectionate regard for their well-being. People who contribute to charitable organizations may do so with two goals in mind: They may contribute money to the orphans of Haiti because they have a compassionate concern for reducing human suffering, or they may contribute to a university because they have a benevolent interest in progress and think that education is worthwhile. Sometimes our deeds are done out of both motives: sympathetic compassion and benevolence—as when a person adopts a homeless child or provides college scholarships for disadvantaged youngsters.

Both compassion and benevolence, if concerned with the good of the recipient, may be said to express *altruism*. An altruistic act is *carried out for the benefit of another person (or persons) at some expense or sacrifice to myself, and without any primary expectation of reward*. It is other-regarding in its objective, seeking to reduce the suffering, or enhance the enjoyment, of other human beings.

What is the relationship of altruistic moral caring to Christianity? The New Testament has emphasized the importance of compassion as a moral virtue; this includes pity, mercy, sympathy, and a desire to reduce suffering. Christianity, however, is rooted in faith and feeling, and it is based on commandments from Jesus, who admonished us to love one another. This is no doubt an important contribution to the development of moral sensibility. It is a significant modification of the pagan virtues of classical Greek philosophy, by emphasizing a moral concern for other people.

Moral caring in humanistic terms, however, is not synonymous with this Christian virtue. First, because Christianity often takes suffering to have some intrinsic moral value, some Christians believe that we should suffer as Christ did on the Cross. Some religious extremists will flagellate themselves in the name of the Lord. St. Bernadette allegedly suffered in silence painful canker sores, never revealing her affliction to others; this sacrifice was said to be morally worthy. For the humanist, suffering is an evil that we should in principle avoid; it can be justified on some occasions for the good that it may engender. For example, if I go to a dentist, and he reports that I have a bad cavity that needs to be drilled, I may decide to suffer short-range pain for the long-range good (though I may hope that the dentist gives me Novocain® to deaden the pain). Or again, a nation may suffer great hardship in time of war in the hope of gaining victory. But this does not mean that suffering or pain has intrinsic merit.

Second, ethical compassion should not be accepted as a blind outpouring of feeling unmitigated by cognition. Not all expressions of compassion are justifiable, for some forms of compassion may be misdirected or inappropriate. For example, persons on welfare may evince my compassion and induce me to provide them with benefits, though perhaps instead I should encourage them to find jobs. A person may feel some compassion for a brutal murderer who tortures little children and may wish him to be freed from prison. I can hardly have any compassion for him, given his past behavior. Thus, there are often limits to be placed on compassion, especially when it conflicts with other virtues and values.

Third, moral caring has a broader range than Christian love. It is not focused simply on the desire to reduce suffering in others; it also wishes to enhance the positive distribution of goods. Accordingly, benevolence is essential to its fulfillment, and this is focused on increasing the sum of enjoyments in this life, not suffering or deferring it to the next. Humanistic altruism is thus more full-bodied than ascetic or self-denying Christian martyrdom. An exaggerated concern for the poor and disadvantaged sometimes is a mask for resentment against the affluent and successful. . . .

ALTRUISM

Are acts of compassion and benevolence a genuine expression of altruistic concern, done without any hope of personal gain; or are they motivated ultimately for selfish purposes? A person may contribute to a charity because he will receive a tax deduction or public acclaim. If so, the motive may be primarily self-interest. Another person, however, may do so principally for the benefit of others, without any expectation of recognition or reward; he may not even request a tax deduction and may contribute anonymously. One may ask: Are *any* acts truly altruistic, or is there an element of self-deception here?

The cynic denies that any acts are purely altruistic in intention, and he endeavors to reduce all such acts to egoism. At this point a theory of psychological motivation becomes relevant. A utilitarian might argue that the motive of an act is irrelevant to its moral quality. The important factors are the consequences to the general welfare, the increase in the sum of pleasure or happiness, and the reduction of pain or unhappiness. There may be some truth to this appraisal. It is not what you say or feel, but what you *do* that counts. This issue, however, is of vital significance to humanism and its conception of human nature. It does matter to us whether the milk of human kindness and the spirit of generosity are genuine and whether human beings are capable of other-regarding compassionate and benevolent caring.

Many theists hold a bleak view of human nature; the doctrine of original sin demeans who we are. Are humans corrupt, brutal, evil, and interested only in satisfying their own selfish desires—as the pessimistic nihilist claims? Or do they have the potentiality for real moral caring? Without being accused of naïve optimism and an unrealistic appraisal of the human condition, I submit that there are wholesome moral dimensions intrinsic to the human species—at least potentially—and that these can be nourished so that they reach fruition.

The theist denies that human beings are capable of such autonomous moral behavior. Only God can redeem man from evil; humans are impotent to save themselves. If this dismal view is mistaken and human beings are capable of empathy, compassion, and benevolence without the sanctions and admonitions of deity or without motives of pure self-interest, then we *can* do something about enhancing the ethical dimensions of life. Whether any human being will be moved by altruistic moral caring is a complex question; it depends on the social and cultural environment in which he or she lives, the educational influences, and the rewards and inducements offered. No doubt we do things for a variety of motives, and these include not only self-interest and altruism, but also a whole host of other complex causes. The challenge to the humanist is whether altruistic motivation is *intrinsic* to our very nature—at least potentially—and whether men and women can mitigate the evils that beset them in the world and redeem themselves. Conversely, the challenge is whether they have to barter their souls for false doctrines of salvation if they are to behave morally. To argue, as the humanist has, that moral impulses and imperatives are intrinsic to the human being requires us to examine their sources in human behavior; and by doing so we have found a naturalistic ground for moral conscience.

Egoism and altruism are both partially true; they are false only if either is taken as a comprehensive theory of motivation. Extreme self-interest theories attempt to reduce all human motives to a single source: the selfish desire for pleasure, sexual gratification, power, glory, or gain. Self-interest clearly applies to patently self-motivated actions undertaken to reduce a person's needs or to satisfy his desires. But does it apply universally to any and all acts, including those that appear to be other-regarding, charitable, or self-sacrificing? An organism surely needs to engage in self-interested forms of behavior if it is to survive and function. It needs to satisfy its hunger for food, protect itself from danger, and seek sexual gratification. Thus, self-interest is a necessary component of any person's life; it can be justified rationally. But the issue is whether *all* motives are self-centered. I think the error lies in the failure to ascertain if the *primary* object of desire is one's own gratification or that of others, for there is a basic difference in the objective or goal of an act. Benevolent acts have *other* persons' interests in mind. In many acts the agent's own interest is involved, but the agent may also be interested in helping others—so there can be a double focus. Surely we should not blur all distinctions and claim that the motivation of a self-seeking hedonist or power-hungry despot is the *same as* an other-regarding parent, educator, or humanitarian who genuinely wishes to devote himself or herself to enhancing the welfare of others.

Conversely, the egoist has a valid case to make against altruists who seek to smother creative initiative, courageous independence, or individuality, and extol self-effacing sacrifice as the highest virtue. Antony Flew protests vehemently against the efforts by socialists and welfare liberals to use the state to impose forms of egalitarianism on society.[3] This can dampen individual initiative, he claims, which is the spark of human creativity. The egoist thus has a right to object to the effort by communitarians to condemn all self-centered behavior as evil. The common good is perhaps best fulfilled by maximizing individual freedom, not suppressing it, thus allowing incentive and enterprise to increase the sum of wealth for society. Promethean courage can likewise be destroyed by the legions of God's disciples imposing their standards of self-sacrifice in the name of compassion as the highest virtue, thereby demeaning courage, independence, and self-determination. Libertarians reject the morbid

Augustinian-Christian view that anything done out of self-interest (including the satisfaction of erotic impulses) is venal and wicked.

This should not, however, deny the capacity for genuine altruistic loving, caring behavior in the human being and the need for communitarian cooperative acts. I submit that there is a need to receive love but also to give it; this is not only the desire to be at the center of affection (an infantile response in itself), but also the need to extend it to others. It is this capacity to bestow love and affection, and to be compassionate and benevolent that expresses among the highest qualities of human morality. The salient point, however, is that there is no contradiction in recognizing that we are *both* self-centered, as we should be, *and* altruistic, which is necessary if we are to live and work together in communities. It is the capacity for altruistic behavior that is crucial to the humanistic eupraxsophy. We need to encourage good Samaritans to appreciate the biblical injunction "Thou shalt love thy neighbor as thyself." We need to extend the range of our moral concern to the aliens in our midst and beyond our borders. But to what extent is this possible, given history's testimony of the capacity of human beings to be cruel and rapacious, particularly toward those outside of one's community?

Critics maintain that humanism's positive appraisal of human nature is too high; they remonstrate that mankind is incredibly selfish and vindictive. The greatest enemy to man, states the cynic, is man. Robert Burton observed that man is like Aesop's fox who, "when he had lost his tail, would have all his fellow foxes cut off theirs."[4] William James maintained that "Man, biologically considered . . . is the most formidable of all the beasts of prey . . . and indeed, the only one that preys systematically on its own species."[5] The lessons from history about the dark side of human behavior should disabuse us of any simplistic romantic ideals about the beneficent nature of human beings. There is a recurring saga of men and women brutalizing those who are different from them. Once a person is reduced to an inferior status, by denigration of his or her race, gender, ethnic or national origin, or class, it is easier to violate his or her moral dignity.

The causes for such cruelty are complex, and they have many sources in our nature and in society. These are rooted no doubt in the fact that we were at one time uncivilized wild beasts, ferocious and cunning, capable of killing and destroying those who were viewed as antagonists. Our capacity to kill is demonstrated in our relationships to other animals, which we are ready and able to hunt, track, kill, and eat, and to use their skin for warmth and protection. We have domesticated some animals and used them as beasts of burden, working them to their capacity. But humans are also capable of extending the range of moral concern to animals within their own circle and to express care, love, and affection for their dogs, cats, cows, sheep, and horses. We express a complex set of attitudes and motives to animals. Some people are vegetarian and will not kill or eat animals. Many feel strongly about defending animal rights. Thus, our relationship to other animal species is ambivalent: we can demonstrate hate and fear or love and affection.

The issue here concerns our relationship to other human beings. It is likewise bipolar, for we are capable of displaying either cruelty or kindness, hatred or generosity. These impulses, no doubt rooted in our evolutionary past, emerged as part of our struggle for survival. Humans are born as naked apes. The entire moral history of the race has to be instilled in every youngster from the moment of birth; each of us is only one generation away from savagery....

COGNITION AND CARING

The roots of caring behavior are biosociogenic; they develop often unconsciously, perhaps even instinctively, and surely they are emotionally charged. At some point in human conduct, however, moral awareness is enhanced by cognition. Ethical rationality is not a superfluous addition to moral caring but can become constitutive of its very form. Because our beliefs interpenetrate and mold our attitudes, empathy and compassion may be reinforced by cognitive reflection. Indeed, it is through the process of deliberative reasoning that an individual's self-interest can be reconciled with the needs of others; intellectual factors enable us to evaluate conflicting demands within situations. In some cases, compassionate actions may be undeserving or foolish; in others, fully justifiable. In some instances, intended deeds of benevolence may be unwarranted in the light of the circumstance; in others, they may be rationally justified.

Is there a rule of reason that will help us resolve complex ethical dilemmas? Yes. There is a key ethical principle that provides us with some guidance. This takes the form of the following general rule of moral caring: *A rational person ought to express some moral caring for the needs of others.*

The first part of the principle of moral caring involves compassion and empathy. Thus, we may state as a general prescriptive rule: *Where it is within our power, we ought to mitigate the suffering, distress, pain, and sorrow of other sentient beings.* This applies to our friends and relatives, for they are within the range of our conduct. The rule also has a wider net. But there may be little that we can do for those outside our range of conduct, except perhaps to contribute to charities or agencies that will reduce hunger, assist handicapped people, and provide aid to the victims of natural disasters.

The second aspect of the principle of moral caring is that *we ought to develop a benevolent attitude toward all persons deserving of it*. Not everyone is deserving of our benevolence; those who behave indecently may be undeserving. Again, we should act benevolently where we can to those who are within our range of day-to-day conduct. And we should try to distribute goods and services in a positive way to enhance the well-being of others. For example, we ought to help children wherever possible to attend school, to learn how to think critically, to enjoy good music and the arts, and to appreciate the diverse enrichments of culture. And we ought to help ensure a prosperous and peaceful society. Thus, we also have a generalized positive moral obligation toward *all* persons. A person may accomplish this by performing little deeds or large ones, by giving gifts to individuals or charities. And he or she may also engage in cooperative social programs for the wider good.

Why do we do so? Perhaps because it is in our self-interest to do so, but also because we wish to see the good of others enhanced and to distribute to as many people who deserve it the fruits of civilized life.

In summary, this rule of ethical rationality states that we ought to act so as to mitigate human suffering and sorrow and to increase the sum of human good and happiness, providing it is possible to do so.

This rule is still highly controversial for many conservative libertarians. They hold that it is a mistake to dole out help to others, who instead should be taught to fend for themselves. Many libertarians oppose the role of the state in providing public welfare to the disadvantaged, the ill, needy, or elderly members of the population. They are especially opposed to the use of taxation by the state to support programs of welfare. Many would not necessarily object to other social institutions, private charities, or individuals providing assistance. Other conservatives, however, are opposed to any sustained effort at altruistic compassion and benevolence because they believe that it may undermine the virtue of self-reliance and thus foster dependency. Egalitarians, Christians, socialists, and others seek to help the weak, the poor, the homeless, and the dispossessed by distributing the goods and services of society more equitably.

Others argue that we should not simply try to divide up the existing pie but bake more and more pies. We should seek to expand economic growth rates, by providing incentives for individual achievement and entrepreneurship. All of this may be granted to some extent—though in the complex corporate world, individual enterprises have been replaced by larger economic units in which individual merit is often lost.

One might still argue on moral grounds that one ought to help those who through no fault of their own cannot help themselves. This would exclude indolent individuals who could work and prefer not to, or those who have been brought up in a culture of dependence and neither develop any independence and autonomy nor seek to pull themselves up by their own initiative.

Still another problem concerning the appropriate extent of moral caring is the fact that many conservatives today have become extremely chauvinistic or nationalistic and wish to limit the range of moral concern. They believe that their first duty is at home, not abroad. Thus, a key issue concerns the question: How far should our moral concern be extended? Should it apply to every person or community in every corner of the globe?

HUMANITY AS A WHOLE

I submit that our moral duty indeed should be extended to humanity as a whole and that this moral rule should thus be generalized. This means that we should be concerned not only with the well-being of those within our community or nation-state but also with the entire world community well beyond our own parochial interests.

Extreme chauvinistic partiality is divisive. Although our loyalty to the norms of our country or ethnic group takes us beyond selfish parochial interests to a wider concern for the good of the inhabitants of the region in which we live, extreme chauvinism between ethnic groups and nation-states can be destructive. Moral caring thus should not end at ethnic enclaves or national frontiers. Ethical rationality enjoins us to build institutions of cooperation and to attempt wherever possible to negotiate our differences peacefully. The broader injunction is that an *impartial ethical rationality should apply to all human beings who have equal dignity and value.* This implies that we should be concerned with the defense of human rights everywhere.

Accordingly, we each have a duty to help mitigate the suffering of people anywhere in the world and to contribute to the common good, thus finding some common ground with all humans. This expresses our highest sense of compassion and benevolence. This implies that people living in the affluent nations have an obligation to mitigate suffering and enhance the well-being, where they can, of people in impoverished regions of the world, and that those in the underdeveloped areas likewise have an obligation to replace resentment against the affluent with reciprocal good will.

Chapter 10

EDUCATING THE WHOLE PERSON

The Liberating Arts

I

We have heard a great deal in the past about the need for general education. The traditional arguments in favor of the liberal arts are no doubt familiar and persuasive. They were embodied in the rationale for the Great Books program, courses or curricula in Western civilization, and the study of the classics. Many of us believe that the reaction against such studies in the sixties—reactions that often denuded or abandoned the liberal-arts curriculum entirely—were narrow and intemperate. Although many students and younger faculty claimed that such studies were "irrelevant" to their interests or to those of the social context, their responses were fundamentally unreflective. For the situation that higher education will face in the decades ahead is such that we need to renew our commitment to the ideals of general education.

However, we cannot go back to the older forms without modifying them. Much of the liberal-arts curriculum was too historical in character and will not meet many of the genuine needs of the future. Thus, general education takes on a new dimension: that is, education must in some way equip both the student and the social polity to deal with the new kinds of problems emerging. The old parameters and guidelines of the past—though they need to be studied and appreciated—are not a be-all and end-all and surely do not suffice by themselves. For example, it is apparent that we can no longer teach courses in Western civilization alone, for the new focus must be on world civilization, not simply on the history of the West, but the future of all humankind. Accordingly, the real question we face is how will education enable students and society to adapt to the rapidly changing world of the future.

Many students, in their boredom with traditional liberal-arts subjects (which we found so exasperating), have turned to vocationalism. "What does one do with the B.A. degree?" we are asked. "It bakes no bread!" Therefore, many students have rejected the liberal arts and the humanities with disdain. Many have also discovered that the completely unstructured, self-actualizing curricula did not enable them to develop a career or function in the outside world. The need to develop skills for a vocation, which the self-actualizing programs overlooked, is important. But one lesson to be learned is that vocationalism or careerism by itself, without supplemental nourishment by general education, is woefully inadequate; the continuing need is for some exposure to what I shall call the liberating arts.

II

The continuing problems that we will continue to face in the decades ahead are the disruptions and opportunities caused by intense social change. We are, in my judgment, living through a new Renaissance, which is expressed by a tremendous burst of creative energy; it is characterized by innovation, dynamism, experimentalism. The most direct expression of this can be found in the explosion in technology and science. The rate of technological invention and application is accelerating very rapidly and will continue to do so in the future. With each new scientific discovery, there are new possibilities and powers, as well as unforeseen by-products and fallouts. In the twentieth century, the automobile, air travel, radar, the Green Revolution, new medical technology, electronics, computers, and space travel have all had their impact. The same scientific and technological growth forces will no doubt continue in the future with powerful implications.

In consequence, we may expect social dislocation and fundamental changes in institutions, structures, and values. Indeed, at the present in this country—and in a good part of the world—we are experiencing a moral revolution, which involves a basic transformation of our values; our very notions of life, work, love, and sex are being radically altered. Given the tempo of technological change, this was inescapable.

The technological explosion and the consequent shift in values places a strain upon both the individual and the social fabric. The old order gives way to the new; all too few of the guidelines of the past seem adaptable to the present, and even less so to the future. The individual is often wrenched from a tranquil background and thrown on his own. Psychological distress and existential despair may overtake him. In a quandary, he looks for sustenance and support. He is often prey to every cult and fad, which feed on his gullibility and promise to answer his quest for security. Given these changing social conditions, rapid political and economic transformations also occur; here, too, most of the traditional parameters break down. Political movements seek both to respond to and to direct the vast technological and social changes going on. On all sides people ask: How shall we act? What should our goals be? What kind of world do we want to bring into being?

If we attempt to forecast the future, we discover that the number of problems we shall have to face as individuals, as a society, indeed as a world community staggers the imagination. On the bleak side are threatening clouds we are familiar with: resource depletion, the scarcity crisis, ecological destruction, the population explosion, political conflict, and—over all—the possibility of nuclear war. The individual faces a loss of values and an increase in his or her sense of alienation and meaninglessness in an increasingly dehumanizing technological society. On the positive side are a number of promises: new explorations and adventures, opportunities for unparalleled technological development, a world of abundance and affluence, the cure of disease and poverty, increase in life-span, increased creative enjoyment and freedom for the individual, and the building of a genuine world community.

There is one possible scenario for the individual, which is already happening and seems likely to continue in the future. First, with increased mobility and travel, the historic rootedness in one place—the commitment to the local community—will be eroded. Narrow parochialism will be overcome. Although this will no doubt expand the horizons of the individual even beyond the nation to the world community, it may also lead to severe trauma, a loss of the sense of belonging.

Second, people will need to change careers, occupations, and jobs more frequently, perhaps several times in a lifetime. New technologies will make some occupations outmoded and residual. The iceman was replaced by the refrigerator repairman, the seamstress by the sewing-machine operator, the bookkeeper by the computer technician. This process will continue. Even seemingly well-established professions—law, medicine, engineering, teaching—will be faced constantly with new demands and methods, often so innovative that they will sweep away and make obsolescent the best-trained but superannuated professionals of the previous decade. Thus the ability to change careers and vocations in midstream becomes a prerequisite of survival, especially the ability to adjust one's skills. If we wish to lead satisfying lives, we must be willing to adapt to new demands.

Third, the old moral values and religious traditions are becoming increasingly difficult to apply to the urgent needs of a new cultural reality: the rules governing marriage, divorce, family, and the role of women in society are being transformed. Breakthroughs in biology lead to new moral dilemmas: cloning, biogenetic engineering, euthanasia, voluntary sterilization, group cohabitation, changing sex roles, and behavioral control are only some of the new adventures in experimental living. The orthodox religions, as defenders of absolute values, have to compete with a number of alternative systems. They are hard pressed and must either stretch and change or become irrelevant. The individual discovers that he must create his own values and personal goals; there are no easy guidelines, and only his own conscience and conviction can help him.

III

It is in this situation that general education inevitably will play a vital role. Indeed, the entire educative process is crucial; the so-called knowledge industry will be the growth industry of the future, the pivotal institution of society. Whether we can meet the needs and challenges of the future as individuals and as a society will depend upon the kinds of educative processes that we undergo.

What do I mean distinctively by education? The learning process, the process of expanding the dimensions of experience and intelligence, the increase in imagination and understanding, the ability to adapt and adjust.

Now let me make it clear that although schools are essential to this educative process they are not the only institutions that should be charged with that mission. Moreover, education is not a commodity to be supplied only to the young, from elementary school through college. As I view it, it is a continuing process for all age groups and at all levels. It is never ending. Perhaps the greatest crisis of the generation ahead will not concern the young but will arise from the necessity of adults adjusting and responding to new and challenging horizons.

Classically, education was the task of the schools, whose chief function was to inculcate the beliefs, values, and basic skills of a society and to train for vocations and professions. It was, as it were, the transmission belt for the traditions of the past. Today, the perennial truths of history no longer seem adequate. The growth of knowledge is intense, and one cannot hope to obtain a degree in a specific field and then rest on one's laurels; there is the ongoing need to keep learning and growing. Virtually all of the institutions of society must have an educative function. The family, churches, labor unions, corporations, business, and industry need to incorporate work-study programs. But perhaps most vitally today the electronic mass media—TV and radio—and magazines, newspapers, and other publications have a role to play. Indeed, the greatest single need that we have, I submit, will be to develop new forms of adult education in society at large.

However, the colleges and universities will no doubt continue to make as their main contribution to society the fulfillment of the tasks of general education; they can do this *best* by providing a rich curriculum in the liberating arts—scientific and humanistic. These studies will help to fulfill one of the chief functions of education: enabling individuals to adapt to the changing future, to withstand future uncertainties and novelties, and hopefully to enjoy them.

It is clear that the curriculum of the future will need to undergo a rather drastic alteration that older forms of general education are unlikely to undergo. It should, in my view, involve several components, many of them familiar: training in the basic skills—reading, writing, computation, for example—professional and occupational preparation, understanding of the nature and practice of democracy, and an appreciation of history and the arts. Yet, the vital element is to increase, by means of the sciences, our understanding of the rapidly changing world in which we live so that *we can develop the ability to make reflective value judgments.*

These later emphases help to realize the ideals of a general education and of the liberal arts that many of our schools have recently abandoned for vocational training or programs in individual self-expression. I believe that we need to return to generalist endeavors but, in a new sense, by explorations in the liberating arts. The chief goal of this kind of education is to clarify our ability to formulate value judgments so that individuals can creatively expand and realize their potentialities in a changing world.

It is curious that in the United States, perhaps the most innovative scientific and technological civilization in history, a drastic critique of science and technology is now under way. Science is blamed for many of our current problems. There is in some circles a neo-romantic flight into anti-intellectualism. This points to a failure in education. For we have not adequately explained science as a great adventure in learning; nor have we succeeded in developing an appreciation for the scientific method: the appeal to evidence and logical criteria in judging hypotheses, the tentative and hypothetical character of knowing, the use of reflective intelligence as a way of solving problems. Given the rapidly changing character of the postmodern world, we cannot retreat from the use of technology and science.

Today, some are overwhelmed by a failure of nerve. If people are to adapt to the future, then education in the sciences—physical, biological, behavioral, and social—must be a required part of every course of study, along with other courses in the liberal arts. But the emphasis must not be simply upon science as a static form of knowledge but rather as an instrument for control: science as a method of modifying the natural and cultural world. It is not scientific discovery that is to be feared but the misuses of scientific applications, their abuses by dehumanizing social and political forces.

Concomitant with this cultivation of scientific imagination is the urgent need for moral education, a continual process of value examination. By moral education, I do *not* mean indoctrination, inculcation, behavioral conditioning, but rather, as the psychologist Lawrence Kohlberg labels it, the process of cognitive moral growth.

Moral values, in the best sense, are the product of a process of evaluation that human beings engage in as they respond to the challenges in the environment: an appeal to traditional standards is never enough, though they be enshrined in religion, law, or custom. Rather, we need to learn how to deliberate about the things that we hold to be good, bad, right, and wrong, worth cherishing and appreciating. Mere emotion or passion is not enough; we need to learn how to deal with our values cognitively, by means of critical intelligence. According to Dewey, values should be treated as hypotheses upon which we act; they grow out of concrete situations and are most wisely grounded when they are fashioned in terms of the needs of the situation and their consequences in the world.

Given the strains of modern life, we cannot always provide young people with ready-made answers, and certainly not ready-made professions, careers, or occupations. No one can anticipate fully the future course of an individual's or society's existence; the best that we can provide is some resiliency, some help in developing cognitive moral awareness, as a way of life, a means by which the person can respond effectively to life in light of a deeper understanding of it. We need a whole new curriculum, one that deals not simply with what is or has been but with what is likely to be, given our effort and persistence.

Thus, surely one of the basic goals of education of the future—perhaps the most important—is the need to develop resourceful people, self-reliant, resilient, capable of critical and responsible thinking, able to adjust and adapt, hopefully with some sense of wisdom, some understanding of their own capabilities and power but also aware of constraints and limitations. Individuals especially need to know how to judge truth claims objectively, how to be skeptical, how to avoid gullibility, nincompoopery, fraudulent and counterfeit promises, how to live with ambiguities and uncertainties. But if we are to cope with the future we also need some audacity and courage—a willingness to introduce new and daring departures. We must dare to dream, to create new visions of what can be. In a sense, we may become what we wish—if the wish is informed and implemented by a firm will, patience, and energy. As we face new problems, we need to introduce new means and new alternatives. Thus, creative imagination as well as deliberation are essential prerequisites for coping.

IV

In talking about education for the future, I am not unmindful of the need for the schools and teachers to deal with the individual learner. There ought to be electives; affective education is important, and we need to develop in students an appreciation for learning. It is not merely dead subject matter that we want to transmit; we want to deal with live human beings who need to be motivated.

But I fear that the recent movement for affective education—sometimes called "humanistic" and which is exemplified by Paul Goodman, John Holt, Edgar Friedenberg, and others—has emphasized the immediate experiences of the individual student to the detriment of his cognitive skills. There has been a tendency to depart from the hard and vigorous cultivation of the arts of intelligence—the difficult effort of mastery and achievement. We need to use our intelligence to judge claims about the world, to describe and explain what we encounter, and to develop normative judgments that will guide our decisions and conduct.

The task of education of the future is to enable us to cope with new and unexpected situations and challenges. But this can be done only if we liberate individuals from repression, discipline, and habits, and encourage impulse, creativity, and exploration. We need to draw forth and nourish innate spontaneity and curiosity, to satisfy a hierarchy of needs and drives. But part of human development and growth involves moral growth. This is not, I reiterate, obedience to dicta or law but a reflective process of deliberation, a recognition and appreciation, not only of our own mature needs but also those of others. Thus disciplined thinking, self-regulating and demanding, is required.

Moral education, as I conceive it, must begin in elementary school, continue in high school, reach fruition in college, but still be part of the ongoing life of a man or woman. Moral education cannot be left solely to religion or the home, as in the past; nor is it solely the task of philosophy departments, but it should permeate the curriculum. In the best sense, value education involves freedom and autonomy, the capacity to think critically and creatively about life's problems, about options, alternatives, and choices. Among the frontiers of moral concern will be the definition and evaluation of the ethics of freedom and equal rights, the implications of scientific discovery, and the creation of a world community in which our commitment to humankind as a whole, over and beyond narrow loyalties and parochial allegiances, is possible.

Freedom from authority, dogmas, ideology, or tradition in the area of morality need not mean subjective caprice, promiscuity, or anarchism in taste. It can lead to objectively relative and responsible judgments, based on human experience and reflection, value judgments worked out in shared experience. But if this is to occur, then it is essential that the *method* of critical valuation be cultivated, not only in the schools, but in all the institutions of society.

In summary, possibly the most important needs for education in the liberating arts in the future will be to develop at all levels, including the area of adult education, the ability to adapt to a changing world; to expand our understanding of our own world, particularly by means of the sciences; to cultivate the skills of intelligence, especially as they bear on moral judgment and decision; and, finally, to develop autonomous individuals capable of withstanding the shock of rapid change and social conflict. The challenges to education have never been greater.

EUPRAXSOPHY

The Unification of Knowledge

THE NEED TO INTEGRATE KNOWLEDGE

We face a unique crisis on the frontiers of knowledge today, and this is not necessarily due to the paucity of knowledge, but, on the contrary, to an embarrassment of riches; for scientific discoveries have grown so rapidly that it has become difficult to assimilate and interpret this vast body of knowledge. Concomitant with this is the extreme specialization that has developed. It is a truism to say that the advancement of scientific knowledge can best be achieved by a division of labor; that is, complex theoretical and technological problems can best be solved by the intensive concentration of efforts. Great progress has resulted, often by a relatively small number of workers in a field who follow the technical literature and are versed in its conceptual framework and the use of mathematical methods, and whose contributions are reviewed by their peers. This departmentalization of knowledge has had enormous success, yet at the same time specialists have so divided their subject matters that members of the same profession often are unable to communicate with one another as fields and subfields proliferate. The dilemma can be readily illustrated by reference to medicine, where general practitioners have declined in influence and where patients are referred to specialists for the diagnosis and treatment of most illnesses. The gap we face is that we do not always know how discoveries in one field relate to those in others. Nicholas Murray Butler, a former president of Columbia University, once defined an expert as "one who knows more and more about less and less." Clearly specialists within the same profession interact with their peers, and there is some interdisciplinary communication. But other scientists and the educated public at large are looking for generalizations that cut across specialties; they are seeking concepts, hypotheses, and theories of broader significance.

It was possible to provide such general interpretations on the frontiers of knowledge in earlier centuries. This often was the task of the philosopher, who had special analytic and interpretive skills. Aristotle summed up the main scientific, ethical, and political wisdom of his day, at least in broad outline; and he was able to synthesize this by means of his metaphysical categories. His doctrine of four causes, substance, form and matter, potentiality, and actuality, gave a comprehensive overview of how nature operated and how we experience and understand it. His idea of nature was organismic: species were fixed, and the universe was intelligible to the human mind. The Greek idea of nature was modified drastically by latter-day theologians, who viewed the universe as God's creation, fulfilling a plan in which Man played a central role. The Newtonian-Galilean world-view rejected teleology and overthrew Aristotle and the organismic universe. The new idea of nature was that it was materialistic, mechanistic, and deterministic. The great philosophers of the modern period, Spinoza, Hobbes, Descartes, Locke, Leibniz, and Kant, attempted to interpret nature in the light of the Newtonian scheme. In the nineteenth century a historical focus emerged, and this led to the sweeping theories of history of Hegel and Marx. This was also the century in which there was a great leap forward in biology, and in which Darwin's evolutionary hypothesis replaced the doctrine of fixed species. There were also important developments in the social and behavioral sciences, which attempted to understand and study human psychology and social behavior. The twentieth century has seen the expansion of quantum mechanics, the modification of Newtonian theories by relativity physics, and the dramatic advance in our knowledge on the cosmic scale in astronomy and on the micro-level in nuclear physics, chemistry, genetics, and biology. Moreover, the new technologies that have been created have enabled unparalleled scientific advances: for example, computer science, space technology, and biogenetic engineering.

Today it is increasingly difficult to develop a comprehensive unified view of nature and of the human species. The philosophy of science has focused more on epistemological issues than on interpreting what we know. So the central questions are: What does science tell us about nature and life? Can we develop a larger cosmic *Weltanschauung*? For any one mind to do so today would require an enormous capacity to understand conceptual and theoretical developments on the frontiers of knowledge. There are literally hundreds of thousands of scientific journals today, and they are expanding at an exponential rate. We would need a super-Aristotle to do so. Are there enough brain cells in any one mind to ingest and comprehend this massive amount of information?

But the need for such knowledge is as pressing as ever. Perhaps we do not need to store the megatrillion bits of information or even to sort or catalogue it; we need only to program and interpret it. What we need to develop today, as in the past, is some *sophia*, or wisdom. This means an ability to coordinate what we know, and/or to synthesize it. Now clearly there has to be an effort within the sciences to develop higher-level unifying theories, from which lower-level theories and hypotheses can be deduced. Efforts have been made to develop highly generalized theories in a number of fields: in physics, astronomy, psychology, biology, sociology, anthropology, and history. Such theories attempt to integrate all that is known in one particular area, and some creative scientists have attempted to do that. We see the bold insights of such endeavors, but also the possible snares: Hegelian, Marxist, and Toynbeean theories of history, generalized Freudian explanations of sexual behavior, Whitehead's *Process or Reality*, and so on. All of these were ambitious programs and all of them had pitfalls. Nonetheless, there is still a need for more comprehensive interpretations of what we know. These may serve for a time during an epoch when certain general paradigms dominate the scientific imagination, but these unifications may eventually give way as unexpected discoveries and unsettling new theories are introduced.

The postmodern intellectual world is in a state of disarray in comparison with previous periods, for we have not found a grand synthesis; and indeed we may never succeed in creating one. To place the burden of providing some integrated cosmic outlook on the philosopher today is inordinately difficult. The special problem with contemporary philosophy is that it has itself become highly specialized and fragmented into separate schools with their own gurus and literatures. Often great divides have been erected across which there is little communication. It was considered to be the task of metaphysicians classically to provide integrative systems of knowledge, but the classical metaphysical enterprise has been thrown into disrepute; for most metaphysicians attempted to spin out speculative theories of reality quite independent of the discoveries of the empirical sciences. They thought that it was possible to analyze the logical and ontological structures of nature without relating their conceptual schemes to perceptual experience. Many philosophical systems were purely formal and had no relationship to the real world, or to the concrete findings of the sciences. Many philosophers indeed were, or still are, anti-scientific, or at best nonscientific, drawing on formal logic, or literature, or the arts, quite independently of scientific inquiry. Existentialists, phenomenologists, postmodern deconstructionists, and analytic philosophers have attempted to plumb the depths of reality or the relationship between language and the external world without considering essentially what science was discovering about it. Some philosophers, such as Heidegger, have disdained any contamination with science or technology, urging a return to the call of Being in a prelinguistic sense. Some have reverted to the literature of theology and mythology to fathom the nature of reality. Yet for any thinker to persistently ignore scientific interpretations of the world is difficult to comprehend today. For it is the methods of scientific inquiry that have been the most effective in developing reliable knowledge; and it is the concepts, hypotheses, and theories of the sciences that should be our starting point.

Nature is encountered by us as pluralistic. We discover what appears to be both order and disorder, chance and chaos. Hence we may never develop a reductive unified theory comprising all of the processes of nature. Corresponding to the variety and multiplicity that we find, however, are levels of description and explanation, and unifying theories in specific sciences. The quest for a comprehensive theory accounting for everything is faced with perhaps insuperable obstacles. Not only is it not possible for any one mind to absorb, let alone understand, the complex kaleidoscopic range of knowledge that we possess, but each of us is limited by the particular spatial-temporal slab in which we exist. We are each culture-bound, confined as it were by the intellectual, philosophical, and scientific paradigms that dominate our age. Yet in spite of the Herculean dimensions of the task and the complexity and finitude of a person's life, there is still some compelling urgency that we at least attempt to make some sense of our collective knowledge.

Any adequate interpretation of the body of knowledge cannot be focused only on our own present temporal-cultural framework, for we need some historical perspective that defines where we were in the past in comparison with where we are in the present. This required some appreciation for the great literature of history to be knowledgeable about the struggles men and women underwent in seeking to explore and learn about the world. This would include some reckoning of their break-throughs and discoveries as well as their failures and blind alleys. Alchemy, bloodletting, numerology, psychical research, phrenology, and astrology are testimonies to the failed pseudosciences of the past, fields in which countless generations of investigators were engaged, and in some cases, still are. Any effort to integrate knowledge must be made with the knowledge of the great conceptual systems of history, many or most of which have been replaced, and of the great civilizations that have had their day in the sun and have also disappeared. But we need also to know of the great achievements that have remained and been incorporated into the body of tested knowledge today. In addition, we also need to have some sense of future prospects of the expanding frontiers of knowledge and the widening horizons of new ideals, goals, and ends to which we may aspire. These are all part of the human adventure in which we can collectively participate. But any world-view we work out will be *ours* at this particular nexus in history, and this will most likely give way in future generations that are faced with new challenges and opportunities.

No matter what the epoch, however, the demand of humans for meaning is perennial. And so we ask: What does it all mean and how does it fit together? What is my (or our) place in the scheme of things? What does this portend for me (or us)?

Unfortunately, some cultural lag is ever-present, for it takes time to digest and assimilate the knowledge that we already possess. It is a paradox that many of the integrative schemes that still dominate human belief hark back one, two, or three millennia. The explanatory tales and parables of God and spiritual forces, woven out of the human imagination by our nomadic-agricultural forebears, still sustain the bulk of humankind. They are the myths of consolation, spawned by the yearnings for the sacred and fed by the transcendental temptation.

The overwhelming fact of life is its finitude and fragility. It passes so quickly. We are each destined to be buried by the sands of time. In the desperate effort to cope with the contingencies and ambiguities intrinsic to the human condition, men and women are led to postulate hidden sources outside of nature. Life in any age is uncertain and indeterminate, fraught with tragedies; and so there is a deceptive quest for eternity, a search for moorings for our otherwise rudderless vessels in the uncharted seas of existence. That is apparently one explanation of why human beings cling to myths long since discredited, and why they are still fixated on their promises. What else do they have to make sense of what they perceive as an otherwise meaningless world? At the present moment, we have progressed rather far in what we know about the universe. We understand full well that eschatological divinity tales are mere illusions that have no foundation in fact. Those who wish comfort can seek out priests and prophets to make their passage through life more bearable. Those who wish truth can find no consolation in self-deception. Skepticism has shattered the idols of the temple.

But if God is dead, what is the human prospect? Must it remain forlorn in a bleak universe? Is it possible to develop an authentic alternative that has some rational support? But to whom shall we turn for guidance? Unfortunately, not to the scientific *specialist* who has divided up the world, investigates only his small portion, and does not know how it fits together. Shall we look to the philosopher who takes as his task cosmic *sophia*? Also, the philosopher, in being committed to examining all sides of questions in the process, is often unable to make up his mind or resolve any of them. Philosophy from the earliest has been interested in analyzing meanings and unraveling mysteries; but the philosopher is often hesitant and indecisive, unable to solve quandaries, unwilling to stimulate motivation or action. Human beings want to know, not only for the intrinsic pleasure of knowing, but so that they may act. And it is the business of life that demands answers. We go to practical men and women to help us solve our concrete problems: doctors and lawyers, bakers and tailors, engineers and architects, business people and politicians.

But we need something more. We need *generalists*, who have a broader view of how the sciences interrelate. We need historians, who have an understanding of past human civilizations. We also need idealists, who have some sense of possible future worlds to create, men and women of inventive imagination. Surely we are mere mortals, not gods. Who among us can claim to encapsulate or plan the entire human prospect? We need to be skeptical of utopianists who offer unreliable totalistic visions of other worlds and strive to take us there. We need some ideals, but we also need to protect ourselves from the miscalculations and misadventures of visionaries.

THE EUPRAXSOPHERS

At this point, it seems to me, we need to make room for *eupraxsophy*, a new field of knowledge and a craft.[1] *Eupraxsophers* will strive to be generalists, able to understand, as best they can, what the sciences tell us about nature and life. Eupraxsophers will thus study the sciences carefully—anthropology and paleontology, psychology and sociology, economics and politics, genetics and biology, physics and astronomy. They will attempt to work with other generalists in developing general systems theory, and in finding common concepts and theories that cut across fields and seem most reliable. They will attempt to incorporate the skills of the historian and the futurist at the same time. But they will also be skeptics, in that they will be critical of pretentious untested claims. They are able to analyze the meanings of terms and concepts and to examine the evidential ground for belief. They will attempt to be objective in their inquiries.

Eupraxsophers will concentrate on two tasks: (1) They will seek *sophia*, or wisdom, a summing-up in a synoptic view of what the most reliable knowledge of the day tells us about nature and humankind. (2) They will also be concerned with *eupraxia*, that is, with *eu* (good) and *praxis* (conduct)—succinctly, good conduct. They will, in other words, attempt to draw the normative implications of *sophia* for living our practical life.

How will eupraxsophers proceed? In the first sense, by applying the principle of *coduction*. If they cannot find a unified-field theory, incorporating all of the sciences, they can at least develop a factorial analysis. They can, in other words, seek to comprehend or explain nature by reference to pluralistic sets of causal hypotheses. There are levels of inquiry in which specific kinds of factual data are described and accounted for. These are drawn from the micro and macro levels, and apply to physical-chemical, biological, psychological, and socio-cultural systems of events. They refer to subatomic particles, atoms, molecules, cells, organs, organisms, persons, cultures, social institutions, and the global system. They are related to our planet, solar system, and galaxy, to other galaxies, and to the universe at large. I have introduced the term *coduction* to describe such an approach to understanding.[2] Clearly, the logic of conductive explanation would allow for both reductionistic and holistic theories. In the human domain they would allow for both physicalistic and intentional explanations of human and social behavior.

As a methodological program, coduction encourages the quest for general physicalist explanatory principles, but it would also allow for teleonomic explanations. For it must deal with the various levels of data under observation and the concepts that are introduced to interpret the complexities of higher-order systems. Coduction thus leaves a place for both bio-chemical explanations and psychological, behavioral, and socio-cultural explanations on the level of human behavior. We must always be prepared to exercise our skeptical criticisms about any such theories that are proposed. Selective skepticism within the sciences is essential to inquiry. Nonetheless we recognize that we have many well-tested hypotheses and theories, and that our cosmic outlook is best informed and constantly transformed by reference to this body of reliable knowledge. Here our *sophia* is not fixed but is a function of the historical-cultural epoch in which we live.

Eupraxsophers will also have a deep interest in ethical and social questions, and will help us to frame reliable judgments of practice. Both individual and public choices can best be *act-duced* in the light of empirical knowledge. Our evaluations of good or bad, right or wrong, are most effectively formulated by reference to a valuational base. Included in the base are factual and technological hypotheses and theories about the world and ourselves. This includes causal knowledge, knowledge or means/ends, and predictions of the consequences of our choices. The valuation base also includes value-laden norms and ethical principles. This incorporates our own *de facto* prizings and appraisings, and our understanding of the normal needs of the human species, the common moral decencies, and the civic virtues that may prevail in our own socio-cultural historical context. What we will decide to do in any context of moral decision-making is open to ongoing criticism. All choices are tentative and hypothetical. Thus some degree of constructive ethical skepticism is intrinsic to our life as reflective members of the community. Nonetheless we can reach some measure of reliable ethical knowledge. Our *eupraxia*—the things we consider worthwhile—is related to our cosmic *sophia*—our understanding of the universe in which we live.

Are there a sufficient number of eupraxsophers in our midst? Regrettably, they are all too few in number. Philosophers like John Dewey, Sidney Hook, and Bertrand Russell exemplified the eupraxsophic life; they were interested not only in knowledge, but action. It was not simply the love of wisdom (*philo*) that they sought, but good ethical practice (*eupraxia*). They were skeptical of occult, theological, and transcendental theories. As free thinkers they drew upon the sciences to understand the world; they espoused humanistic values and defended the free society.

I submit that there is an identifiable need for the universities and colleges to develop a new profession, that of eupraxsophy. In addition to training scientists or technocrats, economists or philosophers, we need men and women interested in the quest for wisdom and its application to the good life. Eupraxsophers are concerned with questions concerning the meaning of life and the relevance of the sciences and the arts to the life of practical judgment. This is surely one of the tasks of liberal education. Students are exposed to a wide range of fields of human knowledge in the arts and sciences so that they can expand their horizons of appreciation and understanding. Unfortunately, the university curriculum today has been emasculated by the demands of the narrow specialty professions. Students have been given a smorgasbord of subjective electives. They are unable to interpret what they have learned, or reconcile it with their system of values. Moreover, few students really appreciate the methods of critical and skeptical inquiry or the nature of reliable knowledge. All too often, in the name of liberal arts education, students graduate as scientific illiterates. Eupraxsophy should be the mark of every educated person: the capacity for reflective judgment and skeptical inquiry, some understanding of the universe in which he or she lives; and some ability to formulate judgments of practice.

CONVICTIONS

The final question that I wish to address is whether persons committed to skeptical inquiry in all areas of knowledge can live fully. Will they be sufficiently stimulated to undertake great tasks; or will skepticism corrode their judgment, undermine their zest for life, deaden their desire for exploration and discovery?

This is a crucial issue that is often raised, but its solution is *psychological* as much as it is theoretical. It deals with the question of human motivation and how to untap the vital potentialities for living exuberantly. The real test of eupraxsophy is whether it can arouse conviction. Will it have sufficient motivational force so that people will consider their lives interesting and exciting, and will they readily embark upon robust Promethean adventures?

What is pivotal here is the recognition that, in stimulating great actions, we must be beyond purely cognitive thought. Human beings are not empty intellectual shells, but passionate centers of feeling, profoundly influenced by the intensity of their inner emotions and desires. Thought cannot and should not dominate everything. We have the capacity to be moved by aesthetic beauty and the arts, and to be inspired by ethical choice. This is testified to by the fact that humans are not only interested in ascertaining whether or not their beliefs are true, but in how to satisfy their passionate desires. A full life is infused with intensity and emotions. It is moved by love and affection, anger and pride, fear and hope, glory and despair. In both our private soliloquies and public expressions, we need to interrelate our thoughts and feelings, our beliefs and attitudes. But although we need to savor the immediacies of the emotional life—the exciting thrills and the subtle delicacies—skeptical inquirers ask that personal beliefs not be deceptively influenced by feelings, and that beliefs be amenable to modification in the light of inquiry. There are constant temptations to sacrifice thought to other passionate interests. At some point we need to regain our cognitive composure. There should therefore be limits placed upon unrestrained temperament and, in the contest between true belief and deceptive passion, the former must eventually win out.

Plato observed that the "chariot of the soul" is pulled by three horses: reason, ambition, and passion. The goal of the wise person is not to allow either passion or ambition to lunge out beyond the lead horse, reason, and to so entangle the chariot that it is overturned; but we need to have all three horses work together in unison. The chariot of the soul should be guided by reason if harmony is to be reached, but ambition and passion still have a place in the full life. For we still are irreducibly men and women of feeling. We fall deeply in love, are moved to laughter or aroused by victory. We need to taste and enjoy the hedonic pleasures of life. We need to be committed to helping others, to be involved in beloved causes. Sometimes our illusions may cloud our clarity of thought. Sometimes we may be overwhelmed by false prophets, grandiose schemes, or illusory projects. We need to be critical of mythic systems of fantasy and illusion and of unbounded goals that are destructive to ourselves and others.

We need a realistic appraisal of the human condition. This includes an appreciation for the positive reaches of life—and here some optimism is warranted. But there are also the sometimes tragic components of death, failure, disease, and suffering—and here some realistic pessimism is relevant. Secular humanists are impressed by the unbounded potentialities of the Promethean spirit and the opportunities for experiencing joyful living, yet we must not overlook the tears and sorrow that we sometimes experience. Eupraxsophers need to offer some consolation to the bereaved, or else they will be outdistanced by the theological purveyors of empty promises of eternal life. The Old Testament admonishes us to remember: "Mine afflictions and my misery, the wormwood and the gall."[3] Or again, the tragedian reminds us: "Preach to the storm, and reason with despair. But tell not Misery's son that life is fair."[4]

Life must go on, responds the practical person, and we should try our best. No doubt we need a realistic appraisal of the human condition, but it needs always to be infused with some underlying optimism, or else the faint-hearted may be tempted to give up, exclaiming "What's the use?" Thus there is a basic principle of motivation that the skeptical humanist insists upon: that life is good, or can be good, and that living is better than dying. Indeed, it can be exciting, full of joy and zest. The empirical evidence that life can be intensely significant has been attested by the lives of countless men and women who have been skeptical, yet were passionately committed to the achievement of great ideals or to the robust fulfillment of joyful living. No doubt this is the first principle of the skeptical humanist: *Life itself needs no justification beyond itself.* The question "*Why* life?" has no cognitive significance. Skeptical humanists and atheists need not be devoid of some form of natural piety, an appreciation of the wonder and magnificence of the cosmic scene—particularly as they stare into the heavens at night. "My atheism, like that of Spinoza," says the humanist philosopher George Santayana, "is true piety towards the universe and denies only gods fashioned by men in their own image, to be servants of their human interests."[5]

The decisive response to the nihilistic skeptic is that we encounter life head-on; and we find it good in the *living of it*. The basic problem of life is not *whether* to live, but *how* to live. The problem of whether to go on living may be raised in some existential situations, such as by persons suffering a painful terminal illness. Here voluntary euthanasia may be a meaningful option. Despair may also overtake individuals living in any overly oppressive society. Here revolt may be the only option. Still, the basic question we face is not whether to live, but *how to live*, and *how to live well*. The lust for life must precede everything else; if it is absent, there is little that can be said. Courage, motivation, affirmation, the intense desire to live is thus the first premise; but this is not imposed on life but is natural to it and at all stages—for the infant, the child, the adolescent, the mature adult, the aging person (providing that the person is not suffering some biochemically induced state of depression).

Skeptical inquiry is our second premise, but this grows out of the first. Life precedes reason, and reason can only minister to it as its servant. Skeptical critics will say, "Aha! another assumed principle! What is the justification for this?" To which I respond: *If* we wish to live, and to live well, *then* the methods of skeptical intelligence and the quest for reliable knowledge are the most effective instruments of our desires. Knowledge can only modify and transform our interests, but the lust for life itself must come first.

Knowledge is surely a good in itself, in that it can give us intrinsic pleasure; but more directly, it has high pragmatic value in helping us to define and explain who and what we are and what is happening in nature; and it best provides us with the instruments for resolving our problems. Knowledge can uncover the limiting conditions within the natural world; it can also discover creative new potentialities, and it can evaluate the consequences of our choices. The justification for knowing is found in the process of living, in helping us to cope with the obstacles that confront us. Practical reason is thus embedded in the very fabric of life. It defines what it means to be a civilized being.

We cannot demonstrate that the kind of skeptical inquiry that I have defended is ultimately provable to the nihilist. Yet it has become central to our lives. To abandon it is to slip back to brute biological existence; to expand its use in all areas of life is to advance the cause of civilized living. Beyond that, perhaps nothing more can or need be said.

Chapter 12

THE EUPRAXSOPHY OF HOPE

Does humanist eupraxsophy offer any *hope* for humankind? For many people this is the ultimate test of the secular outlook.

For theists, the single most important hope is theism's promise of eternal salvation. The term *religion* in its original etymological sense meant *religare*, or "to bind." This referred to a state of life bound by monastic values. Those in a monastic order had the hope of receiving salvation in the next life, presumably as a reward bestowed by God on deserving believers. Unfortunately the evidence for immortality of the soul is totally insufficient. The belief is based on wishful thinking. Human consciousness ("soul") is a function of the body, and as the body dies, so does consciousness disappear.

The belief in immortality should be exposed as a false hope. Death is final for everyone—the believer and nonbeliever, the commander of armies and the lowly soldier, the dedicated teacher and the beginning student, the moral idealist and the profligate hedonist. Would life be truly hopeless, as many theists expect, if everyone accepted the reality that each of us will die some day?

What is the response of secular humanists? What form of consolation can we offer to those who bemoan life's brevity and uncertainty, suffering and tragedy? Is it the case that without God life would be futile? Should we all become nihilists?

Secular humanists are dismayed by the tenacity with which believers cling to their hopes for life eternal. Why are so many people deluded by a false promise of an afterlife? Such individuals lack the courage to become what they wish. They lack the *audacity to create their own world of hopes*. They overlook the fact that life can be intrinsically worthwhile for its own sake; that it can overflow with exciting expectations and anticipations. Our hopes are as unlimited as our dreams of a better tomorrow.

The salient point is that human hope for the individual person *should be viewed pluralistically*. There are so many! A living, vibrant person's desires and wishes, aspirations and purposes, depend on having the *courage to become* what they wish. Living is always future-oriented. Yet there are so many diverse interests that the opportunities for a good life are truly multifarious. This is especially true within open, relatively affluent modern societies that encourage freedom of choice. Indeed, people—at least, those who have financial means—find there are so many interesting things to choose from in modern culture that choosing itself comes to seem a burden. Eupraxsophy can help us to make sound choices in the face of virtually unlimited horizons for enjoyment and satisfaction.

Despite the current downturn, the modern global economy is still productive beyond the wildest dreams of earlier civilizations, offering consumers a staggering range of products and services. So many conveniences and inventions are available to make life a source of comfort and enjoyment! Consider washing machines, refrigerators, central heating and air-conditioning, cell phones and computers, automobiles and airplanes. There are so many exciting activities and hobbies to captivate our interests: We can view dramas, comedies, or spirited debates. We can go to concerts to hear Bruce Springsteen or Liza Minnelli; watch football or baseball games (we hope our team wins). We can get involved in politics and hope that our candidate or party wins out. We can read books by philosopher Charles Peirce, French novelist Honoré de Balzac, or poet Emily Dickinson to increase our knowledge and appreciation. We may aspire to be a good scientist engaged in research. We can seek knowledge for its own sake. We can visit art museums, become a gourmet chef, grow a lovely garden in the back of the house—at least we hope so. We may hope to visit Turkey, Hong Kong, or Paris and finally do so with great satisfaction. We can dedicate ourselves to a new movement and hope it succeeds, such as raising funds to feed the starving people in Africa, or ridding the world of AIDS or cancer. We can invest in the stock market and hope it goes up; we may fall in love with persons romantically and hope that it is requited. We can enjoy erotic sex, and hope that its feelings are mutual. We can take our family to amusement parks, enjoy our kids, and hope they turn out well. We can engage in vigorous exercise every day and hope that we remain healthy. We are dedicated to our careers or jobs—whether in medicine, nursing, education, construction, or sales—and hope we succeed.

In other words the list of things to do today is virtually endless, depending on the culture in which we live. So individuals have a variety of roads to take, of activities to embark upon. It is the fullness of the creative life that beckons us, hopefully a life overflowing with desires, aspirations, and manifold wishes. Life need not be "a vale of tears" that we need to escape from, but a fountain of satisfaction and significance. And if we are somewhat stoical, we accept death at some point as life's natural end. False promises of eternal salvation will get us nowhere—especially if we can truly find life itself intrinsically meaningful and good.

Of course not all of our wishes can be satisfied; and achieving them may depend on strenuous efforts, our economic resources, and luck. In poor economies, a person's choices may be severely limited when he or she has to wonder where the next bowl of rice will come from or who will protect the community from danger. The doctrine of divine salvation perhaps only makes sense in poor and/or unjust societies where people are hungry, sick, or are repressed.

That is why realistic secularists need to do whatever they can to ameliorate the human condition. That is why we need to bring into being societies that are just and economies that are productive in which every person has the opportunities to realize the best of which he or she is capable. Although life is short, it can be lived fully. Our best response to those who deny this life for the promise of the next is to demonstrate that *this life is the only one we have*, and to insist that *we ought not to waste our only lives in fear and trembling*. We should rather summon the courage to become what we want as best we can. It is life that we need to celebrate—not the life of the fetus or the stem cell, but the life of the fully realized person. Life is a precious gift. We should not flee from it! Rather we should affirm its vibrant appeal, in spite of the naysayers in our midst. This is true for every person. But it is also true for those societies that are still constrained by the messianic theologies of the past, which seek to limit the realization of human aspirations, which thwart reason and science, and do not allow humans to become what they aspire to—an attitude which looks backward and not forward. These societies are fixated on death; in the last analysis they are the enemies of life.

The nineteenth and twentieth centuries have seen three dominant secular ideologies of hope. The first was Marxism, which portrayed the ideal of a utopian socialist (or communist) society. This now lies shattered on the rocks of failure and disillusionment, though a qualified form of social democracy has survived. Indeed social democracy stands as the primary modifier of the second ideology of hope, namely libertarian capitalism, which placed its hope for economic prosperity in free markets, and which has survived (in part) thanks to social-democratic reforms.

A third secular eupraxsophy of hope is a form of pragmatic non-utopian meliorism, such as advocated by John Dewey, arguably the leading American philosopher of the twentieth century. Dewey urged us to place hope in the ideals of democratic participation, education, and the method of intelligence to create more democratic open societies. (Please see the remarkable book by Stephen M. Fishman and Lucille McCarthy, *John Dewey and the Philosophy and Practice of Hope* [Urbana: University of Illinois Press, 2007.]) In such open societies individuals have enough latitude to fulfill their unique purposes, yet the government also has an important role in public policy in ensuring personal freedom of equality of opportunity and in defending basic human rights.

A new secular eupraxsophy has now overtaken the world. That creates the need to extend democracy, education, and pooled intelligence to the planetary community at large, transcending any national state. The efforts by 192 countries, which met in Copenhagen in December 2009, to find ways to moderate global warming is the best illustration of the vital importance of an inspiring new planetary ethics that transcends the limits of national sovereignty and attempts to deal with problems that affect everyone on the planet Earth. Such a global focus seeks agreements, treaties, and regulations that maximize the common good for the entire planetary community.

We may not be entirely satisfied by the results of the Copenhagen conference. Yet it marks the recognition by the planetary community that cooperative efforts are essential if we are to solve the serious global problems that we face communally.

MEANING AND TRANSCENDENCE

THE VALUE OF LIFE: THINGS LEFT UNSAID

All living beings undergo continuous processes of replenishment and renewal. Within each species is the constant striving to persist and to reproduce its own kind, in spite of the surrounding forces in the environment that tend to denude or destroy it. All forms of animal life seek food in order to survive and procreate—though most apparently are unaware of the tentativeness of their existence. In the end nature prevails and every single representative is vanquished: the leaf withers and the lilac dies; the sapling that grows into the magnificent elm eventually rots and decays; the young stallion is reduced to a decrepit horse.

And what of human personality? We are creatures of intelligence and imagination. We are aware that his life is finite. We see that the infant, the child, the young person, and the mature adult, all full of possibility and power at one time, eventually grow old and die. Pubescence, adolescence, senescence are all inevitable phases of life. Human beings thus have knowledge of their inexorable demise, and also of the tragic character implicit in the human condition. Life is full of danger: as soon as one is born, one is old enough to die.

There is the sudden accident or the incurable disease that can overtake friend and foe alike. These bitter pills are difficult to swallow. Most people will not or cannot in the final summing up accept this ultimate death. Out of their anxieties about it grows the quest for transcendence and religious faith.

That life is or can be good and bountiful, full of significance and pregnant with enjoyment and adventure, is also apparent to those who have the courage to overcome the fear of death and achieve something in the world. Modern civilization, education, science, and technology have helped us to minimize disease and extend the years of a life of rich enjoyment and harvest, without worrying about our ultimate destiny or God's plans for us. Yet lurking in the background of the consciousness of every person is always the potential for despair, the ultimate dread of his own death. No one can escape it: we are all condemned to die at some time, no matter how we may strive to stave it off.

My father was struck down at fifty-nine of a heart attack, in the prime of life, but he told us at his bedside that he knew he was dying. He kissed my mother and said that his life in summation was happy. My mother, always ebullient, loquacious, beaming with life, on her deathbed at ninety-five told us that she did not want to die. She refused to accept her approaching end with equanimity. Her mother, at eighty-three, suddenly gasped her last breath in her daughter's arms and was dead without warning before she knew what happened. Her youngest daughter died of a terrible cancer at the age of fifty. Regardless of how we feel about death, each of us too will someday reach, even after a life of fullness and exuberance, a point of no return.

Let us reflect on the human situation: all of our plans will fail in the long run, if not in the short. The homes we have built and lovingly furnished, the loves we have enjoyed, the careers we have dedicated ourselves to will all disappear in time. The monuments we have erected to memorialize our aspirations and achievements, if we are fortunate, may last a few hundred years, perhaps a millennium or two or three—like the stark and splendid ruins of Rome and Greece, Egypt and Judæa, India and Perú, which have been recovered and treasured by later civilizations. But all the works of human beings disappear and are forgotten in short order. In the immediate future the beautiful clothing that we adorn ourselves with, eventually even our cherished children and grandchildren, and all of our possessions will be dissipated. Many of our poems and books, our paintings and statues will be forgotten, buried on some library shelf or in a museum, read or seen by some future scholars curious about the past, and eventually eaten by worms and molds, or perhaps consumed by fire. Even the things that we prize the most, human intelligence and love, democratic values, the quest for truth, will in time be replaced by unknown values and institutions—if the human species survives, and even that is uncertain. Were we to compile a pessimist's handbook, we could easily fill it to overflowing with notations of false hopes and lost dreams, a catalogue of human suffering and pain, of ignominious conflict, betrayal, and defeat throughout the ages.

I am by nature an optimist. Were I to take an inventory of the sum of goods in human life, they would far outweigh the banalities of evil. I have outdone the pessimist by cataloguing laughter and joy, devotion and sympathy, discovery and creativity, excellence and grandeur. The mark made upon the world by every person and by the race in general is impressive. How wonderful it has all been. The cynic points to Caligula, Attila, Cesare Borgia, Beria, or Himmler with horror and disgust; but I would counter with Aristotle, Pericles, da Vinci, Einstein, Beethoven, Mark Twain, Margaret Sanger, and Madame Curie. The nihilist points to duplicity and cruelty in the world; I am impressed by the sympathy, honesty, and kindness that are manifested. The negativist reminds us of ignorance and stupidity; I, of the continued growth of human knowledge and understanding. The nay-sayer emphasizes the failures and defeats; I, the successes and victories in all their glory.

The question can be raised: How shall we evaluate a human life and its achievements—in the long or the short run? What is the measure of value, the scale of hope? From one's immediate world there may be boundless opportunities. Look at the things that one can do, if social conditions permit a measure of freedom and if one has developed the creative verve: one can marry, raise a family, follow an occupation or career, forge a road, cure a malady, innovate a method, form an association, discover a new truth, write a poem, construct a space vehicle. All are within one's ken and scope, and one can see a beginning, a middle, and an end. One can bring to fruition the things one may want, if not in one's lifetime, then in the lifetimes of those who follow and their children's children. France, the United States, Russia, China, and the New Zion are social entities that human beings have created. The despairing person groans that they have or will disappear *in the end*, in the long run, if not today or tomorrow, then ultimately. He complains about the ultimate injustice of our finitude. One may know that that is true and even come to accept it. But we are alive today, and we have our dreams and hopes, and the immediacies of experience and achievement can be enormously interesting, exciting, satisfying, and fulfilling.

Can we enjoy ourselves today and tomorrow without worrying about the distant future? No, says the nihilist. He is unable to live in this world; he is fixated and troubled by its ultimate disappearance. "How can life have meaning if it will all end?" he complains. Out of this grows a belief in immortality and ultimate survival.

"Why not make the most out of this life, if that is all we have?" I respond. Indeed, this life can be full of happiness and meaning. We can make a comprehensive list of all the goods and bads and of all the values and disvalues. For every evil that the pessimist anti-humanist presents, I can counter with a virtue, for every loss, a gain. It all depends on one's focus. A person's world may be full of the immediacy of living in the present, and that is what he may find rich and vital. The life-world involves one's yesteryears. This includes a human being's own small world—the memories of one's parents, relatives, colleagues, friends. It also includes the history of one's society and culture—as memorialized in the great institutions and traditions that have remained. But more, one's life-world shares the recorded histories of past civilizations and the memories of great minds, artists, geniuses, and heroes, as bequeathed to us in their writings and works that remain. There is also the residue of things far past, which, uncovered by science, tell of the evolution of the human species, as the strata of earth and rock dug up reveal more of our history and that of other forms of life. It also encompasses the physical universe, extending back billions of years. The eye of the cosmos unfolds through countless light-years in the telescope of the astronomer: the formation of the rings of Saturn and moons of Jupiter, the birth and death of countless suns and galaxies. And what does our present include? Everything here now on the planet and in the immense cosmos investigated by science. But what does the future hold? One can contemplate his own future: tomorrow, next year, twenty years, or fifty. How far may we go? We can make plans, but we cannot foretell what will be—if anything—one century hence. Of this one may be fairly certain: the universe will continue to exist—though without me or my small influence affecting it very much.

Thus one can argue the case from two vantage points. First, there are the life goals or scene of action that an individual, his family, and culture experiences, its dimensions of space-time, its phenomenological range in immediacy, memory, and anticipation. And this can be full of significance. Does life have ultimate meaning *per se*? No, not *per se*. It does, however, present us with innumerable opportunities. Meaning depends on what we give to it; it is identified with our goals and values, our plans and projects, whether or not we achieve them and find them interesting. There is the fountain of joyful existence, the mood of exhilaration, and the satisfaction of creative adventure and achievement—within varying degrees, realism no doubt admonishes.

Millions of people, however, do not find life interesting, are in a quandary, and are overwhelmed by the problems and conflicts they encounter. Life apparently leaves them with a bad taste: it is ugly and boring, full of anguish and sorrow. They bemoan a cloudy day, complain about the humidity, rail against the past, are fearful of the future. The tragic dimension of life is no doubt exacerbated by those who suffer great loss or a severe accident. But nature is indifferent to our cares and longings. A raging fire or cyclone may indeed destroy everything we have built and love; and we are forced to submit to the furies. There is thus the desert of despair, the emptiness of lost zest, the collapse of meaning. In some social systems human beings are their own worst enemies, unable to live or breathe freely, imprisoned in the gulags of their souls.

Yet, within the life-world we occupy, we are capable of intensity, enjoyment, and interest, if we are able to express our proper freedom as independent, autonomous, and resourceful beings, and especially if we live in an open society that encourages free choice. The spark of the good life is creativity—not escape, retreat, or complaint—and the audacious expression of the will to live. *My will be done*, says the free person—not thine. Yes, it is possible—comparatively and reasonably— in spite of the demands and obstacles presented by nature and society, to achieve the good life. I am referring not to a life of quiescent withdrawal or simple self-realization but to the active display of one's talents and powers and the expression of one's creative imagination. One may dig a deep well where none existed before, compose a lullaby, invent an ingenious tool, found a new society, teach a class, pick up and move to another area, succeed on the job or change it. It can be fun; no doubt there may be some sorrow and tears, but basically it may be worthwhile. I am willing to argue the case with the nay-sayer on the level of the phenomenological, contextual life-world. "What is the matter with you?" I may ask. "Are you sexually repressed? Then satisfy your libido. Are you tired and unhealthy? Then examine your nutrition and exercise. Do you hate your work? Change your career, go back to school. Is someone sick? Try to find a cure. Are you lonely? Then find a lover or companion. Are you threatened by your neighbor? Then form a peace pact or establish a police force. Are you troubled by injustice? Don't just sit there; help mitigate or stamp out evil. Enact new legislation. Come up with a viable solution." Human ills are remediable to some extent, given the opportunity, by the use of intelligence and the application of human power.

But it is the second vantage point that troubles so many: the argument from the *long* run. If I don't survive in the end, if I must die, and if everyone I know must also die—all of my friends and colleagues, even my children and their grandchildren—and if my beloved country or society must perish in the end, then is it *all* pointless? What does my life really mean then—nothing at all? This quandary and the despair that such reflections can generate is no doubt the deepest source of the religious impulse, the transcendental yearning for something more. Can one extend his present life-world and those of his loved ones and community indefinitely in some form throughout eternity? People ask in torment and dread, "Why is there not something more to my existence?"

My wife, who is French, sometimes raises these questions when we are alone in bed late at night. And I have heard others raise similar questions. At some point there is the recognition of one's finitude, as one gradually realizes that he or she is growing old and is not eternal. The lines on one's face and the sagging body point to the fact that one's powers are not eternal. Prayers to an absent deity will not solve the problem or save one's soul from extinction. They will not obviate the inevitable termination of one's life-world. They merely express one's longings. They are private or communal soliloquies. There is no one hearing our prayers who can help us. Expressions of religious piety thus are catharses of the soul, confessing one's fears and symbolizing one's hopes. They are one-sided transactions. There is no one on the other side to hear our pleas and supplications.

THE QUEST FOR TRANSCENDENCE

Do human beings *need* to believe that there is something more, something that transcends this vale of expectant promises and ultimate defeat? This is the great challenge for the secular humanist, who is forever beset with extravagant claims of the supernatural, miraculous, mysterious, noumenal, or paranormal realm. Is what we encounter in our perceptions all that there is? Of course not, for we make inferences, develop hypotheses, uncover hidden causes. Knowledge is a product of observation (direct and indirect) and rational inference. Both experience and reason are drawn upon in ordinary life and in the sophisticated sciences to establish reliable knowledge.

We surely should not exclude—antecedent to inquiry—any claims to knowledge about nature or life, however radical they may at first appear. One cannot reject dogmatically new dimensions of experience or reality or refuse to investigate their authenticity. The history of science and philosophy is replete with unwarranted, *a priori* rejectionism. Yesterday's heretic may become today's hero, and today's martyr, tomorrow's savior. One must be open to the possibilities of the discovery of new truths and the nuances of fresh experiences.

The transcendent has had many synonyms. Philosophers such as Plato have sometimes used it to refer to "ultimate reality." Plato distinguished reality from the realm of appearances; sensations and observation only denoted the world of objects and particulars in flux. There was a deeper Truth, he said, which only reason and intuition could plumb: the world of universal ideas, in terms of which the contingent world of concrete fact is dependent. The world of Being remains sheltered to the senses, yet it subsists behind it and can be known only by dialectical investigation and reason. Kant referred to the *noumenal* so as to distinguish it from the *phenomenal*: the noumenal lies beyond the range of our phenomena; the phenomenal is knowable, and it obeys regularities and laws as structured by the Forms of Intuition and the Categories of the Understanding. Science is rooted in the phenomenal world, as ordered by the mind. But the "real" world is itself unintelligible to our understanding. We can only get a glimpse of the noumenal, perhaps in our moral life.

We are able to define and stabilize perceptions and ideas by language. Words clothe fleeting sensations, emotions, and thoughts and give them form and structure. We are able to communicate to others the world we experience and interpret it by relating it to a common world of symbols. But language has many social functions. It enables us to interconnect symbols and to make assertions about the intersubjective world. What lies beyond the rubric of our syntax? Are we imprisoned within walls? Does the mystic intuition enable us to leap beyond the limits of linguistic discourse?

There is some ground for arguing that the world as we experience it, talk or write about it in language, is not necessarily as it appears, and that there is something beyond, which the parameters of the human mind and language cannot presently comprehend or describe. The growth of human knowledge belies any conceit that pretends that what we know is fixed or has reached its final or ultimate formulations. For no sooner is a theory or hypothesis enunciated and maintained as true than its limitations may be seen, and newer, more comprehensive ones may emerge to replace it. Any effort to limit or fix the body of knowledge has thus far met with failure. On the other hand, we cannot thereby conclude that nothing we know is reliable or that the world as we view it in ordinary life and science is mere illusion and deception.

This apparently is the position of those who use the term *transcendence* with a supernaturalistic and divine meaning, as it has been for many latter-day uses of the term *paranormal*. It applies in opposition to two modes of knowing: the appeal to evidence and the testimony of the senses and the use of rational intelligence to develop theories and evaluate hypotheses. It also suggests that there are other ways of knowing—mystical, intuitive, and revelatory faith, all of which claim to give us a glimmer of the transcendent and allegedly supplement our use of experience and logic. Transcendental meditation, prayer, and faith-states allegedly open up the possibilities of a new form of awareness. They supposedly bring us to the brink of a non-ordinary reality. Similarly, for the alleged world of extrasensory perception or psychic phenomena.

By using such techniques, the mystic or psychic claims to be put in touch with another realm that transcends the categories of everyday life, language, and science. This is termed the "higher realm" of being. It shows, the mystic claims, that there is indeed "something more" to life and reality and that this gives proper meaning and perspective to this life. It is the source and ultimate destiny of humans, especially in the long run, says the theist.

The questions then are clearly drawn. Is there a transcendent realm of being existing beyond this world? Is it unknowable to ordinary experience, logic, and science? Is it knowable *only* by the intensive use of methods of transcendental and mystical revelation, nonsensory perception and insight?

It is at this point that the scientific humanist and the mystic are at loggerheads; there are not only different theories of reality but also different methods of knowing. The basic question posed here is: What can be known? Are there limits to human knowledge? Are things that are unknown indeed unknowable? If this is the case, we have two options. First, one may barter one's life to destiny, affirming that because of the limits of knowledge and the need for something more the transcendental stance is a meaningful response. Is this affirmation of belief a reasonable position? Or is it open to criticism and disapproval? The second option is to adopt the stance of the skeptic, that is, suspend knowledge and deny that such forms of reality are knowable or meaningful and to live life fully and on its own terms.

Chapter 14

THE HUMAN CONDITION

Humanist accounts of decision-making in ordinary life have been fairly optimistic, for humanists are confident that rational solutions can be given for many or most problems in life. Ethical judgments are amenable to resolution by reference to given sets of descriptive facts. There is a kind of prudential wisdom at work, and an internal logic governing wise choice. Moreover, a "moral point of view" is reasonable because of man's social nature. For many issues in life one can select with little trouble, and the process of decision is relatively simple. In such cases, the person's choices are usually made by reference to a given framework that is brought into the situation. One refers to his existing values, motives, wants, and desires and seeks to bring these into terms with the social structure of expectations, rules, and norms. Hence some stability in choice is possible. Shall I take the car or walk? Shall I buy a Klee or a Miró reproduction? Shall I vote Labor or Tory? Shall I join the Hay Fever Sufferers' League? What should I send my mother-in-law for her birthday? Should we support old-age medical insurance?

Yet there are times of great trouble and stress when decision problems enter into the very framework of the value structure of a person or society, and when one's most fundamental norms are at stake. At this point one's choices may be said to be both free and in bondage. If one critically questions or rejects the normative patterns of conduct, his own *de facto* valuings and the rules of his community which have guided his life until then, he is left, in a sense, to create a new state of being. At such junctures an individual may recognize the awful character of a voluntary decision that is unlimited and unconditioned by his usual values and expectations. But he can also recognize the frenzied drives that his brute passions and instincts can unleash in the void. Only then might he see that his values and norms in a sense have an irrational basis and that his conduct involves affirmations that seem to be "absurd" in their foundations.

"Practical wisdom" accepts the framework that is given and acts from within, making choices in terms of the existing circumstances. It abides by the golden means of temperance, prudence, and caution. It seeks an equitable solution to its problems. In being "reasonable" one selects the "higher" pleasures over the "lower," and the "moral" life over the "immoral" or "amoral," the "sensible" over the "wild," the "virtuous" over the "vicious." For here one seeks to fulfill oneself in the context of civilized socio-cultural rules. But once we are forced to renounce the standards and norms of social order, or to flout the socially approved character traits, we find that our life is unbounded, yet remains restricted. For, we ask, where else may we turn?

An honest philosophy recognizes full well that the basic structure for our choices is ultimately "arational"; i.e., nonrational, but not necessarily irrational. But if we were to act on this insight—that is, if our choices were to be emancipated from the social-reality principle and be based upon pure impulse and desire—the results might be chaos, and only terror might strike the heart. Fundamental decisions—those concerning death, divorce, choice of a career, war, or national disaster—can call into question the whole basis of our structure of rules and valuings. And this is what the moral skeptic is disturbed about when he demands an "ultimate justification" for his values.

This is the posture assumed by the radical, utopian, or reactionary in politics, who does not accept the given state of values and rules but wishes something entirely different from what now prevails. To the moral skeptic or political reformer who calls into question the whole framework of present beliefs and actions, there appear to be no easy answers. Why accept the *status quo*, as the man of practical wisdom advises? Why not overthrow the whole structure and start anew? For those who have experienced such a state of existential indecision, the problem is real and pressing. For those who have actually wrested themselves loose from their habitual behavior patterns and lived in such a state—by turmoil, conflict, and conversion in their personal lives and careers, or by devotion to political radicalism, or by changing cultures midstream in adult life—such decision problems are all the more drastic. It is well and good for people who have never questioned fundamentally, or indeed have never lived on two sides of life, to advise prudence in choice, to deplore moral or political skepticism, and to claim that existential questions are meaningless. It is possibly necessary to have lived in two cultures to understand one, or to have transvalued and renounced one's former values to understand what they were. For it is in such moments of anguish, when we can discover what appears to be a minimum of guiding lights for choice, that our illusions and myths are seen for what they are, and that we may cry in the night, alone. It is when we become skeptical, cynical, sophisticated, emancipated, or debauched that we may see things in their true outlines. The hobo, bohemian, or deviant is condemned to the social wastelands. But perhaps it is only such nonconforming and anomalous individuals who can see the ultimate irrationality, nonrationality, and sometimes futility of many social rules and conventions.

It is doubtful if our academic professors and philosophers today always see things in a clear enough light, for they have roles to fulfill in society and commensurate statuses, and these frequently destroy their sensibilities. Many have become schoolmarms instilling received opinion in undergraduates. They may succeed, at best, in teaching students to question gently and politely some of the dominant shibboleths and hosannas. They have become men and women of practical wisdom; that is, they are frequently more concerned with the advancement, prestige, and success of their own careers than with truth. Philosophers have become specialists in the division of social labor, and this has determined in part their attitudes and beliefs. The dialogue is within and among philosophers of the same craft.

But to stand outside of the existing framework of values and to look at it critically gives one a different perspective. Socrates was barefooted and bareheaded, a free-roaming intellectual. Spinoza, Kierkegaard, Hume, Locke, Marx, Nietzsche, Mill, and Santayana were, at least, not professors. Our intellectuals today are all too often institutionalized. They are committed to their professional roles within the academies and to corresponding ideologies of prudence. They are not free-floating, but are involved on the inside; all too infrequently do they peer from without.

This negative attitude affects few Englishmen or Americans. "We all know that we have to die one day, why do they have to keep reminding us of it?" complained the English philosopher A. J. Ayer about existentialism. Existentialism by no means presents the whole story. Its attitude on methodology and science presupposes a special moral posture, one that we put to the severest criticisms for its subjectivism, and they minimize or overlook the role of knowledge of nature in decision. Yet European existentialists, such as Heidegger and Sartre, were aware of the revealing moments of human freedom and of the relationship between *Dasein* and nature. They are witnesses to the sand upon which we mortals stand. In the existential perspective, our basic decision problems are not easily resolvable. And in such situations (though any situation, for them, is potentially existential in character), all too few of the usual standards are operative. There are no holds barred, and we seem to be thrown on our own, to make ourselves as we see fit.

If we are honest and receptive to all possibilities and to all points of view, when we find innumerable alternatives—intellectual, passionate, and instinctive—one course of action may seem as good as the next. And the future which is to be made seems to be contingent on nothing but our imagination. Our decisions are engendered and propounded in terms of our commitment to our social and cultural existence and to our habits of character; once a decision is made, a whole line of consequences may follow, changing the entire situation. Yet at any moment, existentially, we can enter the arid desert of nonacceptance; we can suspend and reject all of our commitments. Our basic values and norms in the final summation seem either to represent our conditioned social habits, our unconscious motives and blind feelings, or to be the product of capricious intellectual choice, with one option apparently as good as the next.

This bitter truth about basic things, though seemingly desperate, does not leave us entirely alone. Even here there are some guides available to the individual. There is practical reason, and the norms and standards it presents. There are basic needs which the wise person may seek to satisfy and to take account of in reaching his decisions. Rationality does provide us with some help in reaching decisions, for it can give us understanding of ourselves and our needs. The individual need not be entirely helpless or lost in a sea of subjective indecision; given his desire to live and his social existence, decisions follow. In most of our moments we presuppose our values and act in terms of them. Existential puzzlement occurs only sometimes, perhaps only a few times in life. Life is not riddled with crises to the extent that some would have us believe.

Yet we are capable of entering a mood of desperation, at least philosophically, and we can ask the most basic questions about our existence: (1) Why live? and (2) Why accept social and cultural life? The questions that are framed in this mood are questions of normative justification. In answer to question (1), we must admit that the fact that there should be life rather than death is in a sense an absurdity; that is, we can give no reasons for our existence. We find ourselves here, alive, functioning, without being responsible for our own creation or having given our consent. As I have argued, that we should live is not amenable to rational proof or justification.

That life in the universe at large is better than nonlife cannot be proven. Life has evolved. It is found, given, encountered. From the standpoint of living things, there is a kind of instinctive tendency (in normal cases) to maintain life. For those who do not accept it, the door is always open to leave. Some may grieve our early departure, but nature is indifferent to one more lost soul; we shall return to the dust from whence we came. That there should be life rather than death, hope rather than despair, meaning rather than meaninglessness—these things are of moment only to human beings, not to nature. A person on the verge of suicide or death may seek some consolation for life, and he may yearn for a justification for its continuance. But none can be given, other than that most beings have an instinctive urgency to live. This is its sole justification—that life desires life, and that in living a kind of interest, satisfaction, zest, joy, and happiness may be discovered. It is an odd organism that deliberately seeks its own destruction, although that obviously does happen. Yet even here the death wish is more a distortion of normal homeostasis than anything else. Thus, the option posed between life or death is not between equal alternatives, for there is a primal nonconscious tendency on the side of life. To entertain the idea of death is only possible for a fairly sophisticated being. Hence the balance is heavily weighted that an organism will naturally tend to accept life.

But to accept life—that is, to strive, endure, suffer, and enjoy—already provides some clues in answer to (2) Why society and culture? For if one is to live, to survive and grow, then certain needs must be satisfied. And here society and culture play their functions. Biogenic needs are the products of a long evolutionary process. Sociogenic needs have developed more recently in the drama of human life. Both may be overthrown, though the denial of biogenic needs may lead to disease and death, and the denial of all sociogenic needs may also lead to disease and death or anguish and turmoil. If we fear death, disease, anxiety, then we conform in some sense to the social structure of normative rules and we find it prudent to do so. But it is essential that our culture not be at variance with our biology, and that it satisfy our root nature without unduly repressing it. This is the ultimate test of culture: its long-range ability to satisfy and not to destroy our instinctive life.

Society and culture too, from the wider view, may seem absurd, and that we should willingly be tamed by its restrictions may seem oppressive. Why be civilized? Why adopt the stamp of our age? Why be Etruscan in ways, fashions, attitudes, and beliefs—or Spartan, Hindu, German, or American? What we are is a product of the causal conditions operative in the species at large and of the special historical circumstances and events that have converged upon us. We have little control over the explanatory laws relevant to human conduct, although if we understand the relevant conditions we may be able to act accordingly, circumvent them, or bring new ones into being. Similarly, the social and cultural framework of rules and institutions has already preformed and molded our personalities before we become aware of what is going on. We are its helpless creatures conditioned as babes by society and culture long before we are able to turn upon it, criticize it, or change it.

But can we return to the presocial jungle? This is a live alternative only for the romantic or visionary. To abandon social and cultural rules entirely is not possible. Memory and habit will not release us; we cannot erase language, the social vehicle of our judgments. Of course, there is always the alternative of changing cultures—of moving from one culture to another, from a modern culture to a primitive one or vice versa; or we can move from one sector of a culture to another, we can change classes or cities. But it is virtually impossible for us to abandon socio-cultural rules altogether, for man is now a creature of society and is imprisoned within its walls. There is a root biological dependence for survival on the care of at least one other person: child-dependence seems implicit in the species. It is, of course, possible for people to become disassociated from rules, but extreme instances of this may end up in mental institutions— they are unable to function in their social environments. There have been recorded cases of people who were civilized and then returned to their primitive tribal ways, as in Brazil, for example, where missionaries Christianized some savages, brought them to live in England, and allowed them to return to the jungle again, only to find many years later an almost complete reversion to primitive ways.

No, *we* cannot very well return to the presocial jungle. The question I am raising, "Why be civilized?" is meaningless for the civilized person. It is like the question: Why live? And, as I have aid, there is no rational or ultimate justification for life. One lives because there are tendencies within that strive for survival; when these are not present, one gives up the battle and dies. Similarly, there have developed civilizing tendencies and characteristics that impel expression. To deny them if we could is to accept death in a sense—the death of a new part of ourselves that has evolved and been built upon our basic biological nature. I can no more retreat completely from society and culture than I can from life. Both are enigmas, though we are closer to seeing the evolution of the former than that of the latter, for the processes of accretion are enormously more rapid in the development of culture than in the development of life.

Once I recognize the value of some socio-cultural organization as instrumental for satisfying my basic needs and desires and for creating new ones, the real question I face is this: Which part of society or culture shall I accept and which shall I reject? We know that we can modify some of our practices. There is a hierarchical order of events at work at each level. The individual is a result of vast physicochemical and socio-cultural forces, all of which have converged and left their traces upon him. A person is, as it were, a residue of things past. But one can intervene on various levels, most directly on the level of individual choice and memory. One's nervous system as a particular mechanism bears the imprint of one's own experiences. There are choices to be made, as we have seen. In a sense there are three aspects to an individual's life: physical-chemical-biological, socio-cultural, and individual personality.

The question that the individual faces is usually a proximate one: what to do here and now in regard to this framework? But, once again, he can call into question the whole framework; and I reiterate, there may not be an ultimate answer.

Here philosophy may be relevant. And here an important function of philosophy, and especially eupraxsophy, may come into play—at least it has done so in the past, for it enables us to stand outside the framework and to see things in their proper perspectives. It reveals the presuppositions of our knowledge and action. This function of eupraxsophic inquiry is often overlooked, even though it expresses our highest consciousness and awareness. Most human beings are so immersed in biology and culture, so engrossed in the day-to-day cares of social life, that they forget to stop, take a breath, and inquire: What does it all mean and how does it fit together? They have forfeited their lives to the trivial. Their values are the values imposed by the "they" of social living. The mad pursuit of money, sex, honors, rewards, success can demand all of one's energy and devotion, especially if one operates only within a narrow context of life. Alas, when we take a coductive[1] look at the domain of values, from the outside as well as the inside, we frequently sap these values of some of their potency and vitality.

Spinoza pleaded for the development of an attitude that could see things whole and under the "eye of eternity." Such a perspective, he thought, might emancipate us from the narrow desires and passions of ordinary life. All things, he thought, were modes and affections of the same underlying "substance," "God," or "nature." This is the metaphysical or philosophical insight: once our plans and desires are placed under the focus of eternity and within the broader context of the universe at large, they diminish in intensity; once our present cultural valuings and rules are compared with other cultures past and present, they are minimized in urgency and enthusiasm. Perhaps philosophy is a bad thing, for if taken seriously it may take the wind out of our sails, dry up our gusto, and lessen our conventional motivations. Too much reason may at times hamper rather than facilitate decision, as the Sophists recognized.

The philosophical attitude has been ridiculed precisely because it is hesitant and reflective: while the average person jumps in and acts, the true philosopher sees the futility of haste and may avoid jumping and acting. "Fools rush in where angels fear to tread." I am not here talking about the specialist in philosophy, the logician or analyst. I am referring to the eupraxsopher who is the critic of value and culture and who is aware of hidden presuppositions. For he pre-eminently sees things in the coductive light for what they really are, from the outside as well as the inside. Such an approach also enables an individual to recover himself, freed from the tyranny of the nonessential and the irrelevant.

Such an individual may be able to free oneself from an illusion. One can see, for example, that science is primarily a way of life, one that rests upon the inculcation of a distinctive attitude or that presupposes its own rules of behavior, evaluations, and prescriptions. Reductionism, holism, coductionism, determinism, historicism, and other general methodological principles are really prescriptive rules governing inquiry, even though they are tested by their fruitfulness in inquiry and their effectiveness depends in some way upon nature. Moreover, to be interested, as the scientist is, in clarity, truth, impartiality, knowledge, objectivity, or open-mindedness, rather than music, art, intuition, mountain climbing, or surf sailing, is to affirm a way of life.

To advance the cause of scientific research in society is to express a moral imperative. Scientific research, like most other human enterprises, requires some dedication and commitment. But dedication and devotion are moral qualities, and the whole system of science rests upon decision and choice. The same is true of logical and semantic analyses. Theories of meaning, too, are normative and prescriptive in part, for language rules fulfill human purposes. Logical analysis thus involves instrumental activities. This is not to impugn such philosophical activities; indeed, such strategies of research may be effective. But they are strategic programs, and the deeper truth recognizes that all enterprises, whether philosophy, logic, science, art, politics, or love-making, presuppose basic norms. All systems in perspective, even the most descriptive in intent, may be seen to rest on our valuations. That we ought to lead the deductive, conceptual life rather than the affective, æsthetic, immediate life perhaps is not amenable to any final justification or proof. There are differences in culture and attitude that have conditioned our points of view, and there are sets of values and rules that we already possess and that determine our postures.

The inferences to be drawn from philosophical skepticism may not be precisely as philosophers have drawn them in the past. We cannot deduce a moral conclusion or imperative from our picture of the situation. We cannot even recommend a final attitude. Attitudes and states of character fluctuate with historical circumstances. It may have been well and good for the Athenian gentleman to follow Aristotle's golden mean, to be liberal, temperate, magnanimous, of slow gait, low voice, and proper pride. Or, indeed, for the medieval man to assume the role of the monk or the courtier, or the nineteenth-century educated person to be a hedonist and Utilitarian. It is wise, one may argue, to be rational, intelligent, and objective in one's decisions, no matter what the time or place, as most philosophers have usually claimed. But these are only hypothetical imperatives.

We should not go overboard and claim that the rational life is the ultimate or final ideal. One may also argue that the life of reason is a positive evil if it seeks to deny or reduce the life of passion, and that the substitution of cognitive symbols for emotions and feelings may be oppressive. Reason in a sense may be repressive, for, while ordering our instinctive passions, it may leash them as well. The growth of the cortex and its attendant symbolic power may in a sense be an abnormal growth, for in the place of brute nature it may impose cultural ritual. The life of a virgin librarian may in the nature of things be no more noble than that of the nymphomanic Messalina. I think that we may deny that any one way of life is eternally justifiable, even that of the philosophers. I would explicitly question the sanctimonious admonishments of moralists that we ought to be temperate in our desires, or the impugning of the pleasures of the flesh. If life, at root, is "a tale told by an idiot, signifying nothing,"[2] and if society and culture are like games—sets of rules that we adopt to play at life—then perhaps we ought to get the most out of life.

The pleasures of sex, food, and drink may be as important to a person as the cultural pleasures of art, philosophy, and pinochle. And, if it all means nothing, then any course may seem as good as any other. I am not here necessarily accepting Bentham's remark that pushpin may be as good as poetry. I am merely denying that we need assume that poetry is always better than pushpin. For practical reason, deliberation and calculation about our long-range desires and plans are in order. But, for coductive reason, the deliberative process itself is prescriptive at base, and it is the whole person, not the part person, who must live.

Similarly, while we stand inside of society we may be concerned with social justice—i.e., with providing a set of rules that will most equitably satisfy the distributive needs of the individuals who make up that society, or even within a world community. Here, too, however, from the standpoint of coductive reason there may be something transparent and empty in taking this as the primary end of life. Those of us who are social reformers or socially interested feel compelled to take part in the public affairs of the day. As political men and women we decide and act, and the game of politics may very well take all. There is a kind of religious devotion to the ideal of social betterment. But there seems to be no ultimate basis or justification for moral obligations, either. Our rules in society delimit the rules, rights, and duties that we perform. If we are to perform our functions in a reciprocal way, then we must obey the rules, even if they are only the loose and indefinite ones of morality.

Moral rules, like all others, are teleonomic and instrumental. We build up feelings of sympathy and love for other human beings, and we develop a sense of belonging to a community. We may inculcate a sense of sin, guilt, or conscience about certain acts and support these feelings by custom, education, and law. But we are unable to find any infallible justification for basic moral rules. Their justification is practical and hypothetical, not absolute or categorical. A father or mother feels that he or she must sacrifice for the child, and a grown child for the parent. And this is true as long as we wish to imbibe the game of cultural life, and to live and function. But one can find no ultimate standards or guides that will solve the problem or morality. Because of our social and cultural commitments, some morality is necessary. But society and morality are not intrinsic to the nature of things. And one can, at least theoretically, abandon or resist both.

I have been arguing all along that, within the structure of a level of being, a person accepts events and relations as given. But it is from without that the level is placed in its proper framework. People who have always stood outside of a warm house and peered through the windows cannot fully understand what is being experienced inside the living room by the fireplace, or so we are told; but I fear that people on the inside are equally blind if they never peer out or open their windows.

From inside the house one can say this—science in knowledge, logic in meaning, and reason in practice are the most effective instruments for living. Since we live in a common world of objects and events, and since human beings share relatively the same problems and needs, it is best that our actions and beliefs be based on reasonable methods. Cognition is a need because it enables us to establish our lives in terms of external reality. Theoretical science and practical science at least enable us to find public knowledge and public rules with some objective ground in nature, and in terms of which we can communicate. If all activities are prescriptive, this does not mean that all are equally effective. One cannot defend all systems of beliefs as equally valid because they all rest upon faith, as some religionists have vainly attempted, for there are fundamental differences between the hypotheses of science and those of religion. Faith as tenacity or as will to believe, i.e., faith based on little or no empirical support, is surely different from faith grounded in empirical evidence and experiment. The internal truth claims of the reigning mythologies are not verifiable, but the truth claims of science are. Thus, while both science and religion express prescriptions when viewed from the broader existential context, still in regard to their internal cognitive claims there is a vast difference.

Hence we must defend the marvelous inventions of scientific method, logical clarity, technology, and practical wisdom as being in closer touch with nature than other ways of behaving. We must grant that the scientific method presupposes certain values—which are required in some sense if we are to live and function in nature. From the standpoint of social and national policy and especially for the underdeveloped countries at present, scientific technology is the only hope of competing in a postindustrialist world; it is indispensable for survival. Thus one must defend the scientific method: no matter what our desires may be, if we wish to satisfy them, then science and reason best provide the instruments for satisfaction. Or, at the very least, one may argue in this way: if the way of life that we should adopt is an open question, then we must presuppose conditions of free inquiry in order to resolve the question—but this again is a basic value presupposition of science.

Thus, in the last analysis, science and practical reason have a pragmatic justification and vindication (as Herbert Feigl observed) because they are most instrumental to life activity, individually and socially. Any philosophy applicable to contemporary life must now take them as the main guides for valuational choice. This is the most important commitment of our times. Moreover, in addition to their instrumental values, both science and practical reason have a kind of intrinsic quality and value of their own, an attraction and appeal which only those who have experienced and used them can best appreciate.

Yet we still have two brute facts to face: (1) the fact of life and death, and (2) the fact of society and culture. Who is to speak of them, for them, and about them? Only the existential eupraxsophic consciousness is willing to face the true human condition, of life and death. These brute elements are implicit in human existence—over and beyond our instrumental effectiveness—and this should be apparent to all who are willing to reflect on its nature, and it is especially revealing to all who have divested themselves of their cultural myths, whether those of the ancient god of Immortality or, in our contemporary scene, those of the bitch goddess success or consumer gluttony. These religious myths may serve psychological and sociological functions; they may provide a balm, peace of mind guaranteed, and social cohesion. These functions are often foreign to the literal scientific person who takes these myths (especially the theistic) for literal nonsense, although he himself may worship at his own mythological altars, whether of Determinism, Progress, or some other ideal.

The truly eupraxsophic person is one who dares to face the nature of life and death with courage, the person who has a sense of both the rich possibilities and the inevitable futilities of life—and few of the devotees of organized religions are metaphysically aware in this sense. It is a mistake to think that theism has a monopoly on insight. On the contrary, humanism is capable of a deeper and fuller understanding of the human condition. The true religious response is a response to the demands of the external world. It develops usually when we come to realize in full shock, and usually in times of crisis, the flux of human existence, and when they recognize that, though the fondest human dreams may be realized, alas, "vanity, O vanity," they rest upon quicksand. In the words of the author of Ecclesiastes: "All go unto one place, all are of the dust, and all return to the dust again."

The tragedies implicit in the temporal historicity of life, the death of each human being, the fact that all humans are unclothed, naked, and alone—this is the awesome bedrock fact that confronts the sensitive consciousness. The existentialists were not the first to discover this fact of nature and life or the pathos of suffering and dread. Yet all too few persons are willing to see life and death for what they really are; they put death out of their minds, and, like the other animals, ignore it, or they think that it is a problem only for the old to worry about. We see others die, not ourselves. Yet life and civilization are mere mortal events which will pass like all else.

Along with this awareness of the transience of life—and it takes true courage to face it—there is another fact to be faced: the recognition that there are powers and forces external to and independent of us, the recalcitrant given. There is a source of our being that we cannot control, but that we can only come to terms with and accept. Some mistakenly call this "God," or attribute its power to mysterious demons and mythological entities. Others attribute it to "causal laws" and to the fact that we are only a small part of vast systems of events. In any case, some recognition of our dependence upon the tide of events and the limitations of our powers is present in the eupraxsophic response, and this usually leads to some stoic resignation and perhaps a degree of "natural piety."

These facts of life and death, of transience and dependence, I think that all can accept. They are easily confirmable by scientific observation, and they are as true for the atheist as for the theist. And these facts do not disappear by claiming that the whole problem is a pseudo-problem or cognitively meaningless. True, there may not be a solution, but there is still a real predicament that we face. Yet men and women frequently do not wish to face their transience and impotence. They cover it up or disguise it. The cares of society and culture dominate our consciousness.

Civilization builds symbolic worlds, and we are taken up by new events. We are concerned about making a living, getting married, writing a sonnet, playing the stock market, investigating the causes of a disease, supporting the party, contributing to economic growth, to democracy, or to world peace. And, in our haste, we frequently overlook our brute animal existence.

The existential human condition is often not faced; it is usually forced upon us in times of extreme crisis or change. When it is faced, and faced hard, the truth may chill us, and so we construct false mythologies to avoid it: the immortality myth of the good life promised later on, or the utopian myth of the good life on earth for humankind now. But the scientific method can confirm neither, nor can it guarantee that our vain hopes are inscribed in the womb of nature. The assertions of traditional theistic religions, that God exists or that there is an immortal soul, are at best expressive or imperative utterances that have not been verified and are unverifiable. And the messianic promises of social reformers or psychological therapists that unlimited social progress or psychological happiness is just around the corner awaiting us with certainty are also seen to be idle chatterings in the wind.

We huddle together in society and create smoke screens for the protection of life against the cold wind and death. Nature cannot sustain them—and with the dust they will eventually vanish. As we open the frontiers of space new challenges will confront the human species. Our organic existence will be given new dimensions as we learn to travel in a wider universe. But the new discoveries awaiting us cannot alter the ultimate human condition or the impermanence of life. There are some things we can ameliorate and change, and there are many problems we can resolve—but who except the completely self-deluded can believe in their final solution or in our ultimate salvation? Whether humankind eventually destroys itself or propagates the solar system and stellar systems beyond is the frightful yet exciting options of the future.

I do not wish to seem overly pessimistic. I think that it is important for us to unify our scientific knowledge, particularly our knowledge of human beings. I submit that a science of human beings is both possible and necessary, and that there are no unalterable or *a priori* obstacles, as far as I can see, to the understanding of human nature. Neither the appeal to motive, historical, or teleonomic explanations as special kinds of explanation, nor the fact of free intention or decision, nor any alleged mind-body dualism can invalidate the scientific explanation of human nature. The fact is that the human organism is a teleonomic animal capable of decision and action, and science can trace the conditions of such behavior. Moreover, this knowledge enables us to improve our practical know-how and our power for making decisions. Our prescriptions and rules are more effective if based on descriptive knowledge. Science itself is not purely descriptive, but has a prescriptive basis. But this does not undermine its claims or make it totally unlike other human interests. It merely places it in its proper valuational locus.

Moreover, scientific rationality is probably the most effective value system available in the world today, and it is one that we should be committed to, individually and socially, for the good life. It provides the best means for individual happiness and social progress, and it is particularly the hope of the vast mass of underdeveloped humanity.

Yet in looking at our ethical life we find this paradoxical fact. The human species is a product of nature, and as part of it we are governed by the same causal conditions that are found elsewhere in nature, and that we may be able to understand. Yet we are decision-making organisms—choosing, selecting, valuing. We become aware of our own choices and reflect upon their direction, and we have a creative role in their formation. But here nature is ironic—a cruel joke has been played on human striving. As conscious beings we are able to understand full well the status of our values: they have an animal basis and a socio-cultural fulfillment, yet they are transient, historical, and changing. We can satisfy some of our longings—for love and health, for happiness and equanimity—with various degrees of effectiveness. But the special human condition is that we, through eupraxsophy, can recognize the instability of all human desires and their ultimate terminal character, as well as the instrumental nature of our socio-cultural rules. We should, I suppose, be grateful that indifferent and blind natural processes enable many of us to achieve fourscore and ten, and perhaps more. We should be grateful that, in spite of a nature that is blind, we nonetheless are able to see and understand.

The important power of coduction as a rational principle of understanding is that it enables us to stand both inside and outside the processes of life: we can appreciate things in their proper contexts, but also see their functions and interrelations. Objectivity in knowledge, meaning, value, and decision is contextual; at bottom it is a product of culture, not nature. We can justify, vindicate, or plead our special causes. We can defend our basic ground rules and persuade others to accept them. But prescriptive rules in the last analysis are affairs of a teleonomic animal who has evolved an edifice of society and culture, an animal who, if overly conscious, can undermine his animality altogether. Rather than make us free, the truth may kill us, for it will present to us bluntly and coldly the instability of life and the impermanence of values and social rules. As skeptics we can rise above the illusions of our age. But we can also sink into the well of hopelessness and despair, of instinct and desire.

All that human beings have is life. What we make of it, or what it makes of us, is all that counts. Society and culture have emerged in part to facilitate our animal desires, but they can also be a mask for deception. Humans develop knowledge. Through knowledge we may discover what we are, what we need, what we desire, and what we can have. But knowledge is the instrument of desire, and desire of life; yet life ultimately ends in death. Life while lived can be good and bountiful: love, devotion, kindness, knowledge, achievement, success, well-being, happiness, economic growth, and social betterment are all possible within limits. But all good things must pass, and life has its bitter end. Some may develop feelings of resignation toward these brute facts. Some may panic or lose nerve. In any case, the facts should be allowed to speak for themselves.

The eupraxsopher who has left the cave of illusion can see human nature and life for what they really are. Yet each of us must partake of the game of life. As rational inquirers we must deal with knowledge, meaning, and value, though in so doing we presuppose the rules applicable at the various levels of inquiry. As a practical being one can lose oneself in the whirlpool of life, while as a philosophic being he can understand the ephemeral basis of life (though, unlike Plato, we have no solace in eternal essences). This is the constant paradox of life: reason that is holistic in scope and practical in action is possible, but it is at variance with reason that is coductive and existential in scope. Reason in science and practical wisdom enables us to live and enjoy the fruits of the good life. But reason in eupraxsophy places things in their proper, and broader, coductive focus, and in its revealing light we see full well the opportunities we face yet also the transient character of all human existence and the teleonomic and animal basis of knowledge, meaning, and value.

In spite of all this, life is still worth living and we have within our power the possibility of living fully, even exuberantly. To waste this opportunity or to flee from it is the highest form of human tragedy. The human condition is such that all too often it is fear and trembling (to paraphrase Kierkegaard) that overwhelms us—not the courage to be (Tillich) or the heroic passion to leap over the abyss (Nietzsche). Unfortunately, this tempts many men and women to place themselves in bondage to the false illusions promised by priests and prophets, and to abandon their own sense of power to them.

FROM PHILOSOPHY
TO EUPRAXSOPHY

In my philosophical outlook, one normative prescriptive principle has preceded all others. It concerns a key methodological principle in epistemology and the philosophy of science, namely, the criteria for judging truth claims. My views in political and social philosophy are likewise dependent on this key methodological rule.

The basic epistemological presupposition that has ethical import is my commitment to "the methods of science." I am using the term "methods of science" rather broadly to include empirical, experimental, and rational criteria. I am here referring primarily to the *criteria* for evaluating claims to reliable knowledge, not the process by which we discover truth. And the term "method of science" that is used is plural, not singular. I am not talking about "*the* scientific method." I am leaving the door open to a wide range of research tools and strategies of inquiry but am interested primarily in the standards of validation, confirmation, verification, corroboration, and justification that are used in the sciences— the natural, biological, behavioral, historical, social, and applied-policy sciences—and ordinary life. These methods include the use of mathematics and statistics, technological instruments from telescopes and microscopes to computer simulations, and the drawing upon multilayered coductive explanations from many specialties and fields. The methods of scientific inquiry entail various forms of rationality. That is why I have used, along with others, the terms "critical thinking," "rationalism," and "the method of intelligence" to characterize the quest for objective methods of justification. I reiterate that I have focused in this regard on the question of method rather than classical epistemological issues *per se* about the nature of truth and ultimate reality.

I have been most directly influenced in this approach by the American Pragmatists—Charles Peirce, William James, but especially John Dewey and his students Sidney Hook and Ernest Nagel. The central question for me has always been: What methods have been most efficacious in developing, testing, and advancing our understanding of nature, the biosphere, human behavior and culture, and more precisely our ability to solve problems encountered within the natural and social environment? This question has intrigued me ever since the first course that I taught at Queens College (City University of New York) in 1950 as a graduate student at Columbia University, and it has been the bedrock of my entire philosophical career. The focus on *method(s)* is rejected by many philosophers, such as Richard Rorty, who claimed to be a Deweyan (though many would deny this because of his anti-Deweyan position on method), and the postmodernists, who are skeptical of science and any claims to objective knowledge, and also by those who held a spiritual-paranormal world view and likewise seek to reject or modify science, which they label as "materialistic."

I was influenced early in my philosophical development by the logical positivists, most notably by Nagel (I took almost every course that he taught at Columbia), but also a course that I took with A. J. Ayer, a visiting professor at NYU, and Carl Hempel (of Princeton), who taught a joint course with Nagel at Columbia on the nature of scientific explanations. I was attracted by the efforts of the positivists to use scientific inquiry as a model, especially as a critique of metaphysical (and theological) speculation that had no foundation in experimental verification or experience (following Hume). Clearly the principle of verifiability was too restrictive as a criterion of meaning; yet it was a normative rule that could be useful, particularly in disposing of much metaphysical bombast, because of a lack of clearly definable meaning.

I hasten to add that I rejected the positivist critique of ethics from the start, for I thought that moral and political judgments were *not* simply reducible to expressive or imperative language and lacked any objectivity. I remember arguing one afternoon with A. J. Ayer ("Freddie," as he was called), as an impudent undergraduate on a park bench at Washington Square Park in New York City, that there is a level of ethical discourse that does have cognitive meaning, and indeed had its own logic of justification. *Time* magazine had a story about the time of Ayer's visit to the United States, accusing him and the emotivists of a failure to provide a basis for criticizing Nazi moral imperatives—if ethical judgments were simply a matter of subjective taste, then anything goes. Ayer was offended by this critique, but it was clear to me that the emotive theory was profoundly mistaken. Ayer had modified this somewhat in a new preface to his influential doctoral dissertation, *Language, Truth & Logic*, but not enough in my view. Ayer said that you could argue with proponents of an ethical doctrine, pointing out logical inconsistencies or errors in empirical facts or the consequences drawn from them, but he still insisted that a person's basic values were emotive in essence and may not be open to modification.

I was greatly influenced in my philosophical outlook by another great teacher at NYU, the indefatigable Sidney Hook, who at that time was almost alone in taking philosophical inquiry to the public square, arguing for normative *propositions* that he was prepared to defend contextually, especially his defense of democracy on empirical grounds against totalitarianism. He had of course been influenced by Dewey, his own teacher. When I enrolled at Columbia I tried to read anything and everything that I could of or by Dewey.

My overriding interest was in showing that prescriptive and evaluative judgments were similar to descriptive and theoretical discourse encountered in the hard sciences; and that in any case the latter presupposed a set of methodological prescriptive rules that were normative in character. It was also the thesis of my doctoral dissertation, *The Problems of Value Theory* (Eagle, 1952), where I maintained that there were general normative standards that were commonly recognized by the community of scientific inquirers. For example, concepts had to be clearly defined (operational definitions), theories should be noncontradictory, scientists depended on peer review of publications, plagiarism was inadmissible, hypotheses should be tested experimentally, predictions are confirmatory, laboratory experiments should be replicable, theories should be modified in the light of new evidence and/or more comprehensive theories, etc. I also defended naturalistic ethics. I argued that although ethical judgments cannot be deduced from descriptive ones, the valuational base should include references to scientific inquiry in appraising their adequacy.

My first philosophical paper published in the *Journal of Philosophy* was critical of G. E. Moore's thesis on "The Naturalistic Fallacy" ("Naturalistic Ethics and the Open Question," *Journal of Philosophy* 52, no. 5 [March 3, 1955]: 113–28). I maintained that the sciences presupposed ethical assumptions, as did Moore himself in his theory of definition.

Broadly conceived, by the methods of science, or critical thinking when used in cognate fields, I meant: *rational* criteria (logical consistency), *empirical* tests (observation and evidence), and *experimental* tests (under controlled conditions and in terms of predictive consequences that are reproducible). But it included other aspects: hypotheses should be taken as *tentative* and *fallible* (following Peirce), *skepticism* was a key rule of inquiry (unless we can justify beliefs objectively we should suspend judgment), there was a requirement of *intersubjective corroboration* (within the community of investigators), and the grounds for the hypothesis or theory should be *reproducible* (by other scientific inquirers). This methodology is *comparative, self-corrective*, and its rules of inquiry are not ultimate, fixed, or final.

By way of contrast, other methods of knowing—intuition, revelation, mysticism, faith, emotion, custom, authority—have been much less effective in advancing the frontiers of knowledge. These objective criteria are themselves justified pragmatically by their long-range consequences. They have led to industrial and technological applications, which have had an enormous success in the past five hundred years in transforming the globe, opening up communication and travel, and enhancing human health and welfare. All of this has been for the amelioration and betterment of the human condition on the planet. It is thus *vindicated*, to use a term of Herbert Feigl. This is not a deductive or inductive proof, but nonetheless it appeals to our rationality. The background for this is the pragmatic outlook. Both so-called descriptive and prescriptive sciences ultimately fulfilled human interests and purposes: knowledge thus was a human construct, though it was warranted because it confronted a real world that delimited the kinds of explanations that were effective about nature.

Thus my entire philosophical career was committed to justifying or vindicating the methods of objective inquiry. This was known as "naturalism." Naturalism has many meanings, but its basic premise is "methodological naturalism": we ought to test our beliefs, hypotheses, and theories by objective scientific/rational inquiry. This is distinct from what I later called "scientific naturalism," a summing up of what we know about the universe, based on the sciences at any one period in history. Today "scientific naturalism" means a nonreductive account of nature, drawing its root categories and principles from the sciences. Thus naturalism can find no place for "spirits," "souls," "non-natural" or "supernatural entities," since there was insufficient empirical evidence for them. This drew upon the "principle of coduction," which I introduced in my book *Decision and the Condition of Man* (Seattle: University of Washington Press, 1965; New York: Dell, 1968). This meant that we needed to draw from many levels of inquiry, and thus co-duce explanations. For example, both physicalist and intentional explanations are useful for understanding human behavior. E. O. Wilson in his book *Consilience: The Unity of Knowledge* (New York: Knopf, 1998) uses the term "consilience" (borrowed from philosopher of science William Whewell) to argue a similar approach: We need to develop empirical generalizations about nature and the biosphere, drawing upon different sciences. Wilson believes that we should strive to integrate and unify our knowledge, with which I concur.

Methodological naturalism came under attack by changes within the philosophy of science (from Kuhn to Feyerabend). I never objected to Kuhn, for Deweyites had long held that scientific theories were related to the socio-cultural contexts in which they emerged, but I did object strenuously to Feyerabend, who denied that there were *any* objective methods of science at all. Similarly, I have objected to the postmodernists who emerged to contest scientific objectivity, claiming that science presents mythological narratives (Lyotard, Derrida, etc.) and was an extension of the power structure (Foucault)—undoubtedly true to some extent. My reasons were practical and pragmatic; namely, we have developed a body of reliable knowledge, which is progressively advancing (though constantly modified), and this knowledge is tested daily by impressive technological applications. If the principles of physics were simply "social constructions," as some postmodernists have held, how does one account for the fact that astrophysicists can shoot rockets into outer space with precision, or that biogenetics can create new forms of food? (See my book *New Skepticism* [Amherst, NY: Prometheus Books, 1992] for an account of my epistemological theories, and also *Philosophical Essays in Pragmatic Naturalism* [Amherst, NY: Prometheus Books, 1990].)

Thus my primary interest was in arguing that methodological naturalism not only applies to the sciences but also to ethics and social and political questions, though with far less accuracy and far more disagreements; nevertheless this was a "logic of judgments of practice" (see Dewey's *Logic: The Theory of Inquiry* [New York: Henry Holt, 1938]).

I was distressed when pragmatic naturalism came under heavy attack or was ignored in the 1950s, '60s, and '70s, particularly in American philosophy, and Dewey went into eclipse. I am pleased that Dewey is currently undergoing a revival. I taught courses in American philosophy all those years and was dismayed that analytic philosophers had abandoned any study of the sciences and focused on language. Although analytic philosophy in its day undoubtedly provided powerful logical and linguistic tools, philosophy seemed to lack a subject matter. This was particularly the case with ethics, whose subject matter seemed to many English philosophers not to be *practice* but language about practice. This work was usually on the meta level, whereas I thought that philosophers had missed the main point—there did not seem to be any content to ethical judgments—and that they needed to descend to the concrete and messy world where we are confronted by real dilemmas, not contrived abstract lifeboat illustrations.

Many philosophers prided themselves on the fact that they never bothered with the world of concrete particulars; nor would they make any recommendation. They simply wished to find out how ordinary moral language functioned and left it at that. During that period I was highly skeptical of the use of ordinary language as a guide in determining the rectitude of moral language. I wrote a paper criticizing Antony Flew—"Has Mr. Flew Abandoned 'The Logic of Ordinary Use'?" (*Philosophical Studies* [October–December 1958]). We have been fast friends ever since.

I was influenced by both John Dewey and Marx, who held that it is not enough to understand the world (a theoretical ivory tower or ideal utopia); one needs to enter into the world of praxis and allow cognition to change social institutions. For I was convinced that it was important to move from philosophy (the love of wisdom) to *eupraxsophy* (the *practice* of wisdom), and thus I have labeled myself as a eupraxsopher. I have maintained that we can and should bring the best philosophical and ethical wisdom and scientific knowledge to deal with problems of practice. A similar reticence is found in the sciences; for very few specialists in scientific disciplines are willing or able to interpret their findings to the public and/or make any judgments outside of their narrow fields of expertise. In retrospect, I should have perhaps used the term *eupraxology*—the suffix *ology* rather than *sophy*—because it is science that breaks new ground and gives us knowledge, not philosophy; so it is reliably tested knowledge that we need and not simply philosophical wisdom. Some philosophers have deplored what I do, since they wish to focus on technical philosophy alone—philosophers addressing philosophers—and I wished to relate it to *praxis* and the interests of men and women in ordinary life. I asked, why should religion or political and economic ideologies here provide all of the answers? Why not scientific and philosophical alternatives? Thus I have repeatedly claimed in public that we can live without religion, find life meaningful, wholesome, and significant without reliance upon received opinion. Hence my focus on normative philosophy became central to my activities.

It was because of this in the late 1960s and 1970s that I decided to confront normative questions head on—because the *public square was empty* of philosophical wisdom and philosophers were largely ignored. Instead, politicians, religious preachers and prelates, business leaders, sports champions, and celebrities were the idols of public discussion—at least in America—and the exemplars of wisdom. Only Sidney Hook and Charles Frankel (both Columbia naturalists) seemed willing to deal with questions of public policy and moral conflicts, and a few scattered libertarians such as Robert Nozick.

In 1967, when I was offered the editorship of the *Humanist* magazine, I decided to take it. The explicit editorial policy I enunciated was that we would deal with concrete moral questions of wider concern to the public. At about the same time, I edited a volume for Prentice-Hall primarily on that topic—*Moral Problems in Contemporary Society: Essays in Humanistic Ethics* (1969). I was amused by the fact that my good friend Rollo Handy, then chairman of the philosophy department at SUNY at Buffalo, and a strong naturalist, urged me *not* to assume the editorship. I was an active member of the American Philosophical Association in my early years, and he did not think my colleagues would find it philosophically respectable to do so. But I thought that philosophers had withdrawn from treating two vital areas of basic human interest: first, a generalized account of nature based on the sciences (formerly known as metaphysics) and second, a normative outlook in the ethical and political realm based on scientific naturalism, not ancient theological doctrines.

I have devoted the lion's share of my intellectual life to the application of philosophical analysis to concrete moral and social questions. Students at the universities would ask questions such as "What is the meaning of life?" "How ought I to live?" "What is the just society?" Marxists, Leninists, and Maoists were offering a critique of capitalist societies—Marcuse was especially influential among students of the New Left. As a former student of Marcuse at Columbia, I was perplexed as to how a rather mild Hegelian scholar could be lionized by the students, and how he reveled in it.

The great religions also had answers for the students. Many or most of my philosophical colleagues were skeptical of the regnant religious and ideological dogmas. Many of them taught courses in the philosophy of religion, ethics, or political philosophy. But they rarely took positions. Usually they would present all sides of a question and leave the students in the dark about what their own views were. They simply would provide an analytic presentation of a philosopher's position and then offer criticisms made in the history of philosophy; and not make normative recommendations themselves other than by polite suggestions.

There were two main reasons for this. First, as teachers they did not believe that they should indoctrinate, rather they sought to teach the methods of analysis and leave it at that. They *had* their own strong views, which they were reluctant to express inside or outside class. They would teach the history of philosophy but they would not themselves deal with current burning issues. Second, there was general fear of the repercussions. I decided to take a different approach, to take philosophy to the real world, and to become *engagé* in the real world (like Sartre in France and Russell in the UK), leaving the ivory tower behind, and descending into Plato's cave. My life ever since has not been the same. I have by and large eschewed university committee meetings (the true definition of "academic freedom" is "freedom from committee work!" I quipped). I had really embarked upon a eupraxsophic career, though I had not defined it as yet; it meant the concretization of normative recommendations in practice (*praxis*), offering normative guidelines based on science and philosophy.

Thus I concentrated on normative questions. By "normative" I mean formulating judgments of value in which we evaluate and recommend alternative courses of action, and descending from the meta to the concrete level of moral choices. Valuational judgments are broader than moral or ethical judgments; judgments may be wise or unwise, effective or ineffective, useful or useless, good or bad, and these are not necessarily ethical, but may be economic, political, æsthetic, technological, or instrumental. Such judgments are made in the applied sciences and ordinary life. Indeed, we are called upon all the time to make concrete choices—it is what defines us as human beings. For many individuals freedom and self-determination are burdens, and they seek to escape from choosing. But choices are so essential for life that we need to constantly make and remake them. Thus we ask the question "How shall we choose in any concrete situation?" The root questions for eupraxsophy are these: "By what process shall we decide?" "What are the criteria by which we judge?" and "What values should we accept as intrinsically worthwhile?" At one point, I used the term *act-duction*; we infer actions that are most appropriate to a context, drawing up the valuation base. (See my *Philosophical Essays in Pragmatic Naturalism*, Part II, 1990.)

As a eupraxsopher I was especially interested in the existential questions "Does life have meaning for the secular humanist, atheist, or agnostic who rejects traditional religion?" "Can one choose to live and live well without God?" The dominant religious traditions were undergoing a revival at the end of the twentieth century and so these were live questions, not merely of academic interest. Religious institutions—Christianity, Judaism, Islam, Hinduism, Buddhism, etc.—are among the oldest in human history offering general commandments. They purport to answer the meaning question "Human life had meaning because God, a divine or spiritual reality, bestows meaning on it, including some forms of salvation and immortality." "Our choices," they say, "only assure meaning in a divine framework." Or "the trials and tribulations of this life could be overcome in the next only by a divine lawgiver." These claims needed to be contested by eupraxsophers. Therefore, the first task for the eupraxsophist is to map out secular alternatives to the spiritual-paranormal-theistic conceptions of reality and to show how and why a meaningful life can be lived without dependence on God. Moral choices only take on meaning for human persons capable of decision. It is the challenge of choosing that provides the stimulus for human adventure, exploration, and fulfillment.

PROMETHEUS REVISITED

Here and directly to the point of this volume, the Prometheus myth provides a significant normative alternative to the mythological figures of theism—Jesus, Moses, and Muhammad. None of the latter have a monopoly on truth, nor can the historic claims of revelation survive scrutiny. They are, I submit, fictionalized tales told by ancient poets, who became apologists for faith as elaborated in the Gospels of the Old and New Testaments and the Koran. They are usually encased with impregnable barriers to critical examination. They are held to be inerrant, absolute, and inviolable by many religious believers. Without a detailed discussion, suffice it to say that I have spent decades investigating religious claims and have found them seriously deficient. They lack adequate scientific corroboration and are false in what they purport to be our human destiny (see my *The Transcendental Temptation: A Critique of Religion and the Paranormal* [Amherst, NY: Prometheus Books, 1986]). The Gods of theism are anthropocentric and anthropomorphic projections of human hopes and fears. They have no basis in reality.

The poets Aeschylus, Goethe, Shelley, and Byron understood the insight and power of the Promethean myth. Literary metaphors have the power to extend ideas to large sectors of intellectual culture. And they are still useful today as a competitor with the reigning theistic ortho-doxies. The one difference is that secular humanists know that they are dealing in myth, whereas theists do not, and they are consumed by self-deception.

The naturalistic outlook has been explicated philosophically, drawing upon scientific discovery of the world and the evolution of the human species. Perhaps it is time to clothe it in elegant metaphorical terms in order to dramatize its message. This is the powerful role that the Promethean legend has played historically: a heroic Titan steals fire from the Gods and endows it along with the arts and sciences to human beings. Huddled in caves, overtaken by fear and foreboding, Prometheus provides primitive men and women with the means to create a better life. Hence he is the bestower of culture, and it is this capacity that distinguishes the human species from all others. No longer dependent on their biological drives and instincts to gather food from trees and plants, to procreate at will, to flee from or protect themselves from wild beasts, they can now hunt and fish, create agriculture—and forge the tools to fulfill their ends. They can use reason to formulate their purposes and invent new means for realizing them. They can build shelters and fashion clothing to ensure themselves from the vicissitudes of fortune; and they can develop a division of labor, out of which grows the arts and crafts, the economy, and other institutions.

The meaning of Prometheus for the secular humanist is that humans possess the power to create a better life and thus reap the benefits of socio-cultural development. They can achieve happiness here and now for themselves, their loved ones, for their children's children, and for generations to come. The world that was formerly enshrined for the primitive mind in mystery and awe, controlled by fearful demons and deities, is gradually understood by philosophers and scientists. The world that seemed so intractable is now malleable to suit human desires, not only by satisfying our basic need to survive and reproduce, but also to build a culture that enables us to enjoy the fineries of civilized taste.

Prometheus graphically illustrates a turning point in human history. For Prometheus proclaimed his independence from the Gods. No longer fawning in pious servitude and supplication, he declared his liberation from the false illusions of salvation and dependence upon unseen power, and he decides to build a better life for himself and his fellow humans. His first act is his declaration of independence, but this could only occur because of his courage, the courage not simply to be (Paul Tillich) but to *become* what he wills, and to exert the energy and resolve to achieve his goals and realize his aspirations.

In my book *The Courage to Become* (Westport, CT: Greenwood/ Praeger, 1997), I argue that there are three basic humanist virtues that are Promethean in origin and come into play. The first is *courage*. This expresses the will to endure on one's own, using one's own resources. It is an affirmation of life; and only when it occurred in some mythical past could human history begin. The human species had a biogenetic evolutionary past in which blind and unconscious forces were at work. *Human* history properly began when men and women defied nature and the unknown Gods that sought to keep them in bondage. They sought to understand and master the forces that would dominate them and to create their own futures.

Given what we know about the extinction of millions of species on our planet, the human species lives in constant danger. It is not unlikely that our species may one day become extinct. Thus we are not talking of the death of any particular individual, but of the possible entire death of the tribe, society, nation, or race of humans at some point in the future. Thus courage is an essential virtue for humans, in the present as much as in the past.

A second humanist virtue concomitant with courage is *cognition*. This refers to human reason and to the rational powers that can be developed in order to bend nature to our purposes. At root this refers to our coping capacities. They are the practical tools that we invent and that enable us to survive and to thrive on our own: the discovery of fire, the wheel, the axe, the knife, and the sword, and later the more complex forms of social life, the village, the city, and all the adornments of cultural experience. Reason and science have their origins in practice and technology—enabling humans to solve the problems that beset them and to cope with fires, floods, plagues, storms, wild beasts, and marauding tribes. Humans invented walled cities, the chariot and ship, bridge and reservoir, the steam engine, electric generator, the flying machine and automobile, the computer and rocketship—all promising new capacities and powers. Theoretical science and philosophy, which later developed, added new potentialities for human achievement; for in better understanding nature, we can better forge new tools to cope; thus oral and written language was a supreme invention. The creation of mathematics and the elaboration of theoretical principles of scientific explanation and prediction played a key role in enabling humans to flourish. Both Plato and Marx understood how civilization developed and the importance of the division of labor for that.

In my book, *Forbidden Fruit* (Amherst, NY: Prometheus Books, 1988), I argue that humans need to eat of the fruit of two trees in the Garden of Eden. The first is the tree of knowledge of good and evil, transforming blind obedience to God's commandments to rational choices, using the second virtue of cognition. The second is the tree of life and the hidden powers it provides for realizing the good life. This is the first virtue, the courage to become—to seize control of one's life and to live it fully.

But there is still a third humanist virtue that exerts a profound role in the development of human history. Courage and reason would be misspent by the lone individual unless he shared what he learned in his own lifetime and transmitted this knowledge of techniques and strategies to others. Thus *caring* (benevolence and compassion) enables humans to share the fruits of their endeavors with present and future generations. Man is thus not an arrogant egocentric self-interested being; he is capable of altruistic feelings of empathy. Learning and education are the transmission belt for social-cultural evolution, which now accompanies our biogenetic evolution. For the present generation, humans can engage in biogenetic engineering, which enhances and extends our Promethean powers enormously. Aristotle observed that man is a social animal and that outside of society he would be either a beast or a God. Thus morality lays down the rules of the game. The common moral decencies are learned by every society that wishes to survive and flourish. The above three cardinal humanist virtues are Promethean in origin.

PRAGMATIC NATURALISM AND HUMANISM

Unquestionably, the core philosophical ideas fundamental to my work have been pragmatic naturalism and humanism. There has been an intimate relationship of my thought to the pragmatism of John Dewey and his students. I have been influenced by Dewey's focus on inquiry, problematic situations, the unity of means-ends, the use of cognitive appraisal in evaluating value judgments, and so much else. Dewey was interested in transforming experience by means of the "intelligent," "creative," and "persistent development of the goods of human experience." He sought to discover within experience the regulative norms to guide us. These were best realized by education and democracy and by the "self-corrective method of intelligent inquiry." Here the emphasis is on the process of self-corrective inquiry, where we seek comparative judgments that can be warranted, not ultimate certainties.

Perhaps one aspect of my philosophical career that sets me apart from virtually all other pragmatists is my conviction that the beliefs of pragmatists need to be implemented in action; they may lose their effectiveness unless they are applied. This is not entirely the case for most pragmatists, who are removed from the world, though both Dewey and Hook were deeply involved in the social and political controversies of their day and along with others helped to establish new organizations or issue public statements. I have taken this further, in one sense, as the primary test of my own ideas; for I have said that insofar as ideas have consequences, they will grow in importance only if they are concretized in conduct. I have battled tirelessly in the trenches not only in order to judge whether "x is warranted or worthwhile," but to see whether x could be put into practice, evaluating its efficacy by its personal and social effects.

Thus I consider myself to be a *practitioner* of pragmatism, not simply a theoretician about it. If an idea is a "plan of action," following Charles Peirce, then in a broad sense I have encouraged the formulation of new plans of action appropriate to the post-postmodern world, and I have helped to create new institutions to fulfill these ends. The methods I have used are entrepreneurial and experimental; that is, encouraging new ideas beyond traditional conceptions. I have said that we may need to introduce daring proposals and novel departures, constantly testing them by their effects upon practice. We need always to be willing to abandon strategies that do not work and to try out new ones. In that sense I consider myself to be the pragmatist's pragmatist, testing pragmatism itself in pragmatic terms.

My main interest throughout has been: Can the human personality live a full life without religion, and can society overcome the traditional beliefs and values framed in the infancy of the species? It is one thing to speculate about the possibility of building a new civilization without transcendental religion; it is another thing to test alternatives in the light of practice. It is not simply enough, and surely destructive, to destroy ancient beliefs and customs by negative criticism. It is another thing to develop viable ideals and practices to fill the vacuum. One unintended result of skeptical criticism may be nihilism and cynicism; another, and one that I have always aimed to realize, is to develop constructive, affirmative, and positive new directions. Merely to show that the claims of traditional religion and the other cultural nostrums of paranormal hope and conjecture have no basis in fact or are incoherent is not sufficient. Because even if the existing beliefs are false or nonsensical, we surely need to fill the vacuum and to assuage the hunger for meaning, truth, and value; and we need to test new departures in ideals and practices not simply cognitively, but in terms of human needs, attitudes, and emotions. We need always to ask, what will take its place, and will this be experientially viable? This is not a question of speculative theory but of action taken to achieve normative ends.

Many noble and ignoble social experiments were tried on a mass scale in the twentieth century—from socialism, anarchism, social democracy, or libertarianism to communism and even fascism. These were often concerned with gusts of great expectation; many of them failed abysmally. I have always deplored utopian schemes *per se* as dangerous, especially when they sacrifice human freedom or the principles of moral decency, or compromise means to achieve ideal ends. Instead, I have attempted first to test out naturalistic and secular humanistic ideals on a more limited scale. Can men and women of all ages, children, adolescents, college students, singles, married people, and retirees, once they abandon the transcendental temptation, find life sufficiently rich with significance, capable of stimulating creative intensity, able to throb with motivation, intensity, excitement, and joy, and is it able to slake their passionate thirst for meaning? That is the great test, and it is worthy of our continuing efforts to build a world that leaves ample space for the creative exercise of our diverse idiosyncratic individual tastes and talents, but also allows for mutually shared experiences in small face-to-face democratic communities and on the global scale. This is a vital pragmatic standard by which we need constantly to measure our ideal goals in practice; and that is why I consider eupraxsophy as the next step beyond the philosophical. The public square—often naked of wisdom—needs to be filled by eupraxsophers, men and women of intelligence and knowledge, but also of genuine good will, moral empathy, and caring. Can they bring about significant and enduring change? I submit that eupraxsophic pragmatic naturalistic humanism is unique and different from other philosophical schools that have preceded it.

EUPRAXSOPHY

The key point of the concept of *eupraxsophy* is the centrality of *praxis* or conduct; not *philosophy*, not the *love of* wisdom, but the *practice of wisdom*. Eupraxsophers thus descend to the world of concrete facts, real existential situations, the blood and guts of lived experience; they enter into the world to try to work out courses of action, applying the principles of *sophia* (meaning by that scientific knowledge), whereas *philosophers* are not practitioners; and it is the latter that we need, a new specialty of doers and agents in the world, not separate from it, willing and able to make moral recommendations and to act upon them, not one stage removed on the meta level. By this interpretation neither Kant nor Hegel nor Spinoza were eupraxsophers, though Marx, Dewey, and Russell were.

Philosophers regrettably often withdraw from the world in secluded isolation (usually the universities), whereas eupraxsophers are out there hobnobbing with the facts, the nasty facts! We need *both* theoretical and experimental physicists, *both* research scientists and applied engineers. Eupraxsophers are the engineers of applied science. Truth is, however, we need both philosophy and eupraxsophy, and it is the abdication of the former that I have sought to redress. Unfortunately, philosophy by itself is not enough, having been displaced by science. Philosophy is largely unable to present the principles of sophia, upon which we may act; for its pronouncements are often so abstract and general, and they lack concrete content. They seek to offer principles of logic or dialectic—Hegel is the best illustration of this—whereas eupraxsophy needs to draw upon detailed empirical studies in psychology and economics, politics and anthropology, sociology and the policy sciences, in order to decide what to do in specific contexts under analysis. Eupraxsophers need to get their hands dirty, in the muck of things. Today, priests, ministers of the cloth, psychologists, counselors, and physicians do this work; eupraxsophers need to do it as well. Why? Because religion plays an inordinate role in ministering to human needs, most usually based upon false theologies of hope; they distort the truth, and in the place of sound advice they offer the pabulum and balm of ancient religious nostrums. The great clash in the world is between competing religious worldviews—Islam, Christianity, Hinduism, and Buddhism still persist, whereas scientific naturalism and humanism have been overlooked. Hopefully, eupraxsophers, armed with the tools of ethical philosophy and science, can provide alternative remedies for wise conduct.

One complaint often heard against humanism is that it is too vague and amorphous and that it does not apply its ideal principles to practice. One recommendation is that it become politically involved and that it enlist political activists to the cause (as did the Religious Right and the Roman Catholic Church in the United States or Islam in Muslim theocracies). I am not objecting to this *per se*, since I think that individual humanists need to be politically involved, but we have a far more basic task as eupraxsophers. We need to "minister to the soul" (if I may use a metaphor). We are practitioners of eupraxsophy and of meaning. As an alternative to the medicine men of the past, gurus and spiritualists, soothsayers, rabbis, mullahs, and priests, we need to demonstrate that life can be lived and lived well without the illusions of religiosity, that it can be rich with significance and overflowing with joy, and that concrete choices can be made wisely and satisfactorily. This is the first task of eupraxsophy as practitioners of a different life stance, a life-enriching eupraxsophy of the good life. No doubt philosophers, insofar as they seek to educate students in colleges and universities, may perform these tasks, but often once removed they remain on the abstract metaphysical and historical level. They need to guide their students and society at large, first by rejecting the false ideologies of salvation upon which humankind is still fixated, and second by embracing the positive reaches of human discovery and experience and finding new meaning and purpose. Eupraxsophy in this sense is positive and life-affirming, and it can play a meaningful role. And as such this can have significant social and political consequences for the future of humankind.

NOTES

INTRODUCTION. UP FROM ATHEISM

1. Charles Taylor, *A Secular Age* (Cambridge, MA: Harvard University Press, 2007).

2. These books include Richard Dawkins, *The God Delusion* (Boston: Houghton Mifflin, 2006); Sam Harris, *The End of Faith* (New York: W. W. Norton, 2004) and *Letter to a Christian Nation* (New York: Knopf, 2006); Daniel Dennett, *Breaking the Spell: Religion as a Natural Phenomenon* (New York: Viking Adult, 2006); and Christopher Hitchens, *God Is Not Great* (New York: Hachette Book Group, 2007).

3. Stephen Hawking, "God Did Not Create the Universe," *Times of London*, September 2, 2010.

4. Kimberly Winston, "Secularism Now Being Studied," Religion News Service, August 13, 2011.

5. Two recent volumes examining this phenomenon from a sociological perspective are Phil Zuckerman, ed., *Atheism and Secularity: Issues, Concepts, and Definitions, Vol. 1* (Santa Barbara, CA: Praeger, 2010) and Amarnath Amarasingam, ed., *Religion and the New Atheism: A Critical Appraisal* (Leiden, Netherlands; Boston: Brill, 2010).

6. Philip Kitcher, "Beyond Disbelief," in *50 Voices of Disbelief: Why We Are Atheists*, edited by Russell Blackford and Udo Schuklenk (Chichester, UK: Wiley-Blackwell, 2009). See also Philip Kitcher, "Challenges for Secularism," in *The Joy of Secularism*, edited by George Levine (Princeton: Princeton University Press, 2011).

7. For an extended study on the method of inquiry and the use of critical

intelligence in daily life, see Paul Kurtz, *The New Skepticism: Inquiry and Reliable Knowledge* (Amherst, NY: Prometheus Books, 1992).

8. Kurtz presents his own comprehensive cosmic worldview or theory of nature in his forthcoming volume, tentatively titled *The Turbulent Universe*.

9. The term *normative* refers to concrete, *prescriptive* responses to such questions as "How ought we to live?" and "What is the good life?" For an extended and definitive statement of Kurtz's humanistic and naturalistic ethical theory, see his *Forbidden Fruit: The Ethics of Secularism* (Amherst, NY: Prometheus Books, 2008) and *The Courage to Become: The Virtues of Humanism* (Westport, CT: Praeger, 1997).

10. I borrow this formulation of "spirit" from philosopher John E. Smith. See Smith's *The Spirit of American Philosophy* (Albany: State University of New York Press, 1983), p. 187.

11. R. Joseph Hoffmann, "The Challenge of Neohumanism," http://rjoseph hoffmann.wordpress.com/2011/03/30/the-challenge-of-neohumanism/ (accessed September 9, 2011); Paul Kurtz, *Neo-Humanist Statement of Secular Principles and Values* (Amherst, NY: Prometheus Books, 2011).

CHAPTER 1. HUMANISM AS A EUPRAXSOPHY

1. This is especially true in twentieth-century ethics, among such philosophers as G. E. Moore (*Principia Ethica* [Cambridge: Cambridge University Press, 1903]), the deontologists W. D. Ross and H. A. Pritchard, and the emotivists A. J. Ayer and C. L. Stevenson.

2. E. O. Wilson defends the idea of "consilience," the effort to unify the sciences across disciplines. See Edward O. Wilson, *Consilience: The Unity of Knowledge* (New York: Knopf, 1988).

3. The term *life stance* was first introduced by Harry Stopes-Roe in "Humanism as a Life Stance," *Free Inquiry* 8, no. 1 (Winter 1987/1988).

4. John Dewey, *Liberalism and Social Action* (New York: Capricorn Books, 1955), *The Public and Its Problems* (New York: Henry Holt, 1927), *Freedom and Culture* (New York: Capricorn, 1939).

5. For the most recent statement of planetary humanism, see Paul Kurtz, *Neo-Humanist Statement of Secular Principles and Values* (Amherst, NY: Prometheus Books, 2011).

CHAPTER 2. EUPRAXSOPHY AND NATURALISM

1. See Michael Novak's declaration. At a recent conference sponsored by *Telos* (June 22, 2007), he defended Roman Catholicism and maintained that Jürgen Habermas has wavered on the secularist agenda in his dialogue with Pope Benedict. Many neoconservatives, especially Irving Kristol and his wife, Gertrude Himmelfarb, indict secular naturalism and believe that society needs religion to maintain the social order.

2. Daniel C. Dennett, *Breaking the Spell: Religion as Natural Phenomena* (New York: Penguin Books, 2007).

3. Richard Dawkins, *The God Delusion* (Boston: Houghton Mifflin, 2006); Sam Harris, *Letter to a Christian Nation* (New York: Knopf, 2006) and *The End of Faith* (New York: W. W. Norton, 2005); Daniel C. Dennett, *Breaking the Spell: Religion as a Natural Phenomenon* (New York: Viking Adult, 2006); Christopher Hitchens, *God Is Not Great: How Religion Poisons Everything* (New York: Twelve Books, Hachette Book Group, 2007); Victor Stenger, *God: The Failed Hypothesis. How Science Shows That God Does Not Exist* (Amherst, NY: Prometheus Books, 2007).

4. C. E. M. Hansel, *The Search for Psychic Power* (Amherst, NY: Prometheus Books, 1989).

5. Richard G. Swinburne (*Revelation* [Oxford, UK: Clarendon, 1991] and *The Resurrection of God Incarnate* [Oxford, UK: Clarendon, 2003]) is a theist who accepts revelation on empirical grounds.

6. Edward O. Wilson, *Consilience: The Unity of Knowledge* (New York: Knopf, 1998).

7. William Whewell, *The Philosophy of the Inductive Science* (1840), quoted in Wilson, *Consilience*, pp. 8–9.

8. Quoted in Natalie Angier, *The Canon: A World Whirligig Tour of the Beautiful Basics of Science* (Boston: Houghton Mifflin, 2007), p. 87.

9. See E. Garcia and R. King, eds., *God and Ethics* (Lanham, MD: Rowman & Littlefield, 2008).

10. In the valuation base I have in my writings listed a whole number of normative principles, virtues, and values to which naturalistic humanists are committed: the common moral decencies (integrity, trustworthiness, benevolence, fairness); excellences (health, self-control, self-respect, high motivation, the capacity for love, caring for others, beloved causes, *joie de vivre*, achievement motivation, creativity, exuberance); altruism, impartial ethical rationality, human rights and responsibilities, the aphorisms of a good will, etc.

CHAPTER 5. THE PRACTICE OF REFLECTIVE ETHICAL INQUIRY

1. David Hume, *Treatise on Human Nature* (1739), bk. 111, pt. 1, sect. 1.

2. G. E. Moore, *Principia Ethica* (Cambridge: Cambridge University Press, 1903).

3. H. A. Prichard, "Does Moral Philosophy Rest on a Mistake?" *Mind* 21 (1921); Henry Sidgwick, The Methods of Ethics, 6th ed. (New York: Macmillan, 1901); W. D. Ross, *The Right and the Good* (Oxford: Clarendon, 1930).

4. A. J. Ayer, *Language, Truth and Logic* (New York: Oxford University Press, 1936); Charles L. Stevenson, *Ethics and Language* (New Haven, CT: Yale University Press, 1943).

5. John Dewey, *The Theory of Valuation* (Chicago: University of Chicago Press, 1939), and *The Quest for Certainty* (New York: Minton, Balch, 1929), chap. 10.

6. Ralph Barton Perry, *General Theory of Value* (Cambridge, MA: Harvard University Press, 1926, 1954).

7. For a discussion of "act-duction," see Paul Kurtz, *Philosophical Essays in Pragmatic Naturalism* (Amherst, NY: Prometheus Books, 1990), pt. 2.

CHAPTER 6. THE VALUATIONAL BASE I: THE COMMON MORAL DECENCIES

1. E. O. Wilson, *Sociobiology: The New Synthesis* (Cambridge, MA: Harvard University Press, 1975).

2. Konrad Lorenz, *On Aggression* (New York: Harcourt Brace & World, 1966).

CHAPTER 7. THE VALUATIONAL BASE II: THE ETHICS OF EXCELLENCE

1. For a fuller discussion of teleonomy, see Paul Kurtz, *Decision and the Condition of Man* (Seattle: University of Washington Press, 1965).

2. John Stuart Mill, *Utilitarianism*, chap. 2.

3. A. H. Maslow, *Toward a Psychology of Being* (New York: D. Van Nostrand, 1962); Paul Kurtz, "Excelsior: The Ethics of Excellence," in *Forbidden Fruit: The Ethics of Humanism* (Amherst, NY: Prometheus Books, 1988), p. 169.

4. Paul Kurtz, *The Transcendental Temptation* (Amherst, NY: Prometheus Books, 1986), pp. 63–64.

5. Paul Kurtz, *Exuberance: The Philosophy of Happiness* (Los Angeles: Wilshire Books, 1977), chaps. 5 and 6.

CHAPTER 9. CARING

1. Charles W. Morris, ed., *Mind, Self, and Society: From the Standpoint of a Social Behaviorist* (Chicago: University of Chicago Press, 1956).

2. Emily Dickinson, *Poems*, I, in *The Complete Poems* (Boston: Little, Brown, 1924).

3. Antony Flew, *The Politics of Procrustes* (Amherst, NY: Prometheus Books, 1981).

4. Robert Burton, *Anatomy of Melancholy: What It Is, with All the Kinds, Causes, Symptoms, Prognostics, and Several Cures of It* (Boston: William Veazie, 1859).

5. William James, *Memories and Studies* (New York: Longmans, 1911).

CHAPTER 11. EUPRAXSOPHY: THE UNIFICATION OF KNOWLEDGE

1. I have outlined this concept in detail in my book *Eupraxsophy: Living without Religion* (Amherst, NY: Prometheus Books, 1990).

2. For an extended discussion of coduction, see my *Decision and the Condition of Man* (Seattle: University of Washington Press, 1965), chap. 5.

3. Lamentations 3:19.

4. From *Lines on Reading*, by the young English poet Henry Kirke White (1785–1806).

5. George Santayana, *Soliloquies in England* (New York: Scribner's, 1922).

CHAPTER 14. THE HUMAN CONDITION

1. "Coduction" refers to comparative knowledge drawn from many levels of inquiry.

2. William Shakespeare, *Macbeth*.